Nigerian Foreign Policy:

Alternative Futures

Nigerian Foreign Policy:
Alternative Futures

U. Joy Ogwu

Published by the Nigerian Institute of International Affairs
in co-operation with
Macmillan Nigeria Publishers Ltd

Macmillan Nigeria

First published 1986

Published by
The Nigerian Institute of International Affairs
Kofo Abayomi Road, Victoria Island,
G.P.O. Box 1727, Lagos

in co-operation with
Macmillan Nigeria Publishers Ltd
Ilupeju Industrial Estate
P.O. Box 264, Yaba, Lagos
P.O. Box 1463, Ibadan
Companies and representatives throughout the world

ISBN 978 132 812 6

Printed by Intec Printers Limited, Podo, Ibadan

Contents

Preface

The future of Nigeria's foreign policy predictably came under great scrutiny and generated immense public debate during the 1979 political campaigns. Observers of Nigeria's foreign relations presented often controversial but penetrating arguments for a re-examination and reassessment of Nigeria's foreign policy. The pre-election months witnessed a plethora of newspaper articles, public opinion and essays, all focusing particularly on the likely future paths of Nigeria's external relations.[1]

The new civilian administration that assumed the reins of power in October 1979 is at least old enough now to write its own history. Yet, there is still a continuing debate concerning Nigeria's future in international affairs, and the means by which she must arrive there.[2]

It is, perhaps, immodest to state that this study was undertaken because a need existed to fill the very visible vacuum left in the literature of Nigeria's foreign policy, but there it is. The major purpose of this volume is to lead the reader to the broad alternatives from which Nigeria can choose to shape its future foreign policies.

Although the salience of this essay lies less in the past policies, the idea of envisioning the future summons us to weigh the past and even the present against the future, as all events invariably affect the future. For this reason, the examination of past and current policies and trends are intended to provide a framework or basis for comprehending the futures delineated.

The basic international relations theories employed here do not fit snugly into Nigeria's reality. For this reason, the internal variables have been dealt with according to their salience. Indeed, the emphasis is on the constraints and opportunities in the internal environment as they affect Nigeria's external behaviour.

There is also considerable emphasis on the element of continuity in Nigeria's foreign policy. One does not wish to advance an image of Nigeria with unlimited opportunities for continuities. However, the vital importance of continuity should not be underscored. Perhaps, Ronald Steel, an American political analyst, best explained in the clearest terms the binding connection between continuity in foreign policy, the present and the future. According to him, "foreign policy must have an element of continuity, and the new scaffolding must rest unavoidably on the old foundation".[3]

While this approach served as a pathfinder, that is, providing a coherent view of where Nigeria was in the past, and where it is today, the alternative futures approach serves to explore where Nigeria is heading, explicitly promoting an image of shifts, turns and twists. In other words, the alternative futures advanced take cognisance of the constantly changing nature of the external environment—which is inherently in a state of flux.

The organisation of this volume is designed to aid the reader in understanding: (a) the basic values and norms and major elements of Nigerian foreign policy, (b) the opportunities and limitations under which the leadership is subjected and (c) the prospects of achieving possible and desirable futures. This approach would of necessity force us into a kind of self analysis.

The first chapter examines the figures approach and its increasing relevance to foreign policy. The linkages between the past, present and the future are also explored. More importantly. it focuses on the goals, objectives, interest and values of the Nigerian society summed up as "the national interest". The assumption here is that whatever the national interest represents, it still remains the principal consideration in the formulation and execution of policies. Chapter two assesses the internal environment in which Nigerian foreign policy is made and implemented. This chapter discusses in detail the major forces affecting Nigeria's internal and external behaviour and serves as a springboard or base for advancing the alternative futures. The most salient feature here is the New Nigerian Constitution and its impact on foreign policy. The new Constitution creates and delineates the authority; duties and limitations of both the Federal and State Governments. Indeed, the new Constitution has established a new federal system designed to rectify the deficiencies of the old federal system—which tended to impede a coherent foreign policy.

Chapter 3 briefly analyses the international systemic changes that might affect for better or for worse the alternatives delineated. Attention is paid to Nigeria's African policy—a priority area in Nigeria's objectives. In each area, prognostications are made.

Chapter 4 pulls together Nigeria's extra-African multilateral relations and advances the probable choices.

Nigeria's relations with the great powers deserves a special focus. Some of the disquieting issues about relationships with the big powers are analyzed in Chapter 5.

Above all it must be noted that the futures advanced are essentially hypothetical. No attempt has been made to offer a blue print for the future. Indeed, the range of possibilities could be wider than what is offered. Perhaps what is most crucial in any study of a nation's foreign policy are four vital elements : (a) the aims and objectives of the state; (b) the resources that it possesses to implement those policies; (c) the skill demonstrated in the application of those resources; and (d) the will to implement policy decisions.

The new administration has not been writing on a clean slate for it is heir to the assets and liabilities of the military republic. How and whether the new administration succeeds in placing Nigeria as a ranking power depends largely on factors (c) and (d) outlined above.

Several people have helped either directly or indirectly in the development of this volume and I would like to acknowledge their assistance. For his scrupulous reading of the proposal and valuable suggestions, I thank Professor U.U. Uche. The judgements and suggestions of the three-man committee of assessors who evaluated the original draft were indispensable.

The insights provided by my senior colleagues in the Research Department—Professor Osita Eze and Dr. F. Chidozie Ogene were reinforcing. Very special thanks are due to my friend and colleague, Margaret Vogt, for her personal observations, Emeka Aniagolu for his efficient editing and Moses Bonney for cheerfully typing the manuscript. My friend and Godmother, Antonia Obi-Ezeani, provided her perfect blend of encouragement and gentle, but unreserved criticism. I am deeply grateful to my brothers, Albert and Eddy Maduemezia for their usual encouragement.

My respects to the Director of Research, Professor R.A. Akindele, for his advice and patient assistance through the several stages of preparing the manuscript.

My greatest debt of gratitude is to my husband, Aloy, and our children, Ifeoma, Uche, Chiedu, Awele, and Dumebi, who not only showed great understanding and patience but have also become my 'co-workers', and life-support system.

In addition to public sources, this volume benefitted greatly from a special briefing on Nigerian Foreign Policy, held in Kaduna in 1978. Information derived have been used for background only and not attributed to any of the participants.

The Director of Library and Documentation Services, Mr. A.O. Banjo and his staff have provided invaluable assistance. The comprehensive bibliography in the appendix is gratefully attributed to them.

U. Joy Ogwu
January 1983

For my children, husband and parents
and
every child, woman and man
who
will help to shape a future Nigeria
that is *really* powerful and influential
peaceful and stable
and
genuinely prosperous.

Chapter 1

Introduction

1. The Alternative Futures Approach: Some Considerations

It has been said that 'there is no future except what men make of it'.[1] Fascination with and anticipation of the future as a guide to policy or action is nothing new in the history of man. Concern with the future, whether it takes the form of oracles, fortune-telling, astrology, simple prediction models, scenario building or scientific forecasting constitutes an inherent desire by man to improve his lot, seek, and exercise a more effective control of his own affairs.[2] Eleazu in his discourse on 'African Studies and the Study of the Future', retells the story of an African king, Morgho Naba of Mossi. The king upon learning of the impending invasion of his kingdom by the French, despatched his priests to consult the oracle for some indication of what the future held in store.[3] True, oracles are not in tune with the realities of war or the needs of modernisation, but the action of the Morgho Naba in the context of futuristics not only demonstrated 'rational behaviour' as Eleazu put it, but also the invaluable nature of knowledge and information about the future in the process of decision-making. Peoples' perception of the future has changed considerably over time with the rapid evolution of futuristics from oracles to scientific forecasting. From the concept of the future as unexplorable happenings that are beyond human comprehension and control, the future has come to be perceived as something to be imagined, explored and even created.[4] The imaginative side of furutistics is further explored by Kahn and Weiner who suggest that the study of the future is essentially an attempt to stimulate and stretch the imagination in order to improve perspectives, clarify, define and argue major issues in the design of alternative policy packages in different contexts.[5] It is one thing to say that the future is basically an exercise in imaginative thinking, and quite another to explain policy options and choices exclusively in future terms or long-term planning. This is the fundamental dilemma of the futurist: how to envision the future so that current decisions can better anticipate the new ideas, new alternatives and the goals they help to create.

In contrast, the modern scientist has speculated about the future of science with considerable precision, exploring and creating in more systematic ways new methods of anticipating all kinds of future contingencies. Nowhere are these more focused than in the fields of economics and defence.[6] The serious focus on long-range forecasting of future economic trends and weapons technology emanated from the realization that economic and defence planning are critical to the well-being and survival of nation states. Further, the building of scenarios, forecasting and contingency planning became imperative in the face of new and increasing complex global challenges.

Since the fate of nation states cannot be isolated from these global challenges, it seemed that foreign policy would not escape from the development of futuristics. Perhaps, the major consideration has been the crucial objective of finding a path toward a better future both at the domestic and international levels.[7] There seems to be an increased awareness that the future itself does not merely consist of predetermined events, but rather a matrix of changing aspirations, goals and choices which must adapt to the dynamic nature of the international system. Thus, the changing nature of the international system and the uncertainty about the future suggest the dilemma facing the foreign policy forecaster.

Forecasting or predicting the future usually involves some measure of credibility, and in order to be credible, the shape of the future has to be consistent with the feasibility of proposed goals and the ability of the nation to attain those goals. In the field of foreign policy, futurology has been characterized by predictions and forecasting.[8] Analysts have utilized various approaches, some of them focusing on the questions of how decision makers predict foreign policy events. Some make prognostications from the known and familiar,[9] while other approaches emphasize the specific problems of scientific forecasting—that is, predictions derived essentially from the scientific study of foreign policy.

Stenelo has been one of the leading scholars in foreign policy predictions. The element of continuity in the predictions of foreign policy which he emphasized in his studies is especially pertinent for the purposes of this study. He suggests that 'hereditary mechanisms' tend to encourage continuity and inertia in the foreign policy predictions of policy makers, and attempts to find the relationships between predictions, prediction bases, and the degree of stability and continuity in the foreign policy of a state.[10]

In the first place, he characterises 'hereditary mechanism' as:

> a factor which, in a political context, fulfills two functions in that it, on the one hand, influences the probability that a certain political event will be transferred from one decision-making generation to another, and, on the other hand, contributes to the recipient's maintaining its political heritage.[11]

The above description asserts implicitly that decision makers generally diagnose current events and problems by means of historical analogies in the belief that the shape of the future is not likely to vary considerably. While this method may not eliminate mis-perception of a problem entirely, it does serve to ensure continuity in a nation's foreign policy. As Stenelo pointed out,:

> a foreign policy heritage is normally in itself potentially a stabilising factor over time. Certain parts of its content may conceivably be accepted without objection: other parts are perhaps unwillingly accepted by the recipient because he lacks the possibilities of repudiating them and because the political costs of such repudiation are assessed as being far too great.[12]

Stenelo's hypothesis is that analogies are crucial to predictions; they play the role of providing data for the feasibility of anticipated goals. Empirically, Stenelo highlights the utility of his hypothesis by his adept application of the Domino Theory and the Theory of the Communist Aggressor in American foreign policy.[13] A great deal of analyses in his study show that historical experiences were utilised as prediction basis in American decision-making and planning processes in Vietnam and Korea. Many of his observations and conclusions suggest that policies show a persistent pattern and subsequent stability over time, that decision makers commonly use them to make estimates of what the future is likely to hold. For example, the Domino Theory was a prediction theory—judged from its survival and heritage from one American administration to another. Each administration concerned itself with what would happen if a part of South East Asia became communist. These concerns not only became vehicles of continuity over time, but also the basis for foreign policy doctrines.[14]

The object of this study is not to engage in any 'scientific' fore-casting, rather the approach is to explain the past, identifying genera-lisations and patterns which might serve to provide paths to the future. The focus on the future would entail not only one's vision of the future of Nigeria's foreign policy, but also what choices are available.

To write about the future of Nigerian foreign policy is similar to writing about its past. Indeed, thinking in the future tense in the Nigerian context involves a close scrutiny of the basic trends as they unfolded since independence. According to Patrick Henry, 'I know of no way of judging of the future but by the past!'[15] His comments, written two centuries ago, are remarkably applicable today. Decision makers and futurologists in modern times would readily agree.

A number of analyses of future studies have alluded to the importance of using historical perspectives (the past) in exploring the future. Frankel, in noting the relevance of the past in prediction models, observed that models of the future are based on the notion that the future is simply a function of the past. He further noted that, 'However imprecise, prediction has a bearing upon actual policy'.[16]

Kothari in 'Footsteps Into The Future' made a similar observation. 'Any future' he stated, 'should take into account a long history—the past'. A total break with the past, he admonished, is both an impossible and dangerous proposition'.[17]

Another analyst on African studies and studies of the future was more detailed in his observation. He noted that the study of the future proceeds from the basic premise that the present can do something to shape the future. He clearly observed that modern studies would create alternative futures based on present policies and trends, indicating that some futurologists have suggested that this can be accomplished through the construction of scenarios that identify how each alternative future may be brought to pass.[18]

The above examination of the various views of some scholars engaged in futuristic thinking may seem to the impatient reader a deviation from the basic purpose of this study. In mapping the scope, it is impor-tant to recognise the crucial relevance of history to the future. It is from this springboard that one can advance the central purpose of the study which is 'alternative futures.' Much of the relevance of the past to the future is implied in Josson's editorial on 'Prediction and Forecasting in Foreign Policy'. He concluded that:

> We are all, as it were, driving toward the future mainly by looking
> through the rear-view mirror . . . the safety and comfort of such
> a journey are dependent on the regularity and continuity of the
> path.[19]

This in turn implies that stability and continuity that form prediction basis must not be falsely assumed. Merely transforming from the
past to future would not provide an adequate framework for speculation. Indeed, projection of past events into the future is not entirely
adequate since a great deal of the stimulus to change or continuity
still comes from the external environment. In peering into the future
it is important to emphasize that the future is not fixed; dramatic
changes may occur which may significantly affect policy. So, if
Utopian assumptions are made in this essay, it is based on the subjective
reasoning that both the domestic and external environments may be
subject to sudden twists and turns. Just as Thomas More analysed the
Utopia as a step toward explaining the future, so the student of social
sciences must attempt to examine the complexities of the various
decision-making environments in order to understand the future better.

In addition, to focus on alternative futures is implicitly to express
concern about current policies. Indeed, the relevance of the alternative
futures approach lies in its sensitising us, primarily, to the conditions
and processes under which foreign policy choices are made, and more
significantly, to the character of domestic politics itself. For the purpose of this study, the new Nigerian Constitution will provide the
reference for examining the Nigerian policy environment.

Finally, the whole thrust of the alternative futures approach is to
envision a more desirable environment and raise questions about
possible paths for the nation. But the exercise of speculating about
the future is one that has been perceived as hazardous by analysts
because there has always been a much greater risk of being proved
wrong about the future than about the past.[20] As Stenelo explains:

The problem for a politically responsible predictor is probably to
weigh the strategically desirable encouragement and mobilization of
the recipient by means of positive, optimistic predictions against the
risk of being contradicted by reality and then losing credibility.[21] But
it would be an abdication of responsibility to eschew opinions about
the future for fear of losing credibility. It is presumed that decision-

making itself is a hazardous process, and the politically responsible decision maker or predictor must accept the possibilities of errors in predictions, especially in view of complexities of issues and intervening circumstances.

In the pages that follow, the 'vision' about the future will be based essentially on current trends and the past, presuming that they will provide useful insights into some probable futures and policy alternatives.

In making this assumption, one does not imply that the future should become a mere extension of the past or present. The futures approach of this study is adopted in the belief that Nigeria has the potential and indeed, the ability to shape the future in preferred directions. The shape of the future will depend on the zeal and the responsibility with which the decision maker moulds it. As Kothari succinctly puts it:

> History obliges only those who have a sound perception of the options open to them and have a will to exercise their options.[22]

Closely allied with the above discussion is a further assumption that there is an element of continuity in a nation's foreign policy. It is usually a phenomenon of liberal democratic societies to enjoy an element of continuity in policy. Dent, in his appraisal of the foreign policies of the military in Ghana and Nigeria, established that, there is a certain continuity in the area of foreign policy.[23] What Dent has written of Nigeria and Ghana applies to most nation states and we find this particularly applicable. So far, despite unexpected, sudden and sometimes violent changes in administrations and even the trauma of the civil war, there have been no radical changes in or departures from Nigeria's fundamental foreign policy orientation. This assumption does not imply a total absence of change in the conduct of Nigerian foreign policy. The discernable trend since the end of the first civilian Republic has been a reinforcement rather than fundamental alterations of the basic principles of Nigeria's foreign policy.

Over the past two decades since independence the broad goals and objectives of Nigeria's foreign policy have remained constant. Although the style and conduct of her foreign policy have changed, there have been no profound changes in the content or substance of the foreign policy. The trends that developed since independence in 1960 to the present emanated from the basic formulations of the principles, aims and objectives of the Balewa era. In turn, the basic objectives of each successive administration have been essentially tempered as well as guided by the national interest.[24] What were these interests and how were they pursued to fulfil the aspirations of the society and meet the challenges of a dynamic global system? To facilitate the analysis of Nigeria's foreign policy and present a more realistic assessment of past and current policies, the idea of national interest as an operational concept in Nigeria's foreign policy will be examined in the following sections.

2. National Interest in Nigeria's Foreign Policy.

It is undeniable that the idea of national interest continues to play a prominent role in the foreign policies of sovereign states. It is equally clear that there is no global consensus as to what constitutes the national interest, hence, analysts have not been able to establish with any degree of precision and/or certainty a definition of the term. This lack of a single central definition makes the concept pregnant with intriguing dimensions.

In its classical meaning, the term 'national interest' serves as a convenient base to encompass all the strategies employed in the international interactions of states to ensure the preservation of the stated goals of society. Broadly conceived, the term may either be regarded as a goal or a method of reaching a goal; it may also imply a means to an end.[25] But these goals cannot be formulated without a clear perception of the core values of the society. In his book on contemporary theory and behaviour of states, Frankel discusses the central role that values play in defining the national interest. As he notes, 'value describe the inner element brought to bear by the decision makers upon the process of making decisions'.[26] While it is recognised that the promotion of basic national values remain the principal consideration of decision makers in the formulation of policies, Frankel observes that it is :

> often empirically impossible to determine whether the values found in the formulation of a specific interest had been internalised by the decision-makers or introduced only in response to environmental pressures, generally domestic but sometimes also international.[27]

Implied in Frankel's observation is the possibility that the values incorporated in the formulation of national interest may have broadened ramifications that tend to merge or conflict with values external to the territorial boundaries of a state. In one sense, it means that national interests should not be considered without regard to their global implications.

In making evaluations of past and current trends of Nigeria's foreign policy and predicting its future, it is crucial to recognise, as Frankel does, that national interest falls into two distinct categories—one aspirational and the other operational.[28] In making this distinction he recognises that nations usually have a vision of a set of ideal goals which they may fail to actively pursue or implement because of environmental limitations (external or domestic). In that case, the interests remain at the aspirational level, but capable of being revived toward effectiveness when conditions improve. A state can claim to operationalise its national interest when it possesses the capability to achieve its stated objectives. When proclamations of objectives outweigh capabilities, national interest remains a non-operational aspiration. This consideration is important in assessing and understanding Nigeria's dynamism or lack of it in its foreign policy pursuits.

At different times, in over two decades following Nigeria's independence, successive administrations, from their varying perspectives, have sought to identify the ultimate aims and objectives of Nigeria in its relations within the international system. In a major speech in Parliament in August 1960, the Prime Minister Sir Abubakar Tafawa Balewa, identified what he considered to be the general aims of Nigeria's foreign policy thus:

(1) The promotion of the national interest of the Federation and of its citizens.
(2) Friendship and co-operation with all nations of the world which recognise and respect Nigeria's sovereignty.
(3) Non-alignment to any power blocks.
(4) Assistance to African states in search of solutions to their problems and encouragement of the development of common ties among all African states to foster co-operation among countries of Africa in so far as it is compatible with Nigeria's national interest.
(5) Respect for the sovereign equality of all nations as well as non-intervention in the internal affairs of other states.
(6) Unimpeded decolonization.[29]

Although it is evident from the above that the national interest was not clearly expressed in specific terms, the fundamental aims appeared to serve as guidelines for Nigeria's foreign policy actions. Despite changes in government, the administrations of Generals Ironsi and Gowon pursued essentially the same objectives based on their world view and perception of the hierarchy of Nigeria's interests. Both emphasized Nigeria's active role in the African continent as a prerequisite to attaining its aspiration of greatness. As stated by Ironsi:[30]

> In the whole sphere of Nigeria's external relations, the Government attaches the greatest importance to our African policy. We are aware that because of our population and potentials, the majority of opinion in the civilised world looks up to us to provide responsible leadership in Africa; and we realize that we shall be judged, to a very great extent, by the degree of success or failure with which we face up to the challenge which this expectation throws on us.

General Gowon advocated morality in the treatment of black people under the banner of respect for 'human dignity'.

General Obasanjo's accession to leadership in 1976 witnessed a reappraisal of Nigeria's foreign policy objectives. For the first time, a top level elaboration of the components of Nigeria's national interest was made. The elements of the national interest as enunciated by General Obasanjo include:[31]

(a) the defence of our sovereignty, independence and territorial integrity;

(b) the creation of necessary political and economic conditions in Africa and the rest of the world which will facilitate the defence of the independence and territorial integrity of all African countries while at the same time fostering national self-reliance and rapid economic development;

(c) the promotion of equality and self-reliance in Africa and the rest of the developing world;

(d) the promotion and defence of justice and respect for human dignity, especially the dignity of the black man;

(e) the defence and promotion of world peace.

While these objectives described Nigeria's national interests, they failed to indicate which of the interests were vital to the national well-being. Aluko observed what he believed to be a significant weakness in the objectives:

> . . . most of them are not realisable and therefore, cannot provide a rational and realistic basis for the country's external behaviour.[32]

Instead, he enumerated what he perceives to be 'realistic objectives' based on Frankel's definition of national interests. Delineated in a hierarchical order, Aluko notes that the strands of these objectives can be found in the New Nigerian Constitution. These are:

(i) self-preservation of the country, that is, the defence and protection of her territorial integrity and of her people;

(ii) the defence and maintenance of the country's independence;

(iii) the economic and social well-being of the people;

(iv) the defence, preservation and promotion of their way of life, especially their democratic values;

(v) the enhancement of the country's standing and status in world capitals, especially Africa;

(vi) the promotion of world peace.[33]

Aluko is quite persuasive in arguing that national interest should seek to pursue the 'highest moral ends' in its external behaviour. The question is: who determines the moral values and priorities of Nigeria's interests?

The trends that developed over the period suggests that political leadership at least determined which interests reflect the highest moral values and which were vital interests. In the mid-seventies for example, a new note was heard in Nigerian diplomacy—the key note of moral obligation for blacks all over the world. The idea of moral obligation, to which Murtala Muhammed, Obasanjo and Shagari have appealed consistently in conducting foreign relations has been examined in greater detail elsewhere.[34] This study provides evidence that the principle of the protection of the interests of black people as a conception of national interest not only gained public prominence, but was also very firm in the official pronouncements of the various governments. President Shagari reasserted Nigeria's goal:

> Nigeria shall work relentlessly to uphold the dignity of the black race anywhere in the world.[35]

The hereditary nature of this aspect of national interest and the accompanying element of continuity highlights the level of priority allocated or accorded to Nigeria's commitment to black people. This trend raises the question about the intensity of interests.

In the Nigerian foreign policy process, such familiar interests and principles as national defence and well being, self reliance, greatness and dynamism, freedom and democracy, have often been proclaimed. But it appears that these proclamations run ahead of Nigeria's capabilities. This deficiency cannot be rectified without a systematic evaluation of the nation's level of interest. Neuchterlein's 'new approach' to the concept of national interest offers a framework for operationalising national interest.[36] Neuchterlein's analysis focuses on four basic national interest matrix: survival, vital, major, and peripheral. He argues that these are dynamic and the job of the political leadership is to determine correctly which ones are most important at a specific time and then mobilise the nation's resources to defend and protect them. This approach provides a solid guideline for ascertaining the degree to which interests were considered vital. It will, perhaps, explain why Nigeria's policy on occasion was reticent, just when firmness was needed. For example, the 'response' of the Shagari administration to the Camerounian violation of Nigeria's territorial integrity was not consonant with the mood of the nation.[37] What was the President's perception of the intensity on Nigeria's national interest? Perhaps, the following definition of vital interest would facilitate a more realistic judgement of Nigeria's foreign policy and provide a guideline for the future:

> an interest is vital when the highest policy makers in a sovereign state conclude that the issue at stake in an international dispute is so fundamental to the political, economic and social well-being of their country that it should not be compromised further, even if it results in the use of economic and military force.[38]

Each policy or direction of policy must be judged relative to the leadership perception, national capability, and other relevant variables.

3. Continuities under the Civilian and Military Administrations

As was previously suggested, peering into the future can take several dimensions, (extrapolations, forecasting models—making assumptions about future events, decision theories that indicate how policies take account of diverse alternative futures, etc.). Another important framework for speculations is one that identifies clusters of events that are germane to different time periods and stages of policy. This framework usually serves as a basis for identifying long-term trends and patterns that are likely to continue into the future.[39]

Most observers of Nigeria's foreign policy tend to employ the 'period' approach in their analysis of Nigeria's external behaviour. Delancy, for example, identifies two stages—'civil rule', and 'military rule', characterising them as 'conservative passive' and 'active' respectively.[40] Some have characterised the various periods as 'pro-West.'[41] Others like Anglin perceived the first decade of Nigeria's independence as 'politically non-aligned and economically aligned'.[42] While the compartmentalization can serve to trace the dual processes of continuity and change in a nation's foreign policy, they can be quite misleading. Such straightline labels commonly emphasize the idiosyncratic factor without sufficient regard to the other salient factors and pressures from the various environments which bear upon policies pursued. The most significant advantage of the 'phase', 'stage', or time period approach is that historical analogies can be made—serving as a basis for predictions and future policy directions.[43] For example, stable features in Nigeria's South African policy can be observed in over the two decades of Nigeria's independence. Akinyemi and Vogt have pointed out that the Southern African problem has been one of the continuing pre-occupations of Nigerian governments since the attainment of independence.[44] From the official pronouncements of the Balewa, Ironsi and Gowon regimes, it was possible to discern the embryonic stage of what was later to develop as Nigeria's 'assertive African Policy'.[45] Successive Nigerian administrations have inherited the problem of Southern Africa, and they have to varying degrees pursued policies designed to solve the problem.

The objective here is not to criticise or propose remedial measures to the compartmentalisation approach, rather it is to use the different stages to identify the enduring interests (in this case, the Southern African issue) which dictate continuity and stability in the basic Nigerian strategy in Southern Africa.

Underlying the trends in Nigeria's foreign relations has been the deliberate effort to use foreign policy to achieve the desired goals of prestige and prominence in world affairs. The style, conduct and methods have changed with each new leadership, but the basic national self-image as a rising African leader and a potential actor in world politics has remained constant.[46] Official pronouncements on foreign policy emphasize, for example, Nigeria's 'duty' and 'special responsibility' in ensuring equality of treatment to all mankind.

Nigeria's diplomacy also reflects its world view, namely, that morality is a necessary element of foreign policy which cannot be substituted with stark military power.[47] Various efforts in support of the cause of oppressed peoples and mediation in disputes in pursuit of peaceful solutions essentially reflect strong moral underpinnings. The Shagari administration appears to share its predecessor's perception of morality in foreign policy. In President Shagari's view, Nigeria's national interests would best be advanced by observing morality in dealing with other nations.[48] Perhaps, the shared perception on the role of morality in foreign affairs would serve to explain the remarkable consistency in the various governments' attitude toward the question of apartheid in Southern Africa and South Africa itself as the bastion of the abominable policies.

As previously stated, the Southern Africa issue, for example, has been one of the most constant concerns of the Nigerian government since the attainment of independence. At the first debate on foreign affairs in the House of Representatives in November 1960, the Prime Minister Abubakar Tafawa Balewa in apparent reference to South Africa reassured the Leader of the opposition that on the issue of South Africa, Nigeria 'has a duty to see that there is equality of treatment to all mankind'.[48] The Prime Minister assumed a relatively more aggressive stance on the South African problem in his address to the House of Representatives shortly after his return from the Commonwealth Prime Minister's meeting held in London in March 1961. He stated:

> As for South Africa we shall continue to press in every way possible and at every opportunity for the reversal of their present policy of racial discrimination.[49]

Calling for the withdrawal of South Africa from the Commonwealth, the Prime Minister warned:

> So long as one member openly advocated racial discrimination it was impossible to accept that the Commonwealth was indeed an association of free and equal nations.[50]

The above suggests that the Prime Minister pointedly identified the South African regime as the precursor of the policy of apartheid. The degree of success in dealing with the problem of apartheid and South Africa is a very subjective matter. A more searching examination of the internal constraints that impeded the effective implementation of the administration's policies will be undertaken in the next chapter. The point to note here is that since the Balewa era each new administration has reaffirmed Nigeria's basic commitment to the eradication of apartheid, and the struggle against white minority domination in Southern Africa as one of the fundamental tenets of Nigeria's foreign policy. The perception and vision of Balewa, on the problem in Southern Africa set the tone and provided the basis for the Southern African policy.

Even the brief administration of Ironsi confirmed rather than altered the Southern African policy of his predecessor. In May 1966, for example, the Ironsi administration shut the door on the 'white racists' by announcing that the Portuguese and the white South Africans were prohibited immigrants.[51]

Under the leadership of General Gowon, the official Nigerian attitude toward Southern Africa and African Liberation Movements remained sustained. Reaffirming Nigeria's stance against a possible dialogue with South Africa, the Nigerian Commissioner for External Affairs stated:

> Nigeria will oppose to the last drop of its blood that the OAU as an organisation of all independent Africa should enter a dialogue with South Africa.[52]

Gowon's aid to the African Liberation Movements through OAU channels bears out the continuing commitment of Nigeria to the dismantling of white minority rule in Southern Africa and decolonization in Africa.

With the advent of the Muhammed/Obasanjo administration, a new emphasis and a more forceful Nigerian Southern Africa policy was in evidence. General Muhammed escalated the traditional Nigerian policy toward Southern Africa and decolonisation and, more specifically, took bold a decisive step in recognising the MPLA faction which later became the de jure government in Angola. Nigeria's refusal to bow to American wishes on the Angolan issue is instructive. By this action, Nigeria visibly demonstrated a firm ability to assert its will on the United States over the issue, and General Muhammed's pronouncements sent shocks and tremors throughout the United States. They promptly gave way to Nigeria's desire.[53]

Having been thrust into a position of leadership, Lt. General Obasanjo who succeeded Muhammed, inherited, carried forward, and expanded the Southern Africa policies of his predecessor. Obasanjo stepped up the tempo of support for the legal MPLA government of Angola, and also made massive and constructive contributions to African Liberation Movements. In his frequent pronouncements on the issue, he consistently condemned the evils of Apartheid and foreign interference in Africa.

The 1979 elections reinstated the civilian Republic of Nigeria. The administration is old enough to write its own history, and even in its first two years, there are discernable continuities of unflinching commitment to the eradication of apartheid and decolonisation in Africa. President Shagari has maintained, and even strengthened the diplomatic pressure against apartheid. In a major foreign policy address at the United Nations in October 1980, President Shagari reasserted Nigeria's continuing determination to support decolonisation efforts in Africa and the elimination of the last vestiges of apartheid in South Africa.

The new civilian administration had given vigorous support to Zimbabwe in the struggle towards independence.[54] With pride, President Shagari declared that:

> Nigeria . . . shall continue to assist, encourage and support the struggle against racism, apartheid and minority rule with all our might and resources.[55]

Furthermore, the theme stressed in the President's first annual dinner with the Nigerian Institute of International Affairs, pointedly linked Nigeria's expanded national interest to the preservation of the dignity of black peoples all over the world.[56]

The major inference to be drawn at this point is, that the policy position that was highlighted over the succeeding years in spite of changes in government were basically assumed at independence. Naturally, it is possible to assume that the continuing motivations and actions of the various Nigerian governments on this specific foreign policy issue would offer a sense of direction in exploring the future.

Quite aside from continuities like these, there are also more systematic ways to get to 'future foreign policy'. These perspectives will be discussed at some length in the following section.

Chapter 2

Nigeria's Domestic Environment

In analysing trends and predicting future courses of foreign policy, cognizance must be taken of:

(a) the dynamic nature of foreign policy and
(b) the intricate interaction of the internal and external environments in which foreign policies function.

According to Northedge, 'the foreign policy of a country is a product of environmental factors—both internal and external to it'.[1] This section examines the conditions that helped determine and shape Nigeria's foreign policy. It presumes that the same factors will unavoidably influence the future.

Combinations of political, economic, military and idiosyncratic factors can be viewed as critical variables in the foreign relations of Nigeria and are more likely to have the greatest impact on the future.

1. Political Factors

Like any other developing heterogenous society faced with the challenges of finding unity in diversity, the first civilian republic of Nigeria displayed political inadequacies for pursuing an assertive foreign policy. The Nigerian domestic environment was steeped in the tradition of ethnic politics. Consequently, the political parties that emerged were divided along ethnic lines, most of them owing their principal allegiance to their ethnic groups.[2]

16

Akinyemi for example, observes that:

> the NCNC was for the first and for a long time the only national
> political organisation . . . national in the sense that it had branches
> all over the country and that it was not identified with any parti-
> cular region or ethnic group.[3]

Yet, the 'predominance of the Ibo elements' in the NCNC was still
discernable.[4]

Admittedly, the problem of ethnicity is not unique to Nigeria.
Other political systems like the United States, have to a great extent,
been able to deal with the complex pressures of ethnic influences on
the policy process. In the Nigerian context the ethnic factor has
remained a formidable, not a negligible domestic force. A principal
question is raised by Eleazu in his study on Federalism and Nation-
Building: 'What is it in the Nigerian setting that makes ethnicity so
salient in the direction of disintegration rather than integration?'[5]
He identifies the problem himself thus:

> One basic problem (among many) in the Nigerian political
> system is that the basis of association of these various ethnic
> nationalities is always being called into question: subsidiary to
> this is the question of developing political instrumentalities that
> are congruent with any agreed on basis of association.[6]

Eleazu in his discussion establishes the ethnic factor as a social
fact and rightly focusses on strategies for 'resocialising people' in
spite of their differences, real or imaged 'into the new national consciousness'.[7] While such visions may be realiable, the fact that the
ethnic factor had been and may continue to influence the policy
process in Nigeria cannot be ignored.

The ethnic diversity and the resultant political disunity rendered
political institutions vulnerable, especially in the early years of Nigeria's
independence. The inherent 'feuds' among political parties, and lack
of consensus on vital issues, the fledging political institutions, the lack
of institutionalisation of the political processes, all created an atmosphere of domestic instability. The leadership response to the threat
to stability was naturally to shift overwhelmingly to a concern and
preoccupation with national unity. Nigeria's capacity to actively engage
in a strong, credible foreign policy was thus affected by its inability to

cope with its fundamental domestic political problems.

Related to the ethnic problem is the federal structure of Nigeria at independence. Usually, the structure of a political system is an essential ingredient in defining the scope of a nation's foreign policy. In the Nigerian domestic environment the three and (later four) regions comprising the federation were remarkably powerful relative to the central authority—the federal government. The constitution empowered the strong regional governments to exercise their rights to nulify treaties even those already concluded by the central government. The regional governments also possessed the same powers as the federal government over industrial development. Thus each 'government' exercised its power to seek and secure external loans (where possible) for local development.

The central government was further afflicted by the contradictory provisions of the constitution on coercive powers. While the regional governments controlled their own police, the central government exploited fully its exclusive constitutional rights over the armed forces. In either case, the exercise of these constitutional 'rights' deepened the cleavages in the Nigerian political environment. The regional governments utilised the police to intimidate other political groups and protect their own interests. Similarly, the federal government used the army to its own advantage. Raph Uwechue's Reflections on the Nigerian Civil War points to the most vivid example of what he terms 'constitutional manipulation'. According to him, the most vivid example of this constitutional manipulation appeared during the struggle for power in the Western region in the early sixties, between Chief Awolowo, the Action Group leader, and his deputy, Chief Akintola. Although the matter was nominally the affair of the people of the Western region, it was nevertheless, resolved by influences and interests external to the people of the West. In the 'democratic' contest, it was the strong arm of the N.P.C. dominated Federal Government, not the people of the West, that chose the government of the West.[8]

These internal manifestations of the deep divisions between Nigeria's ethnic groups (euphemistically called 'political parties') and the loose structure of a federal arrangement created a 'free for all' atmosphere in the area of foreign policy where cohesion was needed. To cite an extreme example, Sir Ahmadu Bello, the Premier of the Northern regional government and leader of the N.P.C. had a clear perception of his 'government's' stance on the Middle East issue. While Israel still maintained a diplomatic presence in Lagos (a clear indication that the central government had not taken any decision adverse to Israel); Sir Ahmadu Bello made his contrary pronouncements without due regard for the stance of the federal government.[9]

Much of the basic structure of the first civilian republic was drawn by the British without a clear perception of the complexities of a heterogenous society. Mistrust and fear of domination of one ethnic group by another seemed to have been the basis of establishing powerful regions and a relatively weak centre, a strong centre dominated and controlled by one ethnic group was capable of posing a threat to the development of the regions.[10] The result was that, the regions were actively almost unilateral, virtually eliminating the central government as the principal actor in the political system.

Furthermore, there were divergencies of objectives even on national issues. Nigerian leaders were neither committed to unity nor had coherent policies. Regional polarities however, did not prevent state to state or federal and state interaction on vital issues, but such meetings only served to highlight the fundamental weaknesses of the domestic political structure. In the view of one observer :

> Inter-regional boards composed of ministers tended to be like meetings of the (U.N.) Security Council. Each Government states its position; positive action consists largely in accepting a proposal in principle—which is not normally the end of it—and each goes merrily along negotiating for its own steel mill, even though everyone knows that no more than one mill would be economic . . .'[11]

This picture represents the character and pattern of the political system in the first civilian republic.

A new generation of policy makers appeared with the disintegration of the coalition government. But it took two successive military coups and a threat of secession to dismantle the old structure that had seriously impeded the pursuit of a cohesive foreign policy. The military government's response to the perceived threat was the sudden fragmentation of the regional centres of power from four to twelve in 1967, and later to nineteen, after a careful consideration of the report of a commission instituted by the Muhammed administration.[12] With the substantial weakening of the traditional powers of the old regions, a more solid base for decision making and a unitary approach to foreign policy appeared imminent. The institutional framework provided by the division of states has rectified the lack of political power that the centre in the first republic displayed, in the face of regional interference in foreign relations.

The structure of the Nigerian political system is a fundamental aspect of the policy operational environment. Of at least equal importance is the constitutional framework within which the decision makers operate. It is beyond the scope of this study to offer comparable perspectives on the role of parliament and the role of the executive in the policy process. These roles have been thoroughly analyzed by various scholars.[13] What is relevant at this point is to examine more systematically the implications of the new Nigerian constitution for the conduct of foreign policy.

2 The New Constitution and Foreign Policy

It is clear that the major weakness of the first Nigerian political system had been the lack of a clear perception of the form of political association which will suit the realities of the country. A radical change became indicated and the new constitution was designed to accommodate the special needs of the Nigerian society.[14]

The framers of the new Nigerian constitution clearly set out to utilize federal arrangements to rectify the political problems that threatened the survival of the nation in the first decade of independence, and diverted the attention of the primary decision makers from foreign policy matters. This section is not intended to be a treatise on federalism. Nigerian federalism and its various stages has been studied and analysed extensively by various scholars.[15] The purpose of this section is to examine the foreign policy provisions of the federal constitution and to assess to what extent they will influence the foreign policy goals of the nation.

The major thrust of the new constitution is the promotion of African unity (of which Nigeria is a unit), world peace, international co-operation and understanding. Consonant with the traditional or enduring objective of Nigeria's foreign policy,[16] the constitution specifically states that:

> the state shall promote African unity as well as the local, political, economic, social and cultural liberation of Africa.[17]

Furthermore, the state shall promote:

co-operation conducive to the consolidation of universal peace
and mutual respect and friendship among all peoples and states
and shall combat racial discrimination in all its manifestations.[18]

These were grand objectives, but they left the definition of Nigeria's
interest in its broadest terms. It is not surprising then, that it has
proved difficult at times to develop a national consensus on the methods for achieving these goals. A few prime examples of the diverse
perspectives held by foreign policy experts, the National Assembly and
the enlightened public will shed some light on the problem.

Beginning with the foreign policy provisions of the constitution
itself, several scholars questioned the fluid nature of these goals and
whether in fact they were meant to be hierarchically ordered to reflect
the priorities of the nation, which should rightly be national security
and the protection of societal values.[19] Diversity of opinion on the
broad objectives and the methods for accomplishing them have also
occurred on matters relating to the conduct of Nigeria's African
policy.[20] The Nigeria-Cameroun crisis is a case in point. The fundamental questions raised are: should the goal of African unity enshrined
in the constitution be pursued at all costs? Should African unity take
precedence over Nigeria's defence and security? While these questions
reflect the national mood, they are by no means reminiscent of the
lack of general agreement on broad policy issues that characterised
the first republic.

Perhaps the most significant contribution of the constitution to the
area of foreign policy is the system of power allocation. The system is
organised as a matrix and powers are divided along different arenas—
federal, state and local. Unlike the independence or 1963 constitution
where regions were allowed to share many of their powers with the
central government, the new constitution clearly delineates the powers
of the central government in the formulation and execution of foreign
policy.

By the terms of the constitution, the president (the executive) is the
pivot of the foreign policy process. The formal executive authority
granted in the exclusive legislative list include the conduct of foreign
affairs, defence, negotiation of treaties, (in the case of treaties, a
ratification vote by a majority of the states is required) foreign trade
and foreign investments.[20] On schedule 1, item 7, for example, the
borrowing of money outside Nigeria for the purpose of the federal
or state government is securely under the exclusive legislative list.

The reasons for this can be found in the abuse of such freedoms by the old regions in the first republic.[21]

Although it is clear that the constitution confers on the executive the pivotal role in foreign affairs (as indicated by the list of powers which came under the exclusive control of the federal government), there is some degree of power sharing or 'checks and balances', to limit the abuse of power. The 'sharing' or separation of powers can be found in the relations between the executive and the legislative. The President appoints and receives ambassadors, high commissioners and representatives. The President is empowered to negotiate, sign and implement treaties on matters on the Exclusive list. But the constitution specifies that such treaties must be enacted into law by the National Assembly before they can be regarded as law. Where the treaty relates to matters not on the Exclusive list, then the treaty or act of the National Assembly ratifying the treaty must be ratified by a majority of the State Assemblies. In the view of one observer, this is a serious limitation of presidential power—particularly with regard to multilateral treaties.[22] He surveys the possibility that the President may renege on a multilateral treaty if all the state assemblies do not ratify a treaty that was already approved by the National Assembly because it was found not to be on the Exclusive list. The implication, of course, is that the states could creep into the area of foreign policy an area which appeared to have been the exclusive preserve of the executive.

The President is Commander-in-Chief of the armed forces, but he is not empowered to commit the military resources of the country for war or peace without the prior consent of the Senate. Article 5, paragraph 3 (a) specifies that 'while the President can declare war, only a joint session of the National Assembly can authorise a declaration of war by the President'.[23] This is further reinforced by the provision of Article 53 (b) which states that 'no military personnel shall be deployed on combat duty outside Nigeria'.[24]

While the war provisions of the constitution ensure the dual purpose of responsibility sharing between the executive and legislative branches and a check on the potential excesses of the President, they seriously limit the power of the President to act swiftly in times of national crisis. In addition, it reduces the credibility of the President in Nigeria's relations with its immediate neighbours who expect some degree of security co-operation in times of threat. Akinyemi in an address to the Nigerian Senate on the 'Presidential System and International Relations' built a typical scenario:

> If one of our neighbours who is so friendly with Nigeria sends information at 12 midnight that there is a mercenary invasion about to take place in his country. He sends a frantic 'what are you going to do to help me' message. The President gets in touch with the President of the Senate, the Senate leader or Speaker—relaying the urgency of the neighbour's problem. But under the constitution the President cannot commit his troops because he must wait for the National Assembly to meet to authorise him to declare war. The National Assembly is unable to meet because it is on recess. By the time the help reaches the neighbour, the threat would have been executed for the worse.[25]

There are two problems here: firstly the deliberative process itself, as well as the need for Senate approval would undermine the speed and secrecy needed on such sensitive issues. Secondly, the inevitable reaction of Nigeria's neighbours would be that Nigeria could not be relied upon to respond swiftly when assistance is called for. This attitude in the long-term may even lead to a dimunition of Nigeria's influence in the West African sub-region.

In spite of these limitations on executive power, the formal constitutional sources of executive authority points to a pre-eminence of the President in foreign affairs. The President's immense authority is further accentuated by the lack of specificity on the branch of government that has jurisdiction over such vital Exclusive list matters as arms, ammunition and explosives banks, borrowing of money outside Nigeria, citizenship, naturalisation and deportation of aliens.[26] Also, as noted at the beginning of this section, the constitution has failed to spell out comprehensively the goals, and priorities of foreign policy. The logical and perhaps inevitable direction of this is that the President will have to define the goals and objectives of foreign policy in his own perception of the national interest.

The constitution has been operational long enough to provide a basis for predicting its future in the area of foreign policy. The structure of the presidential system itself as well as the provisions of the constitution have created new political conditions that will strengthen and condense broad national interests against sectoral interests. This in turn will make it possible for Nigeria to achieve a greater degree of domestic political strength and a greater degree of control of foreign relations. But the constitution as a superstructure can only influence and condition the domestic base to a limited extent. For without a corresponding change in the material conditions extant in the system, the political structure and the constitution may be ineffective.

So far, in matters relating to executive and legislative sharing of powers, there have been no spectacular disagreements over foreign policy issues.

The legislature appears to have conceded the role of foreign policy to the President. On occasions such as the deployment of Nigerian troops to Chad and the duration of their stay, the legislative branch has exercised its constitutional powers only in a 'benign' manner.

The unity of Nigeria and the state of the economy are the two key elements that will enhance or undermine the effectiveness of the constitution. Nigeria in the 1980s and beyond may erect a viable political order that could serve as a springboard for the attainment of a genuine, credible middle power status.[27] If the long prevailing ethnic sentiments retain their vigour and intensity, the future of Nigeria's political development could change in the direction of internal conflicts and instability.

The most desirable future shows Nigeria more deeply integrated with the rest of the world, creating opportunities for international influence without undue external pressures. The receptivity of the foreign policy bureaucracies (who implement policy) to the new foreign policy environment will help create the conditions for such a scenario. An important characteristic feature of foreign affairs is the vital role which the foreign policy bureaucracy plays in the formulation and implementation of policies. The Nigerian foreign policy bureaucracy has served as one important mechanism for the advancement of the country's foreign policy goals and objectives, and it is possible that the continuity will not be disturbed in the future. The following section offers a brief analysis of the prognosis of the foreign policy bureaucracy.

3. The Foreign Policy Bureaucracy and the New Frontier

Although the purpose of chapter two is to examine the impact of the elements of the internal environment (within which decision makers operate) on the past, current and future foreign policy of Nigeria, an understanding of the principal instrument for implementing the policies is crucial. Afterall, the test of execution in foreign policy is whether it produces efficiency and effectiveness in the nation's foreign relations.[28]

It is difficult to ascertain with any precision the role played by the Ministry of External Affairs and the degree of influence exerted by the foreign minister in the civilian government. The approach of the Prime Minister, Sir Abubakar did not create much room for initiative or maximum participation for the external ministry. He appeared to have taken a personal hand in the formulation and execution of policy. The evidence are discernable from Aluko's examination of the foreign service. He observes that :

> For the first ten months of independence the Prime Minister remained his own Foreign Minister.[29]

Further, 'the Prime Minister preferred policy papers on foreign relations from the Cabinet office to those emanating from External Affairs'.[30]

Under the military regime, activism in foreign policy created a more visible role for the foreign ministry. The Commissioner for External Affairs, as they were labelled, became integrated with the policy making authority. Okoi Arikpo, Joseph Garba, both External Affairs Commissioners, enjoyed pre-eminence in foreign policy.

The new constitution excludes the Minister of External Affairs from the constitution's list of membership of the Defence Council. This omission underscores his role as the President's principal assistant for the formulation of foreign policy and conduct of diplomacy. However, in practice, Ishaya Audu, the Minister of External Affairs assumed a central role in Nigeria's international policy. He made public pronouncements on the crucial international problems affecting Nigeria, working closely with his ministry. However, it is difficult to discern much difference in the present role of the Ministry of External Affairs from what it was during the first civilian republic. Like the first republic, it is still rigid and ultraconservative, clearly indicative of its colonial beginnings.

The Presidential system of government points to an enhanced role not only for the Ministry of External Affairs, but also for other agencies like the Defence, and Information Ministries, the National Security Organisation, the Ministry of Finance and other Executive agencies that might be remotely connected with the foreign policy

It is generally accepted that foreign policy is power politics—power in all its ramifications : military, diplomatic, information (to put it precisely) intelligence, and even intellectual power. If this assumption is true, Nigeria should equip itself with a foreign policy bureaucracy which would be a useful tool for formulating and implementing foreign policy and carrying on foreign relations. To a great degree, the information, trade and defence ministries have been incorporated into the foreign policy bureaucracy of the present administration. This new style will require co-ordination in planning and implementation to ensure coherence. With Nigeria's increasing role in world affairs, the various agencies enumerated above could assist in the smooth functioning and co-ordination of the policy process—budgetary affairs, military doctrines, gathering and interpreting information, research and analysis of various foreign policy issues.

In addition, a case could be made for a special advisory body in the foreign policy process. By the terms of the constitution, the President is responsible for the conduct of foreign relations. For this function, the National Defence Council and the National Security Council will become crucial in bearing some responsibility in foreign policy making, and fulfilling national security objectives. Given the formal statutory status of the National Defence Council and the National Security Council, much of their time and energy will be consumed by day to day affairs of state, programme decisions, and long term problems. The National Security Council may be limited by the time, energy and skills at its disposal and this will tend to limit the thoroughness of its deliberations on foreign policy issues. Specifically, time pressures may seriously restrict the number of possible courses of action which may be explored in a given situation. Since these bodies have finite time and energy, they will of necessity rely on other agencies to assist in the formulation of foreign policy.

Thus the need would arise to create a select sub-committee of the institutions under review, not only to broaden the base of these Institutions and give it a pluralistic character, but also to expose the executive to expert opinion on foreign policy issues. The utilization of expertise from 'inside' and 'outside' of government, will encourage imput from those who might be able to provide somewhat different perspectives on foreign policy issues. Clearly, in times of crisis, when national security is judged to be gravely threatened, and matters demand immediate attention and action, such a specialised sub-committee would obviously enhance the President's perspectives as well as greatly enhance the information and skills available to the statutory bodies.

It is eminently clear that there are qualities that will distinguish the advocated sub-committee from the normal foreign policy making body.

These are:

(a) Expertise: staffing it with those who are most knowledgeable in foreign affairs; they will bring valuable insights to the formulation of policy.

(b) Proximity to the Capital, that is, the seat of government. The need for speed in decision making cannot be ignored. This body therefore must be available to be summoned for short-run crisis-management. The proposal then is that:

1. Relevant expertise be brought in from institutions such as the Nigerian Institute of International Affairs, the Universities, and individuals of independent mind, integrity and experience, with secure home basis outside of government. The President may also abstract from the NDC and the NSC those members who may contribute technical expertise regarding security and military affairs which the non-military advisers do not possess.

2. Arrangement should be provided for this sub-committee to brainstorm some of its ideas weekly; before taking them up with the National Security Council; they would appraise policy issues, and propose policy strategies. These weekly meetings can play a highly useful role in providing an opportunity for the President to set the tone in foreign policy.

3. The President would bring in others as needed, ad hoc.

4. Contacts with the NSC and NDC would be regular, preferably as often as two days of intensive meetings bi-monthly. In this regard, establishing linkages is imperative for the effective co-ordination of the various inputs.

5. Individual members of this sub-committee would exploit their home bases, whether research institutions such as the Nigerian Institute of International Affairs or Universities, to bring to the notice of members of the committee specialised knowledge about potentially useful and relevant work done elsewhere. On the whole, the significance of this sub-committee is that the executive branch will have a resource group, where issues of foreign policy will be debated and hammered out before being presented to the President through the NSC, or directly to the President.

While it is eminently clear that the President must ultimately choose the course that is finally adopted, as the constitution naturally placed that responsibility on him, it is vital that the President listens to different well-prepared advocates making the best cases for alternative options and amply providing perceptions and insights.

Perhaps the United States blockade of Cuba during the 1962 missile crisis provides a classic case of how rational decision making by an ad hoc executive committee was perfected. It was a crisis decision by a small group of fifteen men assembled by the President in the context of ultimate threat to the security of the United States. The Committee spent about five days in session canvassing all the possible tracks and weighing the arguments for and against each course of action. Finally, the U.S. government's choice of the blockade was the best option available from six categories of action considered by the Executive Committee of the U.S. National Security Council. In situations of extreme urgency such as the one described above, (and in fact, Nigeria may not be immune to such crises) the executive branch would need a committee, that is informal, perhaps ad hoc, but nonetheless authoritative.

4. Economic Factors

In general terms, economic development has remained for a long time one of the principal objectives of the various Nigerian administrations. The result is that Nigeria's foreign policy has been conditioned by economic considerations. In the sketch that follows, some salient economic factors influencing Nigeria's pursuit of low-keyed policies in the first civilian republic and the subsequent vigorous, assertive foreign policy in the years that followed will be examined. Economic influences on foreign policy in the new civilian administration and their likely consequences for the future of Nigeria will be discussed.

Two major economic factors inevitably affect the capability of a state to pursue its stated goals :

(a) the ability of the economy to mobilise and deploy its productive forces and

(b) the degree of external dependence of the economy.

Nigeria at independence was well endowed with human and natural resources. By its sheer geographical size and comparatively large population, it possessed a greater development potential relative to most African countries.

Agricultural products accounted for over 61 per cent of the total value of exports. The possession of key raw materials would have provided a relatively stronger economic base for development, but there were strong forces impeding any form of accelerated economic development. One of them was the economic pull of Britain. Britain's intense need for Nigeria's agricultural resources and raw materials was manifest in the colonial pattern of trade established during the years before Nigeria's independence. Nigeria provided continuity by maintaining the character of its colonial economic structures which was designed essentially to solidify Nigeria's dependence on Britain for trade. The inevitable consequence was the heavy dependence of Nigeria's economy on the fluctuating British prosperity. The leadership believed that the most effective means of achieving national economic and social development objectives was to develop the economy along the capitalist path.[31] Consequently, Nigeria found its external trade very dependent on British economy and deliberately minimised trade with the communist bloc. During the period 1960-1962 for example, over 50 per cent of Nigeria's foreign trade was transacted with the Commonwealth. In 1965, over 53 per cent of foreign investments in Nigeria were owned by British enterprises. Similarly, the developed industrialised western nations made their appearance on the Nigerian economic scene in the first decade of independence. They not only dominated Nigeria's external trade, but also controlled the sources of foreign aid. The tables below illustrates the overwhelming pro-western bias of Nigeria's economic orientation during the period under review:

Table I

Nigeria's Foreign Trade: 1960 – 1970 (in millions of US $)

	Unit	1960	1966	1967	1968	1969	1970
Exports to:							(7 mo.)
1. United States	Million US $	45	63	53	49	112	71
2. United Kingdom	,,	226	295	199	174	246	211
3. Netherlands	,,	60	73	87	76	120	111
4. Germany (Fed. Rep.)	,,	36	78	71	50	54	45
5. Communist bloc	,,	2	9	21	28	29	25
Imports from (c.i.f.)							
1. United States	,,	32	116	78	62	82	77
2. United Kingdom	,,	256	214	181	168	242	179
3. Japan	,,	78	40	53	20	26	33
4. Germany (Fed. Rep.)	,,	43	77	71	59	74	50
5. Communist bloc	,,	11	27	38	33	38	28
Totals:							(est.)
Exports, f.o.b.	,,	475	793	680	587	9051	235
Imports, c.i.f.	,,	−604	−718	−626	−541	−6961	100
Trade balance	,,	−129	75	54	46	209	135

Source: USAID., Economic Data Book, Africa. Revision No. 257, April, 1971, p. 6.

Table II

Nigeria's Foreign Trade: 1960 – 1970 (in million pounds)

Importing countries		Exporting countries	
Great Britain	402,2	USA	1,583.5
FRG	264,7	Great Britain	978.3
USA	213,1	The Netherlands	794.1
France	114,6	France	581.8
The Netherlands	81,0	FRG	413.8

Source: Apter. D., Africa South of the Sahara, 1976 – 1977, (London 1976, p. 644).

Table III

UK – Nigeria Trade (in million pounds)

	1977 £m	1978 £m	1979 £m	1980 £m
UK exports	1,069	1,133	637	1,204
UK imports	219	286	186	151
Balance	+850	+847	+451	+1,053

Source: West Africa, March 23, 1981, p. 607.

Nigeria's weak economic standing necessitated her inescapable dependence on foreign aid and investments to finance a substantial part of her development projects, for example, 44 percent of the gross capital required for the implementation of the First Development Plan (1962-68) were derived from external sources.[32]

This over-reliance on the industrialised countries of the West for a critical supply of technology and capital for development was one of the major factors influencing Nigeria's pursuit of a conservative foreign policy in the first decade of independence. Nnoli, in his analysis of Nigeria's Southern Africa policy, has suggested that Nigeria's pursuit of its national objectives was constrained by a strong dependence on western capitalist nations. He cited as a prime example , Nigeria's inability to implement the 1965 OAU Ministerial Council's resolution to severe diplomatic relations with Britain for maintaining a benign silence over Ian Smith's rebellion in Rhodesia. According to him, 'Nigeria was incapable of paying the political and economic costs of such an action'.[33]

Nigeria appeared to have entered the second decade of her independence with greater economic potential, showing more confidence and greater political will than it did in the first. As Nigeria's economy gained in strength, the economic policies shifted to what appeared to be toward more self-reliance. For example, the Gowon administration immediately set out to accelerate this process with the promulgation of the Nigerian Enterprises Promotion Decree of 1972. This decree appeared to have been designed to develop the economy at home, assert greater control over the process of development through substantial indigenous participation and reduce dependence on foreign sources. It was a response to a serious concern about the dangers and consequences of becoming too dependent on external sources for national development. Various explanations have been offered for the failure of the indigenisation decree, however, its adverse impact on foreign policy need only be mentioned.

Ake's 'Revolutionary Pressures in Africa' and Eze's 'Multinationals and Manpower in Nigeria . . . ' point out that the indigenisation concept in African economies, and in Nigeria in particular has been subordinated to the consolidation of the ruling class.[34] Implicit in this is the establishment of a new accommodation with neocolonial dependence rather than its elimination. In sum dependence is incompatible with an assertive foreign policy.

By the end of the civil war, Nigeria acquired a new economic strength. The boom in the oil industry not only accelerated the economic growth rate, but also greatly enhanced its potential standing on the international arena. Petroleum output at the end of 1970 rose from one and a quarter million barrels a day to two million barrels a day in 1976.[35] Similarly, the economic growth rate rose astronomically from 3.5 per cent in 1966/67 to 12 per cent in 1971/72. In addition, the spectacular success of OPEC oil price increases in 1973/74 and the resultant rise of Nigeria as a potentially rich country was clearly reflected in the nation's earnings. The value of exported oil rose from ₦2,914 million in 1970 to ₦5,523 million in 1974. Between 1962-74, petroleum as a proportion of total exports rose from 10 per cent to about 40 per cent. In fact the Federal government realised a surplus of over ₦3 billion. of revenue in excess of expenditures of 1974 fiscal year, making it possible to finance the Third Development Plan (1975-1980), an expenditure of ₦30 billion without the traditional dependence on external funding[36].

The primary interest of any sovereign state is to avoid dependence by establishing a strong economic base for development and utilize such a base as a political leverage to act in its external relations. Nigeria did not expand its agricultural sector as fast as it did with its import substitution industries. Here again, the vital importance of food for a large and accelerating population is highlighted by the increasing food import bill and import substitution business. This means that the economy cannot maintain a self-sustaining growth.

The sudden changes in world economic conditions occasioned by the enormous increase in oil prices in the early 70s gave Nigeria a new kind of 'independence'. The improved state of Nigeria's economy essentially resulting from its vast oil earnings bestowed on it a leverage which it did not possess in the first decade of independence. More significant perhaps, was the government's ability to determine its own policies independent of external influences. As Aluko observes:

> The phenomenal growth of the economy largely as a result of the oil boom . . . has strengthened Nigeria's position in relations with the super powers . . . . Neither of the super powers can now use foreign aid as a means of political leverage on Nigeria . . . Heavy American dependence on Nigeria's oil (means) that Nigeria is free not only to criticise the United States but also to put pressure on her.[37]

The observation above describes the conditions influencing subsequent foreign policy decisions and indeed, Nigeria's external behaviour. Beginning with General Muhammed's rebuff of United State's President Gerald Ford over the issue of Angola, the subsequent recognition of the MPLA faction as the legitimate government of Angola, the Nationalisation of Barclays Bank, and British petroleum for sanction bursting over aparthied South Africa, to a 'strong neighbour' role in the Chad conflict; Nigeria became poised to act with more self-confidence on 1 October, 1979.

The Shagari administration became heir to the strong economic position and confidence of its predecessors. To that extent, it maintained the tempo of Nigeria's assertiveness in its external behaviour. The continuity was reflected in Nigeria's active participation in the Lancaster House proceedings that led to the independence of Zimbabwe. A firm note of protest from President Shagari to the British government on the issue of Zimbabwe, reminiscent of the Murtala Mohammed era, was an indication that Nigeria would not relent its efforts to ensure justice and dignity for Africa in the liberation process. The President warned that :

> Unless agreement is reached on the transitional arrangements, no agreement should have been deemed to be reached on the constitution . . .[38]

Nigeria's peace-keeping role in Chad, even though futile had drained a substantial portion of the resources that would have been otherwise committed to other goals. The President has also given renewed emphasis to the liberation of Namibia and the eradication of apartheid in South Africa. It may be stated that this renewed commitment, perhaps, springs from the President's perception of the domestic economy. The liberation of Africa requires a commitment of resources and the President seemed to reaffirm it.

> At independence, when economically this nation had so little Nigeria did not hesitate to commit itself politically as well as financially to the struggle for the liberation of Africa. Today, Nigeria is economically better of and the present administration has no hesitation in furthering the commitment of this nation to the struggle . . .[39]

This official pronouncement in November 1980 presumed that Nigeria's oil revenue would accelerate and that the new administration will be able to manage the domestic economy and use it to project a firm foreign policy. However it presently seems that the period of the Nigerian oil prosperity or 'boom' is virtually over, and this could present a major economic constraint on Nigeria's foreign policy if a. less fragile base for national economic development is not urgently developed.

It is noteworthy that Nigeria's earnings since the middle of 1980 to the beginning of 1982 have not matched its commitments. Although petroleum production fluctuated from 700,000 barrels per day in August 1981, to 1.6 million barrels per day in November 1981, to 1.4 million barrels per day in January 1982, informed guesses place future oil output at less than the August 1981 figure.[40] Allied with the low level of oil production is the diminishing foreign exchange reserves which has not kept pace with the total import bill. The foreign exchange reserves declined from ₦5.1 billion in the middle of 1981 to ₦1 billion in March 1982.[41] The Fourth National Development Plan, (1981-1985) estimated to cost ₦82 billion was based on an oil output of 2.1 million barrels per day at $36. Specifically, the 1982 planned budget presumed an estimated 1.3 million barrels per day of oil at market price of $36.

With the sharp decline in world oil demand,[42] the budgetary and long-term economic plans of the administration are bound to suffer reversals. Infact, the President's response to the economic crisis underlined the vulnerability of the Nigerian economy. Strict remedial measures were announced including the reduction of travel allowance for all categories of citizens, and a reduction of imports.[43]

The conclusion to be drawn from the above examination of the state of the domestic economy is simple; a chronic trade account deficit, inflation, a rising foreign debt and particularly an umbilical dependence on one source of revenue for expenditures, promises to keep the country undeveloped and dependent for a long time. This is not to imply that the prospects appear hopeless in the long run. The main point is that Nigeria's dependence on oil will be a source of weakness in future, for it is inevitably a wasting asset. The Nigerian economy has a traditional dependence on oil for revenues. All sectors, including agriculture, manufacturing and mining (especially coal) have not expanded to meet the increasing needs of both the internal and external markets. The economy has not diversified its area of growth, and therefore has become less resilient than in the early years of indepencence. The President confirmed the debilitating nature of the global oil glut:

> Since the government depends on oil revenues for 83 per cent of
> its expenditures, the sudden decline in the oil sector has had
> serious impacts on our domestic finance.[44]

He said further:

> The painful truth is that since we can only hopefully wait for the
> developments in the external sector to change in our favour, a
> slow change which we cannot really influence . . .[45]

Implicit in the President's statements is that Nigeria's ability to
meet its obligations in and outside Nigeria may be heavily dependent
upon successive booms in oil. Substantial petroleum reserves have
been discovered in other strategic areas of the world such as Latin
America, the North Sea, the South Atlantic and Alaska. Alternative
sources of energy are increasingly being developed by the industrialised
states in their quest for 'independence' from oil cartels, and oil itself
as a source of energy. Thus, it becomes possible to imagine Nigeria
a 'fragile giant' in the future.

A worse scenario involves a continuation of the current economic
trend to the end of the 1980s: the world economy continues the
inflationary spiral and the industrialised states maintain the 'squeeze'
on OPEC. Import bills rise because the domestic economy cannot be
sustained without capital goods imports. The foreign exchange reserves
maintain a steady decline. The government is forced to borrow from
the Western banks thereby increasing its indebtedness. More stringent
austerity measures are imposed on the domestic fund and government
spending is reduced. The unemployment thus created and the burden
of the economic measures create discontent and social imbalance—
destabilising influences. The fragile domestic environment of the first
years of independence resurface, not only undermining Nigeria's ability
to act assertively in its external interaction but also compelling it to
divert attention to the domestic arena. A country which had been
distinguished by its successes in the international arena loses its credibility.

A more favourable scenario would be the diversification of Nigeria's
economy. President Shagari has rightly identified the present problem
as 'the global economic and geopolitical calculations of the major

industrial nations to break OPEC.'[46] Having identified the problem, it is fair to assume that the government will diversify its domestic economy especially in the agricultural and manufacturing sectors, produce much of its own machinery and reduce dependence on external loans and foreign investment. A heavy emphasis on agriculture will increase prospects for agricultural exports and meet domestic needs. A dynamic economy will provide the government with an enduring basis of political legitimacy at home and credibility abroad. These pre-requisites of power will only be achieved when it is perceived that the future of Nigeria is largely in Nigeria's hands. As in the past, the economy will be a factor of critical importance in determing Nigeria's future course.

5. Military Factors

The basic aims of national security, defence and self-preservation have been one of the priorities of Nigerian governments.[47] The military resources of the country in the first civilian republic were abysmally low. The Nigerian armed forces consisted primarily of the 'officer' cadre, performing a ceremonial role and could at best play only a limited role in either the strategic defence or security of the nation. Perhaps, the low level of military resources can be found in the threat perception of the leadership. Usually, defence and security planning are based on threat perception and the nature of possible military threats. It appears that there was almost an absence of a strong perception of external threat to Nigeria's security in the Balewa era. If the possibility existed that anyone may threaten, it seemed the Anglo-Nigerian Defence Pact signed in 1960 would guarantee Nigeria some immunity from possible threats. This paternalistic attitude of Britain toward Nigeria was conceived at the Constitutional Conference in London in 1958 when it was agreed that after the attainment of independence, Nigeria would be subject to intense communist pressure.[48] The vulnerability of the Nigerian defence apparatus became clear during the 1962 and 1964/65 riots in the Western Region and among the Tivs. Local police practically unarmed or armed with tear gas and battons were almost overwhelmed by rioters. The armed forces itself could at best only contain internal upheaval.

However, the civil war (July 1967–January 1970) necessitated the expansion of the military establishment. The ardous, but successful prosecution of the war required a redefinition of Nigeria's military capability needs. In providing the armed establishment with the capacity to deal with not only internal but also external threats, it was necessary to include several means to cope with the problem. Thus, Nigeria acquired between 1967 to 1977 a substantial standing army of over 230,600 men.[49] Defence expenditures also increased from ₦314.8 million in 1970 to ₦1,166.7 million in 1975-1976, an astronomical increase of about 400 per cent.[50] Partly prompted by its new found strength and its concern for the security of its West African neighbours, Nigeria extended military support to Guinea in 1970 when she was faced with the threat of a mercenary invasion. In the intervening years, the Nigerian military establishment has performed peace-keeping roles— in Chad and Lebanon, specifically. But these are not in any way indicative of Nigeria's capability for defence.

This raises the question of defence planning to meet the security needs of Nigeria and especially to support its foreign policies. The primary, vital questions of all defence planning are: who might threaten the peace and security of the nation? What would be the purpose of the threat? In what form could the threat be executed? The Libyan military presence and involvement in Chad and the affront to Nigeria's security and territorial integrity in May 1981 by Camerounian security forces offers the clearest answers to the above questions. As one Nigerian newspaper put it, 'the events in the Nigerian Cameroun border conflict has highlighted several deficiencies in the conduct of Nigerian foreign policy'.[51] One of those deficiencies is the absence of a defence policy. Of course, even if the possibility of an external attack did not exist, security for the country should be assured.

Indeed, a crucially important component in any leading role for Nigeria in the future must be military and security development. The need to strengthen the combat effectiveness of Nigeria's army was stressed by Akinyemi in his analysis of the essence of a leading role for Nigeria. He observed that Nigeria is still a paper tiger with neither paratroopers nor other facilities to 'toughen up' the army; 'Unless these shortcomings are rectified,' he noted, 'Nigeria will not be able to play the role of a first class power in Africa'. Akinyemi further observed that Nigeria's weak defences will make it more difficult to pursue a strong domestic programme of economic nationalism, since she will be open to military blackmail by even a third rate European power .[52]

Defence capability assumes that international coercion is not declining. The accelerating military expenditures of governments at the global level is an indication that governments place a premium on self preservation and expect interventions even from their neighbours. In the case of Nigeria, its defence capability remains low relative to other 'Middle Powers' like Brazil and India or Argentina. Manwaring has produced a detailed study establishing the relative military capability ranking of selected countries like Brazil, Nigeria, Turkey South Korea and Argentina. In his view, these countries represent major geographic regions, have a wide range of military strategic defence requirements, and importantly, they represent the large cluster of 'lesser' or 'emerging' powers.[53] The results of his analysis shown in the tables confirms the low level of Nigeria's military capability.

Nigeria's armed forces consisting basically of the army, the navy and the airforce, could with a long range defence planning become a potentially formidable force with an army of approximately 160,000, and a navy of only 7,000. But the army has been characterised by its profound lack of modern military equipment to meet the needs of external threats.[55] The army is equipped with only a limited number of light tanks and armoured cars and personnel carriers. Vogt, a Nigerian defence strategist noted:

> The Nigerian army does not possess medium or heavy tanks of the T-54, F-55 and T-62 varieties that are in the arsenals of several North African countries.[56]

At a glance, it may be noted that in spite of Nigeria's armed forces strength in terms of size (AFT); its relative military capability especially in terms of quality (RCM) scores in terms of potential is expectedly low. This deficiency indicates an urgent need to accelerate its (RCM) faster than most of the powerful states of the world.

This picture is demoralising when compared with Brazil's army equipped with 60 medium tanks, 550 light tanks, 150 armoured cars, 600 armoured personnel carriers, 105mm, and 90mm artillery, Cobra antitank weapons, Roland surface-to-air missiles and Oerlikan antiaircraft guns.[57]

The Nigerian navy had been the most disadvantaged arm of the forces, but in recent times has began to modernise and acquire equipment. The principal equipment include two frigates, three corvettes,

Table 4:

Graphically, Max G. Manwaring presented the model as follows:

Armed Forces Strength

Number of Personnel in Armed Forces	(AFT)
Theoretical capacity to produce 20kt	
weapons	(NUC)

Reach

Merchant Marine Tonnage	(REI)	MILITARY
Number of passengers carried by		CAPABILITY
domestic airlines	(RE2)	

Infrastructure

Defence Expenditure per Capita	(DEP)
Arms Exports	(AEX)
Government Revenue per Capita	(GRP)

In addition, the relative military capability (RMC) of each country was scored and computed according to the following equation:

$$RMC = (^PAFT_{aw} - ^PNUC_{aw}) \times (^PRE1_{aw} - ^PRE2_{aw}) \times$$
$$(^PDEP_{aw} - ^PAEX_{aw} - ^PGRP_{aw})$$

RMC	=	Relative Military Capability
P	=	Percentage
aw	=	Adjusted Weight.

Table 4.1

Position of Relative Military Capability (RCM) of World Sample Countries 1968-1977

Rank	Country	RCM Scores
1	U.S.A.	7,533,000
2	U.R.S. (U.S.S.R.)	4,575,000
3	U.K.M. (United Kingdom)	558,000
4	F.R.A. (France)	320,000
5	F.R.G. (Fed. Rep. of Germany)	100,000
6.	J.A.P. (Japan)	99,000
7.	P.R.C. (Peoples Rep. of China)	57,000
8	S.P.A. (Spain)	16,376
9	C.A.N. (Canada)	14,584
10	I.T.A. (Italy)	13,981
11	N.E.T. (Netherlands)	3,506
12	I.N.D. (India)	3,493
13	G.D.R. (German Dem. Rep.)	3,069
14	S.K.O. (South Korea)	2,727
15	P.O.L. (Poland)	2,128
16	BRA (Brazil)	1,889
17	TUR (Turkey)	1,230
18	A.U.S. (Australia)	,796
19	A.R.G. (Argentina)	,417
20	E.G.T. (Egypt)	,363
21	I.N.O. (Indonesia)	,335
22	C.U.B. (Cuba)	,284
23	P.A.K. (Pakistan)	,227
24	M.E.X. (Mexico)	,171
25	A.L.G. (Algeria)	,147
26	N.I.G. (Nigeria)	,117
27	S.A.F. (South Africa)	,106
28	L.I.B. (Libya)	,102
29	S.U.D. (Sudan)	,024
30	Z.A.I. (Zaire)	,003

Table 4.II

Numbers in World Sample Armed Forces, 1979

Rent	Country	Number	Paft$_{aw}$
1	PRC	4,360,000	1136
2	URS	3,658,000	0953
3	USA	2,022,000	0527
4	IND	1,096,000	0285
5	SKO	619,000	0196
6	TUR	566,000	0147
7	FRA	509,000	0133
8	FRG	495,000	0129
9	PAK	429,000	0117
10	EGT	395,000	0103
11	ITA	365,000	0095
12	UKM	323,000	0084
13	SPA	321,000	0083
14	POL	317,000	0082
15	BRA	281,000	0073
16	JAP	241,000	0063
17	IND	239,000	0062
18	NIGERIA	193,000	0051
19	CUB	189,000	0049
20	GDR	159,000	0041
21	ARG	133,000	0034
22	NET	115,000	0030
23	MEX	100,000	0026
24	ALG	89,000	0023
25	CAN	80,000	0021
26	AUS	70,000	0018
27	SAF	63,000	0016
28	SUD	63,000	0016
29	LIB	42,000	0011
30	ZAI	21,000	0005

Source: Max G. Manwarring, 'Brazillian Military Power: A Capability Analysis of Brazil in the *International System: The Rise of a Middle Power.* Edited by Wayne A. Selcher (Westview Press Inc. Boulder Colo: 1981) pp. 65-98.

eight patrol crafts, two 1,300 roll-on-roll-off (RORO) tank landing ships. The quantity of ships is expected to increase this year.[58] The size of the navy appears too small to be effective in any naval operation. Numbers alone do not assure the fighting capability of a force, but they may indicate its effectiveness.

> The air force has an inventory of 24 combat aircrafts, 10 Puma and 10 Alouette III helicopters. Like the navy, its numerical strength is low and would need to be increased in terms of quality as well, to make its contribution significant.

This sketch of the size and strength of the armed forces has been presented to provide a picture of what Nigeria's military forces is like. Other variables such as the quality of training, equipment, morale, the ability to mobilise at short notice, the capability of intelligence service, technical skills and industrial capacity cannot be analysed in a short monograph.[59] In addition a lack of a comparative approach in this area makes the determination of Nigeria's military weakness more difficult. However, the future-oriented analysis is based on the normative assessment that Nigeria is still militarily unprepared to meet its perceived role in international politics, particularly in security affairs. In August 1975, Akinyemi stated in a Nigerian newspaper:

> Given the nature of the threat Africa is faced with, I believe that the target of Nigerian military preparedness should be parity with French military forces as a condition of minimum deterrence.[60]

This observation made over six years ago is still entirely applicable today.

The realities of international politics require that Nigeria re-examine its military preparedness, for foreign policy cannot be successful without the attributes capable of protecting national interests. In this regard, Nigeria in the future will have to increase the size of its armed forces and begin a long-term modernization programme in terms of education, training and equipment. Secondly, and perhaps most vital is for the country to develop a national military industrial complex. Its critical role in creating a viable productive capacity and military capability cannot be underscored. Brazil is one country where the positive effects of the development of the armaments industry has been most visible. In the case of Brazil, they have utilised economic growth to promote military power. The military future for Nigeria cannot be realised in the absence of a healthy economy. The economy cannot sustain an armed establishment that spends nearly 75 per cent of its budget on personnel.[61] If more resources are diverted to the military, the economy will suffer. Some Latin American countries have utilised the army for civic purposes—engaging them in peaceful pursuits. This strategy may show a long-term positive effect on the economy in terms of reducing costs of civil duties.

The most desirable future is one in which Nigeria would conceive a clearer direction of its defence policy and needs; and employ genuine strategies to fulfil those needs. The recent debate on Nigeria's defence routinely raises the question, 'Does Nigeria have a defence policy?'. The following excerpts from a daily newspaper editorial reaffirms the question:

> There is absolutely no doubt about it that the thinking of Nigerians about defence policy is obsolescent. The ordinary Nigerian has no concept of integrated defence. His idea of defence policy is that of bullets and guns and the uniformed individuals who live in the barracks . . . .
>
> How can we evolve a good policy when our bureaucrats have a colonial conception of defence and see the army as a hostile, alien force which should be isolated? These bureaucrats even seriously think they are helping the nation by feigning security cover on defence proposals and refusing to discuss or debate such a mundane issue as the defence budget . . . .
>
> We believe that the best way of evolving a sustaining defence policy is to look beyond the armed forces to the whole gamut of the national economy, our political and cultural background our weapons system and industrial base so that through integrated planning we may be able to arrive at a policy . . . .
>
> Though Nigeria may play no more than a minor role at the world level, it is likely to take a major part in the drama on the African continent and our policy should therefore aim at ensuring that we do this effectively.[62]

There appears to be a consensus among observers that the summary above is the preferred future for Nigeria if it is to be taken seriously by the world. It would not be going too far to remind the reader that Nigeria has a valuable resource (oil) that is both critical and political in today's world in spite of the current superficial 'oil glut'. There is the possibility that Nigeria may be vulnerable to attack from frustrated industrialised states.

The geopolitical realities of the West African sub-region also lead many observers to anticipate a possible French threat to Nigeria's security. Nigeria is surrounded by Francophone states most of whom are militarily weak, but have defence arrangements with France. Nigeria therefore must contend with foreign military presence along its borders.[63] While acknowledging that military power is no longer, in itself, a solid guarantee of influence and authority in global politics, the armed forces of a state can still be effective even when not militarily engaged.

6. Interest/Pressure Groups

In most organised polities, there is usually a built-in influence system—a term used as a synonym for interest or pressure group politic. Influence may take the form of demand on or support for government policies.[64] Nevertheless, it provides the basis of interaction between the rulers and the citizens, particularly the citizens who have basic interests to project. Viewed from a broad perspective, the policy-influence system serves variously as a barometer, a mirror, and pillar for the decision makers. What is the relevance of influencers or interest groups in governments? The remarkable insight of Coplin perhaps provides a succint answer to that question:

> The decision maker needs policy influencers because they are a source of support for his regime. In both democratic and autocratic states, the leaders depend to a large extent on the willingness of the members of society to provide support. Whether this support takes the form of loyalty of the army, the financial backing of businessmen, the electoral support of the people, or the willingness of the people not to take up arms against their government, it is vital to the decision maker because it makes his stay in office more certain and provides him with the resources to carry out his policies.[65]

Coplin indicates that policy influencers also make demands on the policy maker, which, if not satisfied in one way or another may lead to a 'partial or total withdrawal of support.'[66] The decision maker may choose to respond to these demands or ignore them; the important assumption here is that groups formed on the basis of shared values or attitudes exist in every state, and they make demands and attempt to influence policy decisions through various means.

Although Nigeria is a relatively young nation which has undergone the twists and traumas of changing political systems, it is clear that the policy makers have been subject to varying influences from diverse segments within the society. In the following perspectives on the past and present, the range of the types of interest groups that have emerged over the years and the degree of their impact on Nigeria's foreign policy will become visible.

Nigeria at Independence was characterised as a 'constitutional democracy.' In the public perception of a liberal democracy, it is logical that interest groups should naturally be prominent in the policy process and vociferous in their demands on the policy makers.[67]

Although it has been observed that the first Prime Minister, Sir Abubarka Tafawa Balewa essentially conducted foreign policy,[68] a number of interest groups did attempt to exert some influence on the foreign policy stances of the government. These groups ranged from political groups who were very critical of Nigeria's apparent pro-Western orientation to intellectuals, students, labour organisations and professional groups, notably the press. Their interests and demands were as varied in scope as in intensity. In the political realm, for example, Akinyemi has noted that;

> the attitudes taken by political system, which had their roots in the different religions of the Federation, and their methods of influencing were also conditioned by the country's federal structure.[69]

In the Congo crisis (which was the first foreign policy issue facing the Balewa government) the remarkable divergence of the views of the political parties, notably—the NPC, NCNC and AG greatly reflected the ethnic divisions and interests within the Nigerian society.[70] Akinyemi observed that:

> The Congo crisis was not only a foreign but was a domestic crisis for Nigeria as well. The Nigerian political groups had always differed ideologically on the structure of the Nigerian state, nation

building, and even economic programmes. This controversy was continued in their various attitudes to the Congo crisis. The support they gave to different factions in the Congo was ideologically determined.[71]

However, when there is a policy confrontation like the one between Nigeria and Ghana on the Congo issue, these political groups tended to present a united front with the Federal Government.[72] Other interests such as the trade unions, academics, student organisations and the press, who criticised the government's Congo policy derived such criticisms from their various perceptions, definition and interpretation of the problem. They ranged from a view of the United Nation's stance in the Congo as an impediment to African progress, to the Neo-imperialist scheme of the Western powers in the Congo. Although no visible impact was made on government policy by these pressures, Balewa and his foreign minister, Jaja Wachuku found themselves on several occasions making pronouncements in defence of government position.

Dissent and pressure on the Arab/Israeli conflict during the Balewa era reflected essentially the concerns of religious, and regional interests. While the NPC, a major and Northern dominated party urged the Federal government to severe all relationship with Israel, the Southern regional governments (consisting of the East and West) reaffirmed their friendship with Israel. Pronouncements by the leaders of the regions, Sir Ahmadu Bello, Dr. M.I. Okpara and Chief S.L. Akintola included such utterly partisan statements as, 'to my mind, Israel does not exist,' (Sir Ahmadu) 'I am myself an Israelite, I love and admire Israel,' (Okpara) and, 'you can be assured of our friendship and support at any place.'[73] It is possible to conclude that the views of these interests exerted considerable influence over the policy adopted toward Israel: the Federal government adopted an accommodation-centred policy—encouraging the diplomatic presence of Israel in Lagos with a reciprocal move in Tel Aviv.

The interpretation given the visible role of the political parties and their leaders in attempting to exert influence on policy, is that foreign affairs were salient to them. This was perhaps, the result of the considerable latitude they enjoyed in sharing foreign relations with the central government.

For the most part, it was almost impossible to ascertain precisely the degree of influence that any of the other non-political interest groups brought to bear on the policy-process, except in the case of the Anglo-Nigerian Defence Pact where the heightened pressures led to an immediate abrogation of the pact. One thing is clear however, as Idang observed, Nigerian foreign policy debates had strong 'ethnic and regional undertones' which 'undermined the interpretation and transmission of foreign policy issues throughout the society in meaningful terms.'[74] Foreign policy issues, therefore, usually became controversial and often lacked cohesion.

However, the unitary nature of the foreign policy body in the military era, (especially the Gowon period 1966-1975) limited to a considerable extent the role of interest groups located outside of government. The trend in the Gowon administration had been the influence of powerful bureaucratic and military institutions on the foreign policy process. The Ministry of External Affairs, the Super Permanent Secretaries and the Supreme Military Council were not only dominant in designing foreign policy, but also served as powerful interest groups on pressing for interests and policy prescriptions of their own.[75] Because the military needed expertise in the policy process, the bureaucracy became most effective in filling a vacuum of influence particularly in areas where long-standing policy was not clearly defined, and also in the implementation of policy.

The pre-eminence of bureaucratic policy influencers did not diminish with the advent of the Muhammed/Obasanjo regimes, rather a different style was adopted by the decision makers. From time to time, trade union leaders, academics, businessmen and relevant educational institutions were 'consulted' in an attempt to provide a pluralistic character for the foreign policy process. The Commissioner for External Affairs, Joe Garba, in stressing the pluralistic nature of his administration's foreign policy process stated:

> . . . since the attainment of Nigeria's Independence in 1960, no administration, civilian or military, has taken as much pains as this present administration, to take into full consideration, the temper of Nigeria's domestic public opinion . . . Indeed, I can say without any fear of contradiction that no government has done as much as this government in involving various categories of individuals and national institutions in its policy decision-making whether on domestic policies or on foreign policies.[76]

Influence was exerted by academic/institutional groups, such as the Nigerian Institute of International Affairs through formal channels often behind the scenes providing information and analyses for decision on a number of vital issues through policy papers.

For example, the decision of the Head of State, General Obasanjo to visit the United States in 1977 after a long freeze in Nigeria-U.S. relations and the highly visible and effective involvement of the Nigerian Institute of International Affairs during the 1978 Carter visit, demonstrate the ability of the Institution (aided essentially by the close personal association between the Director General and the military leaders) to exert sufficient influence to review or change policy. While it is true, as Garba stated, that his government 'allowed' the expression of diverse opinions on foreign policy issues, evaluating the extent of the influence of such opinions is a difficult problem.

In view of the nature of Nigeria's new system of participatory democracy (the Presidential system of government), it is to be expected that there will be an increase in politically active interest groups and a new preoccupation with pressure group politics. As in the past the foreign policy bureaucracy—comprising the ministries of External Affairs, Information, and Trade have been influential in the implementation of foreign policy if not in the initiation of policies. The minister for External Affairs, Professor Ishaya Audu, and the ministers in charge of the above ministries have direct access to the chief executive providing essential information for decisions, and advising on the diplomatic implications of policy options. Because most of these interactions occur behind the scenes, it is difficult to acquire data on the policy positions that these Ministers advocate to the President. However, one is left with the situation that the senior staff of the above ministries inevitably implement foreign policy decisions and they could have enormous impact on the shape of the policies.

The Nigerian Chamber of Commerce and Manufacturers Association have attempted to influence government economic policies. These groups believe in self-reliance-centred economic policies. Indeed, their basic foreign policy position can be viewed as self-preservative, seeking to influence government decisions on imports that could not only hinder the growth of their infant industries, but also decrease their projected profits.[77] The efficacy of this group is unclear, but because their belief and interests are generally shared by the government, (the national interest of self-reliance as a condition for development) the policy decisions on foreign economic issues appear to reflect their views.

As in the past, Nigerian political parties have to a lesser extent reflected the interests and divisions within the larger society.[78] There still exists dissonant positions on foreign policy issues, but the archetypical political positions that was displayed during the Congo crisis has diminished. Typical of the presidential system, political parties have cut across tribal and ethnic frontiers, the colossal Northern region has almost ceased to exist as a 'bloc' interest. In a few cases, however, some newspapers attempt to reflect in their demands or support the interest of the political parties, ethnic groups or individuals who control them. Thus, while the *Nigerian Tribune,* (a UPN controlled daily newspaper) utterly condemned President Shagari's 1981 visit to the United Kingdom as 'unpatriotic, ill-advised and a complete sellout,'[79] the *Daily Times* (that has federal government, participation) welcomed the visit as 'symbolic' . . . coming at a time when 'dynamism has become the key word in our foreign policy.'[80] Although this divergence appears to be the reaction of the press, considerable experience from the past indicates that they were responding to politically entrenched interests.

Central to any consideration of interest group activity in the present administration is an examination of the diverse demands on the government during the Nigeria/Cameroun border crisis. With the killing of five Nigerian soldiers on border patrol duty on 16 May, 1981, various segments of the public including political parties, the press, labour unions, student organisations, individuals, and even the armed forces advocated a confrontation with Cameroun. Details of the myriad of demands have been adequately analysed by Macebuh.[81] The pressure generated by the groups was sufficient to propel the country into war, but it was remarkable that it did not contribute significantly to President Shagari's decision to strenuously avoid a state of belligerency. Inferred from this observation is a question mark on the degree to which interests groups shape and limit Nigerian foreign policy. As a practical matter, Nigerian decision makers have often formulated policies on an exclusive basis, relying mainly on the *'Kitchen Cabinet'* of the bureaucracy, and perhaps the political military leadership. On the broadest level, group pressures have not heavily influenced policy. In the case of economic pressure groups, the options that appear to be a response to economic interests may be coincidental or the parallel response of the ruling elite to its own interests or as claimed, 'the national interest.' Perhaps, the abrogation of the Anglo-Nigerian Defence Pact of 1962 represent the unique exception of government 'response' to group pressures. But so far, that assessment is subjective and speculative, for no one could say precisely what conditioned the decision of a Prime Minister who 'made his own' foreign policy.

If Nigeria survives a few more years of participatory democracy, it is possible to say that there will be an enduring effort by motivated groups seeking to influence the making of Nigerian foreign policy, especially in the area of security, rather than just reacting to policies already formulated. It appears that the problem is not one of lack of articulation of demands, but essentially one of response from the decision makers. The potential for harnessing the remarkable human resources of Nigeria to achieve a more dynamic foreign policy lies in its utilisation of the various policy options openly or discreetly advocated, and also in the incorporation of serious, well-meaning groups into the policy process. As previously suggested in chapter 1, one of the greatest sources of important ideas is probably still in the academic community as they provide not only information but the 'scientific' bases on which to utilise such information. Greater participation in the policy process cannot come unless the decision makers demand it.

A greater political orientation in the future will necessitate more interest group contact with the centres of power, to change policy making an exclusive basis. The points at which the quest for a new orientation in the policy making environment will be influenced are: the National Assembly, the Office of the President, and to a lesser extent the Ministry of External Affairs. Through the process of lobbying, various interest groups can make policy suggestions. What seems to be required in addition to the lobbying strategy for policy input, is an effort to politicize the articulate and enlightened Nigerian public on issue areas. This is essential not only because it is desirable to involve people in a pluralistic society, but because their total imputs would add substantially to a more national and cohesive policy, rather than the compromise among ethnic/religious groups evident on the Israeli-Arab issue in the first civilian administration.

7. Idiosyncratic Factors

According to Akinyemi,

constitutional provisions form the skeleton: they are the bare bones. It is the personality of people running the system that puts the flesh on the skeleton giving us the recognizable form.[82]

The crucial importance of personality and psychological factors as a determinant of foreign policy appears to be succinctly articulated by Akinyemi. What Rosenau calls the 'idiosyncratic variable,'[83] should not be under played in any analysis of Nigeria's external behaviour, especially in view of the previous assertion in this chapter that foreign policy was largely determined by the Executive almost to the exclusion of other relevant groups. Also implicit in this observation is the possibility that the personality of the leaders (especially the Executive) had a substantial bearing on the policies formulated. Thus, the policies of the successive adminstrations can be explained by examining the personal traits of the leaders. It must be pointed out, however, that this is not intended to explain the course of Nigerian foreign policies exclusively in terms of personalities. It will be seen that the personality cannot be divorced from all the other variables examined so far in this chapter. The external environment of the decision maker which is no less an important factor of policy formulation will be examined in chapter three.

Decision makers are human beings and every human being perceives things differently depending on his cultural setting, genetic traits, religion or ideological orientation. The contention that Nigeria's foreign policy in the Balewa era was 'low keyed' and 'conservative' is based to a large extent on the Prime Minister's personal traits. Observers of his administration have variously described him as a 'calm and moderate man,' with a knack for compromise, 'his personality being more calculated to placate than to provoke',[84] Balewa's personality and perception of communism affected his attitudes toward communist countries, literature, or even any association with them. The controversial Kuti case and the banning of communist literature from Nigeria are prime examples of his undisguised dislike for communism. According to Idang, the Prime Minister regarded all types of radicalism and militancy as immoral.[85] There was a tendency, therefore, to view communism in strictly moral terms. Whereas Nkrumah's view of Pan Africanism tended to be highly radical, revolutionary, and anti-Western or anti-imperialist as exemplified in the clash of ideas between Balewa and Nkrumah, Balewa's view was marked by cautiousness, restraint, conservatism. and western oriented with a clear reluctance to confront the western powers. Therefore, Balewa's position on foreign policy seemed to be both conservatively moralistic and gradualist. His arguments, attitudes and positions of non-interference and recognition of Tshombe in the Congo crisis was illustrative of the moral principles guiding his perception of problems. His advocacy of gradual transition from colonial rule to independence for dependent African territories to insure adequate preparation, was reflective of both his gradualist orientation and conservatism. One observer noted that this attitude was also influenced by the Prime Minister's experience of British colonial rule in West Africa. He was believed to have considered his own advancement from the Native Authority system to Parliament and then to leadership of the country as a model.[86] Furthermore, Balewa's views on the need to promote African unity first on the basis of functional co-operation was reflective of a conservative's concern about the clear and present danger of militant or radical strategies for achieving African objectives. This dependent African territories to insure adequate preparation, was reflective of both his gradualist orientation and conservatism. One observer noted that this attitude was also influenced by the Prime Minister's experience of British colonial rule in West Africa. He was believed to have considered his own advancement from the Native Authority system to Parliament and then to leadership of the country as a model.[86] Furthermore, Balewa's views on the need to promote African unity first on the basis of functional co-operation was reflective of a conservative's concern about the clear and present danger of militant or radical strategies for achieving African objectives. This attitude perhaps made Balewa less militant about training liberation movements on Nigerian soil. He preferred to give moral and financial assistance much to the disappointment of the attentive Nigerian public who were less satisfied with the symbolism of 'aid' to oppressed African brothers.

In sum, much of what seemed to be lack of adventurism may be attributed to the built-in restraints of the Nigerian domestic political environment and a fragile, infant economy. In the face of the political weaknesses and Nigeria's vulnerabilities, it is doubtful that Balewa's margin for manoeuvre was as great as his critics like to believe.

The military leadership was subject to less of the weaknesses and vulnerabilities of the Balewa government. Nigeria's political structure was suddenly transformed to 'abort' the threat of a regional recession, a civil war was fought and concluded, leaving Nigeria intact, and the sudden economic prosperity aided the self-confidence of the leaders.

The individual who emerged as the 'star' in this period of transformation was Yakubu Gowon, the Head of State. Gowon's appeal and charisma, 'magnanimity' and 'sense of fairness' were believed to have generated an international respect not only for him, but for Nigeria.[87] To have won a war of national unity without inflicting reprisals on the defeated was seen as his greatest personal attribute. While Gowon's benign, christian nature was useful in maintaining internal unity, they proved almost inadequate in fulfilling the coercive requirements needed for pursuing an assertive foreign policy. One respect of this problem is evident, for example, in the sacrifices, concessions, and altruism displayed by Gowon in initiating the *ECOWAS* (Economic Community of West African States) system.[88] Similarly, Gowon's concessions to the Cameroun on the Calabar channel and the extension of the delineation of the maritime boundary between the two countries from point 12 to 'G' on the British admirality Chart No. 3433 bespoke of his conciliatory nature. 'This concession', noted one observer, 'involved a large stretch of high economic area which ordinarily should have been unacceptable even to a 'reverend negotiator'.[89] At some later date, when the Cameroun gendarmes attacked and killed five Nigerian soldiers on the common border, historians and political scientists alike pointed out the conciliatory nature of Gowon as accounting for the neighbour's aggression.

There were obvious personality limitations on the ability of Gowon to pursue an assertive foreign policy reflective of Nigeria's new improved economic situation. In broad terms one might conclude that 'patience', 'caution', 'humility' and all the moral attributes credited to Gowon are not compatible with the firmness and pragmatism that power politics demands.

By 1974, the mood of the nation toward Gowon began to change. Gowon's postponement of the return to civilian rule alienated him from the people and he inevitably had to turn almost entirely to the domestic front. His overthrow in July 1975 ushered in an entirely new character into the Nigerian political scene: adventurous, activitist, pragmatic, and realist by conviction. He was Murtala Muhammed. Having virtually no experience in government or foreign affairs, Murtala Muhammed given his view of the world was forced to initiate a policy based on the conviction that Africans, particularly Nigerians will simply not tolerate the South African and Western power designs in Southern Africa.[90] His taste for adventurism as exemplified by his disastrous civil war crusade to take Onitsha—(a 'Biafran' bridgehead) was sharpened by the conviction that there would be a moral imperative for deploying Nigerian soldiers to assist the liberation forces in Southern Africa. When the South African troops moved into Angola to support the Western backed UNITA/FNLA factions in August 1975, Murtala Muhammed swiftly recognised and supported the MPLA faction as the legitimate leadership of Angola. No doubt the decision was characteristically risk-taking, but he felt the choices were limited given the threat posed by the South African invasion of Angola. Such a decision which seemed threatening to established Western interests might well have pitched the United States and South Africa against Nigeria in the form of a security threat. Many nations were dumbfounded by the decision. But it was a bold decision that was generally acclaimed and accepted by friends and antagonists alike, perhaps, because it was not characteristic of African or smaller nation's foreign policy decisions. It put Nigeria on a pedestal. According to Davidson, 'this event was the onset of a new development of African independence.'[91]

General Olusegun Obasanjo, took over the leadership of Nigeria with the assasination of his predecessor. He assumed office with the commitment to carry out almost to the letter the policies already laid down by his predecessor. But Obasanjo pursued them and attained the same objectives with a different style. He was both calculating and reflective. His approach to the communist involvement (on Africa's side) was realist in orientation. This realistic approach to the liberation of Southern Africa was predicated on achieving the objective of total liberation with the aid of any power willing to assist in the African struggle. Hence, he did not view as immoral the communist involvement in Southern Africa. For example, he justifies the Cuban involvement in Angola in precisely this way.

> In every case where Cuba's intervention was established, they intervened as a consequence of the failure of Western policies and on behalf of legitimate African interests . . . . We have no right to condemn the Cubans nor the countries which felt they needed Cuban assistance to consolidate their sovereignty or territorial integrity.[92]

It was also an acknowledgement that Nigeria was unwillingly to be identified with any ideological camps and that its goal was to minimise their influence. He however, admonished that the Cubans should not 'overstay their welcome.'[93]

General Obasanjo did not necessarily seek to make the area of foreign policy his exclusive preserve. Within the decision making structure, the commissioner for External Affairs, Joe Garba, emerged as an equally astute aide in pursuing foreign policy objectives. An apostle of Murtala Muhammed's Africanist aspirations, he was young, alert, charismatic and willing to tap outside sources for inputs into the foreign policy process. The scores of foreign policy pronouncements of both General Obasanjo and Garba lead to the conclusion that there were no basic disagreements between the two people. Each reinforced the other's position.[94] If anything, their cordial working relationship contributed immensely to the climate of cohesion in Nigeria's foreign policy—a climate which was absent in the first civilian administration.[95]

President Shehu Shagari came to the presidency with a great deal of experience and expertise in administration and an avowed commitment to the foreign policy objectives of his predecessors. Shagari inherited a foreign policy which called for firmness and dynamism especially in African affairs. He is an ardent believer and supporter of the basic principles, goals and objectives of his predecessor's international politics. To that extent, the President in formulating foreign policy was faced with ultimate choices rather than goals; for the goals are already clearly defined.

President Shagari has been characterised by some observers as 'courteous,' 'gentle,' 'soft-spoken' and 'self-effacing,'[96] It is believed that there is, at least on the surface, 'nothing about Shagari to suggest that he is in any sense a militant politician, let alone a radical.'[96] A teacher by training, and philosophical in his views, his foreign policy perspective is held to be deeply influenced by his world view of morality and decent leadership. This is especially evident in his first foreign policy address which took place at the Nigerian Institute of International Affairs annual dinner. He emphasized the human element that appears to be lacking in the pursuit of the international objectives of nations and called for a stronger component of morality in the exercise of foreign policies.[98] The argument about morality in foreign policy is a long-standing and never ending one. In every foreign policy issue the first question that often arises is what would have been the moral thing to do? One wonders if the right path is ever clear in the exercise of international power. Whose morals, for example, should Nigeria rely on? It seems clear that establishing moral principles and values for assessing or judging policies and actions will be an extremely difficult task, especially in a world devoid of absolute moral principles. For example, a moral case can be made for the President's restraint in the face of Cameroun aggression. Yet such *inaction* cannot be justified to the Nigerian public who were jingoistic in their emotions for a military action against the aggressor. The real problem is that a foreign policy characterised by high moralism is likely to always leave little room for manoeuvre.

The images, world view and personal idiosyncracies of President Shagari are only a part of the consideration here. A point no less relevant is the President's scope for initiative in the new Nigerian system of government. In the first place, the President is unencumbered by the inadequacies and political limitations of the first civilian administration. Secondly, his constitutional position, prestige and authority project an aura of invincibility. This implies that he must use his sweeping powers to achieve the purposes which he has pledged to pursue. But this does not appear to be compatible with President Shagari's seeming distrust for 'popular leadership.' He does not as he once stated, 'believe in playing to the gallery for the achievement of cheap popularity all in the name of dynamism.'[99] This perhaps explains why the President has used his immense powers with a minimum of stridency. Yet he has so far succeeded in maintaining the continuity of the military republic. That in itself is an important achievement, for it is essential to preserve in some form a considerable degree of continuity in foreign policy, as the lack of it, or even uncertainty about it could undermine Nigeria's credibility in the international scene.

It must be pointed out that great caution is required in assessing the degree of President Shagari's impact on foreign policy since he is only serving his first term in office in a system that is completely different from the systems in which he had been part of since 1960. He may become surer of his position if he is re-elected for a second term. Only then will his conception of his authority and the manner in which to employ it become more visible.

In the briefest possible form, the salient domestic variables affecting Nigeria's international behaviour have been presented. However, none of these variables should be considered in isolation. In other words, the cause and effect relationship must always be considered. The interplay of a stable political system and a prosperous economy is crucial to a rewarding foreign policy. Similarly, economic growth can be used for the pursuit of military power, but such power cannot be attained with a weak economic base.

The idiosyncracies of the leadership cannot be considered in a vacuum either. Despite the weakness or strength of the characters of the leaders, it is important to take cognisance of the fact that they operate within specific environments and different time periods. For example, the mood of the nation was responsive to General Muhammed's boldness and assertiveness and sometimes impetuousness which he carried on to the external sector. The public receptivity is easily explained. The time was ripe. General Gowon was overthrown for being 'inept', presiding over a corrupt administration for nine years. An 'active,' 'forceful' leader who could employ his power boldly to stem the wave of decadence seemed to be applauded by the Nigerian people, but it lasted only a short while. Why General Muhammed was eliminated after a relatively brief reign is beyond the scope of this book.

President Shagari has assumed the presidency in a period of change and transition after thirteen years of military rule, but the conditions under which he assumed office are more normal than the 1975 scenario presented above. The domestic and external receptivity to the new and complex political system that Nigeria has adopted introduces an element of calmness, expectation and less hurry about judging its performance. But while the present circumstances make it almost unfair to judge the Presidency and foreign policy too soon, the future expectations of the Nigerian public can be easily discerned from their reactions to events since 1979. More than ever before in Nigeria's history, the psychological need of the public for an assertive, clearly identifiable and trusted leadership, capable of taking decisive action in times of crisis has become increasingly visible. The President's great political skill will be judged by his ability to combine the demands of his domestic environment with those of the external environment that is constantly in a state of flux. Furthermore, the President, no matter what flexibility or authority he possesses is not going to revolutionise Nigeria's foreign policy. His decisions will be subject to both internal and external considerations and these come into focus especially when considering alternative futures.

Chapter 3

Nigeria's External Relations

In addition to the domestic factors examined in the previous chapter, political changes and the realities of the global system constitute major variables in the conditioning of Nigeria's external relations. At the time of independence in 1960, Nigeria as a new nation sought, perhaps, unsuccessfully to pursue policies that were not identifiable with any ideological camp. The world order in this period [the 1950s and 60s] was one of bipolarity in which the two super powers emerged from World War II facing each other in a global confrontation that seemed to embroil other nations, especially the newly independent African nations.[1]

Although the United States as the Western super power was not directly involved in Africa, the ideological dimensions of bipolarity seemed to 'seep' through the other Western imperial powers, such as, France and Britain. The issues that bipolarity raised were coloured by the protagonists to represent either good or evil depending on their interests. Despite Nigeria's protestations of non-alignment to any ideological camp, it did not escape the tensions and consequences of the cold war. This position is explicitly explained (in chapter 2) by both the personal attitudes of Prime Minister Balewa toward communism and Nigeria's undisguised political Western leaning. As tensions between the East and West relaxed in the late 1960s, development issues came to the fore. This flowed from the international sympathy for decolonisation in the early sixties. The establishment of UNCTAD in 1964 was the natural result of both the developing countries consciousness for economic independence and the total global quest (even though rhetorical) for interdependence. By the 1970s, the rise of new centers of power such as OPEC, the Republic of China appeared to undermine or render obsolete the previous pattern of bipolarity. Developing countries suddenly became aware of their freedom of action and this was manifest in the increased activities of the non-aligned group, pressing for decolonisation and an equitable redistribution of the world's wealth, OPEC oil power politics, and other Third World Non-governmental Associations—all making demands on the international system. Nigeria was not divorced from these developments in the international environment. In fact, if the variables analysed in the previous sections are correlated with the period described above, then the actions of Nigeria under General Murtala Muhammed and Obasanjo can easily be appreciated. In the future, the policies of Nigeria will still be largely responsive to:

(a) the international environment;
(b) the foreign policies of other states, and
(c) Nigeria's view of itself and the world.

In the world view, Nigeria's size and resources [material and human] place it among the most fortunate of nations. These vital characteristics have led to the belief that Nigeria has an important leadership role to play in African and world affairs. The perception of Nigeria as a candidate for a leadership position has shown its greatest impact at the continental level.

The reasons are clear cut: firstly, because Nigeria has concerned itself primarily with African affairs; secondly, Nigeria's most immediate international relationships have been those with its immediate West African neighbours. However, the leadership role requires the establishment and maintenance of friendly relations with diverse countries, irrespective of differing ideological and political differences.

In addition to the world perception of Nigeria's role in international politics and the limitations of its domestic system, cognizance must also be taken of contingent situations outside the powers of Nigeria. These include essential characteristics of the contemporary period; a thorough knowledge of the international environment, and the realities of the global system. For example, the existence of the great powers is the most inescapable reality of contemporary times. Even more important than the knowledge of the international situation is the realistic assessment of the intentions of other states with which Nigeria interacts. Nigeria could find itself embroiled in diverse conflicts particularly on the African continent if it lacks the capacity to assess the intensions of other states. It is conceivable for example, that Nigeria's emergence as a

major continental leader may run into conflict with the intense economic and political thrust of the French in Francophone Africa.

Similarly, conflict with South Africa over its apartheid and anti-
decolonisation policies may present a future challenge to Nigeria's
basic national interests and security if it decides to respond militarily
to South Africa's hostility. As the international system becomes progressively politically multipolar, the rise of new and powerful potential
major powers will enhance greater economic, political and cultural
inter-dependence among the nations of the Southern hemisphere,
perhaps increasingly isolating the North.[2]

The process of change in the international system characterised by
the increased significance of Third World countries may continue to
endure in spite of the pitfalls and problems imposed by the preponderant influence of the super powers. Systemic changes in the international system are inevitable and they must of necessity accompany
the futures to be considered. As the alternative futures are delineated
later in this study, explicit prognoses about the future of the global
system will be provided concurrently.

Nigeria's external envrionment has been viewed in concentric circles
namely, the West African sub-region, the African region (as the middle
circle) and the international community.[3] The rationale of this model
is that success in sub-regional relations, for example, in ECOWAS will
provide a great spur for success in other areas. It is believed that if
regional co-operatiön flourishes through Nigeria's deep involvement,
the chances of a more credible role in the international area will be
greatly increased.[4] But the approach adopted here is neither one of
priority, nor proximity. The emphasis on African affairs emanates
from the enduring concern of the successive Nigerian leaders on
Nigeria's perception of its role in Africa. As Garba once put it,

> In placing primacy on African issues, we are not merely seeking
> to fulfill our historical role, but also to carry out our OAU Charter
> responsibilities which is to help in achieving the liberation of those
> African territories still under colonial and racist regimes.[5]

Despite the accelerated priority which the Muhammed/Obasanjo era
assigned to African affairs, the position of Nigeria on African issues is
not new. Indeed, concern with attaining and playing a leadership role
in Africa dates back to the pre-independence period. At the zenith of
the struggle of African states for the dominance of their respective

political principles over one another, Nigeria took opportunity to assert its leadership. Perhaps the clearest statement of this concern is found in the 1960 new year message of Balewa, who believed that Nigeria was providing peaceful, sensible leadership by its advocacy of functionalism in Pan Africanism. He stated:

> During the past few months as I have watched events occurring in other territories in Africa, I have come to realise that Nigeria has not only a right but also a tremendous duty to become independent so that she may play her proper part . . ., as the country of the African continent having by far the largest population we shall inevitably occupy an important position . . .[6]

Thus, it can safely be stated that the basic outlines of Nigeria's African policy were drawn at independence. In the Nigerian view, an African environment already beleaguered by dependency was not to be subjected to further loss of power and dignity to a supra-national body such as advocated by Nkrumah and the Casablanca group of countries. That was why Nigeria specifically stated that the promotion of functional unity through the practical steps of economic, educational, cultural, scientific and technical co-operation shall form one of the fundamental tenets of its foreign policy.[7] This policy in recent times has been expanded to include the attainment of security through regional co-operation, policies designed to minimise and where possible, counter French penetration of West Africa. This was basically the raison d'etre for ECOWAS.

Judged against any reasonable criteria, the first civilian administration in Nigeria played a moderate but vital role in continental affairs. In fact, it has been suggested that one of the greatest successes of the Balewa administration was in the area of African affairs. Ardent critics of the Balewa government would disagree with this assumption, but it would be improper to measure the performance of successive Nigerian administrations with the same yardstick. The play of domestic forces analysed in the previous chapter becomes relevant here in assessing and comparing past and current policies. For example, at Balewa's time, Nigeria did not possess the resources, especially the economic resources, that subsequently became available to the military regimes to pursue a vigorous assertive foreign policy. Since it is reasonable to maintain a balance between the country's resources and the policies pursued, it would have been utterly absurd for Nigeria before the oil prosperity to assume commitments beyond its immediate or potential capabilities.

An attempt will be made in this section to analyse and sketch future paths for policy in Africa with particular reference to Southern Africa, the OAU, conflict resolution/pacific settlement, Nigeria's military role, and ECOWAS.

1. Nigeria and Southern Africa

The Southern African problem has always been at the heart of Nigeria's diplomacy. Indeed, Nigeria's general policy toward Southern Africa derives from its commitment to help achieve accelerated decolonization in Africa and to uphold the dignity of the black man.[8] Implicity, Nigeria was faced with all the ramifications of the Southern African problem namely: minority rule in Zimbabwe, South Africa's colonisation of Namibia, a former United Nations territory illegally annexed by South Africa on the expiry of its mandate in 1966 apartheid and racial discrimination in the areas mentioned above and in South Africa itself.

Thus, in the early years following independence both the Nigerian government and the attentive public displayed an ardent concern over the blatant denigration of the dignity of the black man by the minority settler regimes in Southern Africa. The Prime Minister, Alhaji Abubakar Tafawa Balewa, set the pace for the political and diplomatic offensive against South Africa at the first Commonwealth Prime Minister's conference when he called for the 'withdrawal' of South Africa from the Commonwealth on the grounds that South Africa's open endorsement and practice of racial discrimination was detrimental to a free and equal association of member states.[9]

The Sharpeville shootings of 1960 and the Soweto massacre of 1977 evoked a great deal of furor among the enlightened public.[10] The various public reactions and the immense pressure that was brought to bear on the government to act decisively have been adequately treated in other sources.[11]

In keeping with its avowed policy of termination of colonialism and white minority rule in Southern Africa, the Balewa government provided aid to Southern African refugees and gave financial assistance to African Liberation Movements. Nigeria's financial assistance to the special fund of the OAU Liberation Committee progressively increased from £10,000 in 1963/64 to £84,000 in 1965/66.[12] In sum, it may be stated that Nigeria's persistent concern for the situation in Southern Africa was glaringly illustrated by Balewa's hosting of the first Commonwealth Prime Minister's conference in Lagos to discuss the rebellion of the white minority in Rhodesia against the British government. There is no need to reiterate the reasons why the Balewa government could not pursue a relatively more aggressive policy in Southern Africa. It is evident, however, from the foregoing that from the outset, Nigeria identified the problem of the black man in Southern Africa, and sometimes explicitly sought to dedicate itself to solving those problems. However, the leadership was always conscious of the limits within which it could operate without alienating the support of Western, especially British interest which it considered vital.

Successive Nigerian governments have not only continued to reaffirm Nigeria's original commitment in Southern Africa, but also have heightened that commitment. In this regard, the Gowon administration assumed a new forcefulness in its Southern African policy, and spoke vociferously in support of the Southern African Liberation Movements. Specifically, the administration vehemently opposed the supply of British arms to South Africa, led the campaign both at the OAU and in the Commonwealth against the Anglo-Rhodesia proposals, and on the issue of a 'dialogue' with South Africa, Nigeria made it clear that it was not prepared for such talks, and even went further to propel the OAU member states into adopting a common stance against 'dialogue'[13] A *New Nigerian* editorial, 'Free Namibia Before Dialogue', was illustrative of the extreme revulsion of Nigeria over South Africa's violation of the sacred trust to the Namibian people.[14]

A significant channel for promoting the freedom of movement of Namibians was created. The Federal military government concluded an arrangement with the Council for Namibia on the question of recognising the international status of Namibia and the validity of travel documents issued to Namibians by the United Nations Council for Namibia. By this action, Nigeria became the first West African country to honour Namibian travel documents.[15] It appeared that Nigeria's concern over Namibia was sharpened by the (June, 1971) International Court of Justice opinion placing South Africa on notice that it had illegally violated the prerogatives of its mandate and that authority for Namibia must be rightly transferred to the United Nations.[16] But South Africa could not be persuaded or coerced into loosening its iron grip of the territory. In turn, South Africa's intransigence aroused increasing concern for the open institutionalised denial of the basic principles of human rights and self-determination. Nigeria, within its limits at the period under review, attempted to infuse material and moral support to the Namibian people under the leadership of SWAPO (South West African People's Organisation) to achieve freedom and self-determination.

While the Namibian question burned, the imminent crisis in Angola triggered off a heightened commitment from the new military administration of General Murtala Muhammed. It appeared that a decisive step to support the MPLA faction was the only viable alternative in view of South Africa's involvement in the crisis. Indeed, South Africa's military intervention and support of UNITA and FNLA precipitated Nigeria's decision to recognise the MPLA.[17] The Nigerian initiative in Angola signalled to the great powers that it was not only capable of taking on an independent stance on issues vital to its national interest, but also was poised to pursue and attain its declared objectives of ensuring self-determination and majority rule in Zimbabwe, Namibia, and the elimination of apartheid in South Africa itself.

It may be argued that in the history of the nation, few foreign policy issues have aroused such support as has the landmark decision on Angola.[18] The support of the general public was well exemplified in their willingness to contribute generously to the South African Relief Fund set up by Nigeria to alleviate the plight of South African refugees.

The Federal government itself began to adopt a firmer posture on the Southern African problems and indeed, demonstrated an explicit dedication to its commitment. For example, General Murtala Muhammed broke through the relative conservatism and caution of his predecessors and admitted the liberation movements, opened its doors to refugees and exiles from Southern Africa, admitted their displaced students into higher schools and universities and embarked on manpower educational programmes for citizens of the conflict torn areas who could benefit from such technical training.[19]

Another and perhaps even more significant aspect of Nigeria's involvement in the Southern African problem is the diplomatic offensive launched by Nigeria against the white minority regimes in various international fora, especially at the United Nation. It was specifically designed to shape and influence world opinion on the evils of apartheid and the urgent need for self-determination in the colonised areas of Southern Africa.[20] Beginning in 1960, Nigeria at the United Nations advocated vociferously for the independence of Angola, Namibia and also voted for the condemnation of apartheid as an evil against humanity.[21] In addition, Nigeria's chairmanship of the United Nations Committee on Apartheid in the 70s provided a strategic location from which Nigeria could launch vigorous international campaigns to stir up global moral indignation against apartheid. It may be noted that the World Conference For Action Against Apartheid held in Lagos in 1977 was a profound manifestation of Nigeria's commitment to eradicating apartheid.

From the platform of the UN Committee mentioned above, Nigeria has also specifically sought to exert pressure on prominent Third World Groups in the UN such as, the Non-Aligned and the Afro-Asian groups to effectively isolate South Africa and Rhodesia and support the liberation movements in more tangible terms. Even more significant is Nigeria's persistent attempts to bring pressure to bear on the great powers that have sustained the minority regimes with massive infusion of armaments and development capital. Nigeria employed the use of threat during the Obasanjo administration to pressure Britain, for example, into reconsidering its role in Zimbabwe and South Africa, and translated that threat into action when it nationalised Barclays Bank for doing business with South Africa and British Petroleum in Nigeria for selling Nigeria's oil illegally to South Africa.[22]

It is also noteworthy that Nigeria identified the United States corporate interests as one of the most important sources of support for South Africa's prosperity and sought to apply political pressure on the United States administration.[23] By 1976, Nigeria's bilateral relationship with the United States had faded and waned to the point where the military government of General Obasanjo could refuse the US Secretary of State, Dr. Henry Kissinger an official visit to Nigeria during his African tour.[24] The Carter Administration took the cue on assuming office in January 1977 and set the pace for a thaw in US/Nigeria relations by repealing the controversial Bryd Amendment which flouted United Nations economic sanctions against Smith's illegal regime in Zimbabwe. Carter's Human Rights Crusade, his visit to Nigeria and his subsequent major foreign policy declaration supporting one-man one-vote in South Africa, were illustrations of the new twist in US policy toward Africa and Nigeria in particular, and yet another indication of the results of Nigeria's efforts to influence the opinion of the key countries that made the minority regimes in Southern Africa capable of resisting international pressure.

It is clear that Nigeria has scored valuable successes in its commitment to the liberation struggle in Africa. Nigeria's *final* position on the Anglo-American proposals for a constitutional settlement in Zimbabwe and its crucial role in the Lancaster House talks on Zimbabwe bear out its ardent dedication to a just solution. Brigadier Joe Garba, Nigeria's then External Affairs Commissioner stressed this role when he stated that:

Nigeria fully supports the position taken by the Presidents of the Frontline States that . . . Zimbabwe is an inalienable and non-negotiable right of the people of Zimbabwe which must now be exercised as a logical sequence to the acceptance of the principle of majority rule.[25]

Despite the transition from military to civil rule in October, 1979, the new civilian administration adroitly assumed a key role in the Lancaster House negotiations on the constitutional future of Zimbabwe. Nigeria remained strong enough in the negotiations that when Margaret Thatcher's British government appeared to block efforts to reach transitional arrangements, President Shagari sent a firm protest to the British government. More important, and perhaps more illustrative of Nigeria's commitment were the strong delegations sent not only to observe the Lancaster House proceedings, but also to monitor closely the elections that followed. The attainment of Zimbabwe's independence since 1980 has not prevented or caused a dimunition of Nigeria's concern for Zimbabwe's domestic political, social and economic needs. Shagari's offer of ₦10 million at Zimbabwe's independence celebration though not decisive for Zimbabwe's economy showed a marked interest in the survival of Zimbabwe.

In like vein, Nigeria is infinitely interested in the long-range stability of Southern Africa with the decolonization of Namibia. In this regard, Nigeria is becoming increasingly involved in drawing up long-range plans with the Frontline states of Tanzania, Zambia, Angola, Mozambique, Botswana and Zimbabwe. This concern for the future of Southern Africa has been marked by a resolutely firm position on the status of Walvis Bay as Namibian territory and especially on the conduct of fair and free elections in Namibia. Almost all pronouncements of the Nigerian leaders on the Namibian issue tend to reinforce the country's commitment to ensuring Namibia's independence. In fact, Nigeria is now not leaving any room for Western manoeuvres or the kinds of pressures that Great Britain attempted to exert on the Patriotic Front during the Lancaster negotiations. Nigeria's Vice President, Dr. Alex Ekwueme stated quite succinctly the limits:

> Nigeria will accept either the proportional representation system of voting or the single constituency system in respect of independence for Namibia, because both systems have been well tested.[26]

In addition, in financial terms, Nigeria's contribution so far to Namibia's independence fund has amounted to about $666.6 million.[27]

The brief discussion above provides the prediction basis for the future paths of Nigeria's Southern African policy. In outlining the paths, cognizance is also taken of the domestic environment and the stimulus from outside. For example, a future that intensifies or escalates Nigeria's Southern African commitment presupposes that the nation possesses adequate, parallel economic and military resources backed by a willing public and a less hostile external environment. The solution to the Southern African problem still remains a cardinal tenet in Nigeria's foreign policy. It is however, possible that dramatic changes may occur that would alter the level of priority of Southern Africa. The following broad alternatives are open to Nigeria.

(i) Continue to Champion Liberation Movements

For years Nigeria has tenaciously given support in varying degrees to the liberation movements in Southern Africa. The Murtala/Obasanjo regimes had through the recommendations of the Adedeji Committee (which reviewed Nigeria's foreign policy in 1975) synthesized the fundamental tenets of Nigeria's foreign policy in a new orientation and doctrine that links the liberation of Southern Africa and the interest and dignity of black peoples all over the world. This doctrine has not only been largely fruitful in advancing Nigeria's leadership role, but has gained the greatest strength in providing continuity on a specific policy issue. In the linkage paradigm, the oppression and bondage of blacks, especially in Southern Africa was tantamount to oppression of Nigerians. General Obasanjo once stated that:

> We in Nigeria believe that so long as one inch of African territory is occupied territory, we remain in bondage, and . . . wherever any black or African is oppressed, we share the indignity.[28]

On another occasion, he pledged that:

> Moral support for liberation movements is a duty in the interest of the black man all over the world.[29]

It seems therefore that there is no alternative to this policy as long as Nigeria continues to espouse the linkage between black oppression and Nigeria's national interest of self-preservation. Embracing this future, Nigeria would continue to maintain and sustain its commitment to the liberation struggle and the eradication of apartheid. Nigeria would devise strategies to enhance the strength of African Liberation Movements to make them more effective; substantial military, material and economic support would be extended not only to the liberation groups but also to the frontline states who have borne the strains of the problem. Conventional military arms and units would be mobilised and stationed in the Frontline states. The South African military dominance in the area could be weakened by augmenting Cuba's military presence in Angola with military supplies mobilised from sources sympathetic to the African cause.

This policy assumes that armed struggle against South Africa for the liberation of Namibia will be on the rise if it continues to display intransigence on Namibian independence. A crucial aspect of the armed struggle and an alternative to conventional warfare and open confrontation is guerrilla resistance. If this strategy is efficiently co-ordinated and given adequate support, tremendous impact could be made from within the South African domestic front. The primary objective would be to change the system from within.

A highly organised intelligence gathering machinery would be set up in cooperation with the Frontline states, essentially utilising their manpower, but with substantial technical and financial assistance from Nigeria to monitor closely the activities of the 'enemy'. Neither the Frontline states nor Nigeria can afford to relax their guard over an enemy that incessantly seeks to weaken the morale of the freedom fighters by military raids and incursions. This approach, while providing an essential support for the freedom fighters, would keep the physical involvement of Nigerian troops to a minimum.

Another facet of this support would be to expand the open door policy granted to liberation groups to include bases and military training facilities. The establishment of military training camps (with a provision for training in urban guerrilla warfare) would greatly enhance the operational capability of the liberation groups.

Nigeria's commitment to armed struggle in Southern Africa perhaps provides the main focus for assessing the degree of tension between Nigeria and the racist regime of South Africa. In reiterating Nigeria's commitment President Shagari in a foreign policy pronouncement stated that

> We are supporting and we will continue to support the liberation fighters . . . we will not sacrifice this commitment to any other cause.[30]

It may be presumed then, that Nigeria and South Africa are mutually antagonistic. Indeed, the hardline approach rests on the mutual perception of Nigeria and South Africa as common enemies; therefore, relations between the two countries are bound to be tense and hostile. It is conceivable that Nigeria would be vulnerable to potential South African infiltration in an attempt to thwart Nigeria's efforts and weaken its domestic political machinery with a view to distracting it from its external commitments.

Since the scenario for the near future that emerges, is one of intensification of support for liberation movements, a necessary corollary of this support, would be a parallel intensification of vigilance on the domestic front. The Federal government should continue to emphasize the depth of its concern for the security and stability of the nation. A keen awareness of the possibility of an indirect South African offensive and a machinery to confront it would help Nigeria to overcome the gaps and weaknesses of its intelligence system. Finally, linking the security of the Nigerian people and the liberation struggle would serve to escalate the anti-apartheid fervour of the Nigerian public—a spirit which had provided invaluable moral support for successive Nigerian governments in their involvement in Southern Africa.

(ii)   A Regional Collective Defence Arrangement

South Africa is a relatively credible military power in the African context. In addition to its own technology and armaments industry it has guaranteed access to arms and other material assistance from its Western supporters.[31] To confront and compel South Africa to free Namibia, abandon its evil system of apartheid rule and respect the sovereignty of the Frontline states, African countries, especially those in the fore of liberation efforts must possess an equivalent or greater military capability to back up their policies. But African countries are relatively unarmed. The possible threat from South Africa highlights the urgency of a collective defence system, and the need to take a longer perspective at the security interests of the African continent.

The principal challenge to Nigeria would be to champion a revitalisation of the concept of an African Common Defence system which Kwame Nkrumah desperately advocated in the early 1960s. Nigeria would vigorously encourage all African states to eschew narrow parochial interests and to conceive of their political future and independence as being predicated on the security of the African continent. Thus, political and economic co-operation among African states which is already manifested in the OAU framework could be expanded to 'spill over' into a common defence arrangement, with African states progressively advancing toward a Pan-African Security Organisation. As implicitly suggested by General Obasanjo:

> One thing that is clear is that right now most of us at the helm of affairs in Africa have come to realise the absolute need for the proper co-ordination of efforts in the struggle to liberate Africa.[32]

By calling for a 'co-ordination' of efforts Nigeria rightly recognises the inherent limitations of individual African efforts and the necessity for a better concerted strategy to deal with the problems not only of the South African threat but especially of various external threats. Africa has always been faced with the threat of external aggression and subversion. The convulsions of Shaba, the incessant raids on sovereign Southern African states by South Africa, the attempted mercenary invasions of independent African states as in Guinea in 1971, and the Republic of Benin in 1975, are significant signals that a common defence system is imperative. A primary objective of an inter-African defence system would be to protect its members against external aggression (by deterrence) rather than a primary goal of operational confrontation with South Africa itself.

The linking of national security and collective African security would foster conditions that would propel African countries to a high degree of military preparedness. In advancing this strategy, Nigeria would tactfully and regularly consult with sister African countries on the most feasible methods for mobilising troops. It is vital to be aware of the inherent fears of other African states about such a concerted military effort. Among the many arguments advanced against the concept of an

African High Command is the fear that Nigeria's pre-eminence in the region would tend to dilute the sovereignty of other states and render them vulnerable to Nigeria. But the advantages of collective defence far outweigh the perceived dangers. In the first place, it is assumed that African states share mutual security concerns. It follows then, that a credible continental security arrangement would provide the basis for resistance to any threats that might be directed toward individual African states or the African continent. Secondly, African states would consequently develop some measure of bargaining strength to bring pressure to bear on South Africa to acquiesce on Namibia's freedom and establish social justice in South Africa.

A regional defence community would entail a coalition of members or special units of the armed forces of individual states that would operate under a unified command system. Indeed, Nigeria could promote the idea with greater success in the ECOWAS defence arrangement. This would serve as a foundation on which a broader defence command could be constructed. Although this alternative would be a slow incremental process, it should by no means be dismissed as an unfeasible future. An African defence system even in a nucleus form would provide some measure of deterrence and a possible 'no entry' sign to potential imperial powers who exploit the vulnerability of African states to impose their will. This later advantage is particularly necessary for thwarting the type of paternalistic reaction which Western countries (led by France) displayed in establishing the pretentious 'Pan African Defence Force', triggered off by the invasion of Shaba.

The formidable military presence of Cuba (a small Carribean nation) in Africa and their relative impact—instilling some fears on Angola's enemies, underlines the necessity for African states to organise a defence force and increasingly assume their own destinies and responsibilities. The presence of Cuba in Angola, although gratifying, appears to suggest that African states are incapable of defending their own interests. It is clear that the principal objective of an African Security Community would be the establishment of a credible deterrence that could dilute potential external threats and provide Afrcan states with the credibility to enforce common pronouncements.

The advantages of an African Defence System have by no means been exhausted in this sketch.[33] The important point to note is that a credible defence organisation is vital to Africa's security. The conditions and threats that existed when Kwame Nkrumah made the call for an African High Command almost two decades ago still exist and cannot be erased by parochial interests, fears of rivalry and loss of national sovereignty. Since the issue of South Africa is perceived in security terms, this alternative becomes imperative.

(iii) Intensified Diplomatic Offensive. Propaganda and Firm Economic Sanctions

South Africa's intransigence over Namibia and its apartheid policies is sufficient confrontation for Nigeria to intensify and propose dramatically new ideas (even at great economic costs) for exercising optimum sanctions against South Africa. This path assumes firstly, that South Africa is, and will continue to be perceived by Nigeria as a crucial dimension of its foreign policy and would continue to receive profound, specific attention. Secondly, it also assumes that change in South Africa is not only inevitable, but desirable in Nigeria's national interest. If change is inevitable, then the question is: what should be the agents of this change? Is it by armed tactics as the first alternative suggests or a combination of strategies?

Nigeria would accelerate its campaign designed to isolate South Africa from the world. To accomplish this objective, it would design its own system of monitoring South Africa's collaborators, exercising its powers to reward or punish countries that respect or negate sanctions efforts. This strategy is especially relevant in the economic realm. Despite the boom and burst nature of Nigeria's economic environment, it has emerged in the world economic system as a fertile and viable climate for investments and trade. To that extent, Nigeria does possess considerable leverage if efficiently employed to shape the attitudes and policies of other states which interact with it in desired directions. If Nigeria imposes and enforces its own trade weapons as it did when it nationalised British Petroleum and withdrew government accounts from the Barclays Bank in 1978, it would signal to multinationals and investors who have parallel relationships with South Africa and Nigeria, that a disengagement from South Africa is indicated if they wish to maintain their investments in Nigeria.[34] Indeed, an application of quid pro quo conditions and demands on businesses seeking to share in Nigeria's prosperity would force them to chose sides. But the proposals of dramatically new ideas for exercising sanctions against South Africa is not new. In his opening address at the conference for Action Against Apartheid in January 1978, Lt. General Obasanjo declared Nigeria's intent to set up an Economic Intelligence Machinery that would monitor the activities of multinationals operating in Nigeria.[35] The monitoring unit promised to deal seriously with multinationals which collaborated with South African countries. It is evident today that the results of this monitoring machinery, if it was ever implemented, have been rather sterile and unsatisfactory. British Petroleum and Barclays Bank were perhaps, scapegoats caught on the path of Nigeria's march toward the liberation of the remaining colonies of Southern Africa.

No doubt, the difficulties encountered so far in implementing total sanctions against South Africa reflect largely the contradictions between the rhetoric and actions of the Western industrial powers who link their national economic survival with the political economy of South Africa. The evidence shows that the Western powers led by the United States and Great Britain have not only contributed to, and sustained the South African economy, but have bolstered their military capability to resist increasing international pressure against South Africa.[36] Similarly, Nigeria in its quest for technology and development has developed almost umbilical linkages with the same capitalist centres—the United States, Western Europe and Japan. Beyond the utility of serving as 'warning shots', the trade weapon may not be completely effective as Nigeria may subsequently alienate those countries on whom it is greatly dependent for the transfer of technology and much needed investment capital.[37] In other words, a stringent application of the economic weapon may have a reversed repercussion for Nigeria. In the years ahead, the Capitalist centres, condemnation of South Africa will remain largely rhetorical as they continue to transact substantial levels of trade with the apartheid regime. As Eze explains: [38]

> Massive disinvestment (by the multinationals) is not feasible because in the present world economic recession both the multinational and the Western governments have a greater desire to maximise their returns from their investments from South Africa and to preserve a market which offers them large profits. (This is not to imply) that withdrawal of Western investments in South Africa will not contribute to the undermining of apartheid but that the Western investors for obvious reasons are not willing to take such a measure.

For economic weapon to be credible or remain formidable, Nigeria and the African countries imposing sanctions would have to strengthen their economic growth, diversify their economic relations, pursue progressive economic policies and maintain political stability to reduce their economic vulnerability to the industrialised powers. Without rejecting economic sanctions, arms or trade embargoes, it seems that this alternative will of necessity have to go hand in hand with the first alternative. The lessons of Angola, Mozambique and Zimbabwe illustrate the potency of armed struggle as a significant instrument for wresting power from the illegal, minority racist regimes. In this connection,

> . . . the independence of Namibia and the intensification of armed struggle in South Africa (will compel) Western interests to seek ways of reconciling their interests and those of the newly liberated countries. Their economic interests would have been sufficiently threatened to bring them to seek a realignment of forces.[39]

The limitations inherent in persuading or coercing entrenched Western interests to join in applying economic sanctions on South Africa should not be allowed to hinder real progress in the fight for the African cause. Nigeria today, has largely distinguished itself as a politically powerful and influential nation in international politics. Even those who measure power in terms of military capability appear to concede Nigeria's position as a potential major world actor, whose opinion on African affairs is pre-eminent.[40] Despite United State's power and pre-eminence in world affairs, it respected the value of despatching lobbying missions seeking Nigerian influence on African issues. The United States inspired Kissinger mission on Angola in 1975 and the Mohammed Ali mission on the boycott of the 1980 Olympics are aptly illustrative. Nigeria could utilise this position to advance intensively the African cause by seeking to exert political influence both on a bilateral and multilateral basis. Even more significant is the fact that Nigeria's role in so many international organisations, its diplomatic presence in over one hundred capitals of the world, would enable it to lobby and present the African cause to a wide audience.

The key to this strategy is a diplomatic offensive, propaganda and information against South Africa; a diplomatic offensive that appeals to morality, peace and the security interests of the world-perceiving apartheid as a threat to a global peace. The objective would be to isolate South Africa from the world. The advantages of this alternative to Nigeria are considerable. In its pivotal position as a leader of one of the most vigorous United Nations Committees, that is, the Committee against Apartheid, Nigeria, for example, would make use of its position to exert pressure on diverse group representatives at the United Nations to effect a total psychological isolation of South Africa. Nigeria was in the forefront of the African group lobby at the United Nations General Assembly to have 1982 proclaimed as the International Year of Mobilisation for Sanctions Against South Africa.[41] This proclamation is itself a considerable indication that world opinion could be effectively mobilised to generate effective sanctions against South Africa.

But one point must be kept in mind in envisioning changes in South Africa's policies. South Africa operates a formidable propaganda machinery. Part of its political warfare tactics is to employ the services of Black Americans at huge sums to carry out its public relations activities.[42] This strategy is designed to sway the Black American public opinion in favour of the racist regime. South Africa must not be allowed to carry out schemes (among unsuspecting blacks) that would dilute the considerable gains made so far. Nigeria has natural constituencies in areas of the world where black people reside.[43] In large political centres as the United States, Great Britain and Brazil, this advantage could be put to great use if information is efficiently disseminated to them.

In addition, Nigeria would continue to maintain an 'eagle eye' especially on the issue of Namibian independence. While reiterating its commitment to the implementation of the Security Council Resolution 435 of 1978 which embodied a United Nations plan for Namibian independence, Nigeria should simultaneously seek to keep the celebrated Five Western Nations Contact Group from derailing from the set track. The close relations that Nigeria has had and may continue to have with the Western Contact Group consisting of the United States, West Germany, Britain, France and Canada, may be an asset in influencing them to effect the desired change. Part of the strategy would be to help the Western Group overcome the dominant perception of the Southern African problem in ideological terms. Reagan's East-West orientation in the negotiations should not be allowed to sway world opinion. An International Herald Tribune editorial in March 1981, noted that there is a suspicion in some quarters that the Reagan administration 'intends to make Angola its African E1 Savador. an anti-Communist project'. An Angolan solution it is suggested, would be a pre-requisite for a Namibian one. If this scenario shows the faintest indication of becoming real, then the pendulum would have swung back from where it started and Nigeria's task in Southern Africa would have just begun.

(iv) Develop a Nuclear Alternative?

A dramatic change has occurred in Southern African politics since the struggle for liberation began. The change was brought by South Africa's possession of a nuclear bomb.[44] Implicit is the fact that South Africa possesses a formidable weapon that would enhance its security, consolidate its domestic political base, and frighten off real or imagined threats emanating from African states.

Some astute observers argue that the South African atomic bomb explosion was timed and designed to weaken Nigeria's stance at the Lancaster House Talks.[45] Admittedly, the Nigerian military government may have been surprised and concerned by South Africa's newly acquired lethal weapon, but it did not appear to have had any noticeable impact on Nigeria's unflinching position in the negotiations. However, the significance of the nuclear explosion cannot be overlooked. Firstly, it has increased the possibility that South Africa possesses the potential to gain and deploy nuclear capability in the future. Secondly, even if South Africa strictly adhered to a policy of utilising its nuclear power for peaceful purposes only, it would serve to enhance its technological development and self sufficiency in energy. In either case, the South African initiative will affect Nigeria's behaviour.

The challenge posed by the South African device does appear to confront Nigeria with the choice of moderating or radicalising its policy on decolonization and the elimination of apartheid in Southern Africa. South Africa does possess the weaponry with which to deter any radical policies that might threaten its security. Since the issue of South Africa is perceived in security terms, Nigeria would come to regard the acquisition of nuclear weapons as imperative both to counter the potential threat of its South African enemy and to enhance its own international status by maintaining strategic deterrence.

President Shehu Shagari had a good reason to declare to the world that Nigeria would not hesitate to develop and build its own nuclear weapons if South Africa possessed atomic weapons. With the growing South African military power, the only credible response by Nigeria is an urgent development of its own nuclear weaponry. The pilot project established in 1976 as the Atomic Energy Commission could indeed serve as a nucleus of a nuclear development. A nuclear research programme would not only provide the essential stimulus to acquire scientific knowledge in the nuclear field, but would also greatly supplement national energy requirements. In sum, not all the attention of policy makers should be focused on the military dimension of adopting a nuclear option. They must also think ahead of what is feasible in terms of the nation's ability to do so in the near future.

Although the acquisition of nuclear weaponry may not be decisive in determining the successful outcome of the South African problem or even enhancing Nigeria's international status, it is still a necessary step toward diluting or neutralising South Africa's advantage, and perhaps, serve to redress the regional imbalance with South Africa. A nuclear option as part of Nigeria's deterrence policy assumes that South Africa will continue to be perceived by Nigeria as a crucial dimension of its foreign policy and would devote considerable attention to it. Furthermore, the Nigerian initiative to mobilise and influence other African leaders to share its motivations for going nuclear should begin in the near future. This option assumes that Nigeria is considered the leading African state, and that having nuclear weapons on Nigerian soil was the answer to South Africa's nuclear monopoly. Perhaps the clearest statement on this strategy was made by Mazrui;

> These African countries which signed the Non-proliferation Treaty should review their positions and consider setting up a continental nuclear consortium allied to a strategy of developing a small military nuclear capability first in Nigeria and later on Zaire and black ruled South Africa.[46]

But the decision to start nuclear building both for black Africa and Nigeria would suffer from two major drawbacks. Development of nuclear capability must of necessity accompany generalised and specialized development of technological capability. Neither Nigeria nor its African neighbours possesses the strong national bases and discipline to sustain the tremendous safety demands imposed by a nuclear responsibility. Second, even if Nigeria were the only African country which could independently carry forth a nuclear option, it would need to obtain external support for its nuclear plans. Nigeria would need to take intensive diplomatic steps to convince its nuclear friends to assist in such a programme. The problem is accentuated by the inherent misgivings in the industrialised West about the dangerous use of such weapons by under-developed states. While India acquired its nuclear technology from Canada under a false pretext in 1974 to produce the Third World's first atomic explosion, they may not be willing to impart the knowledge to Nigeria. The Schmidt government of West Germany was severely critized in 1975 for providing nuclear reactors and a complete nuclear cycle, with technology for Uranium enrichment and plutonium separation to Brazil.[47] Nigeria could negotiate with friendly Third World nuclear nations like India or Brazil to obtain support for its nuclear strategy. But, there is little doubt that if India or Brazil wished to sell nuclear technology to black Africa, it would not have some difficulty in doing so. The Western nations claim to have every good reason to fear that under-developed non-nuclear nations might want to make use of nuclear materials to make weapons and 'terrorise' the world.

In spite of the apprehensions of the industrialised nations about nuclear technology transfer to the Southern hemisphere, the prohibitive costs of developing such technology, the balance of terror or regional catastrophy that it would bring; a peaceful nuclear device at least, would provide modern technology required for Nigeria's economic development. If in the future Nigeria feels its security increasingly threatened, a nuclear option as part of its deterrence policy would be imperative.

It seems that in the foreseeable future, Nigeria will continue to revel in its declared strategy of going nuclear through, statements, public pronouncements and speeches. The actual strategy should begin with problem. The assumption is that such a line of action may be based on domestic considerations—namely to preserve domestic stability and coherence.

Although this alternative may appear to satisfy a public that wants its social needs fulfilled, the costs and risks to Nigeria's international image and status would be immense. In the first place, it would mean that Nigeria will abandon responsibility for ensuring the freedom and dignity of the blackman, and this would in effect mean opening the corridor for the enslavement of the Nigerian to the oppressor. Secondly, given South Africa's new nuclear capability, she would seek to terrorise Nigeria and indeed the continent if she perceives that Nigeria has become complacent about developing the capability to defend its foreign policies.

Black Africa looks up to Nigeria for leadership and prestige. If Nigeria withdraws its commitment to liberation in Southern Africa, the integrity and credibility of Nigeria would not only be thrown into serious question, but the region would be subject to the mercy of the big powers. The consequences of adopting the position of an unaffected bystander are by no means exhaustive; the important point to note is that such an alternative would not only pose a grave threat to Nigeria's security interests, but would negate and nullify the process of decolonisation in Africa, for long the raison d'etre of Nigeria's African policy.

One of the supporting arguments for a passive policy in South Africa include the possibility that Nigeria will face a real predicament if liberation is achieved. It is possible that a *Black* South Africa will become a rival and a competitor for influence and power. Given South Africa's enormous human and material resources, Nigeria may experience a progressive dimunition of its influence in Africa if the newly independent nations catch up with it in development terms. Would it not therefore be in the national interest to ensure perpetual enslavement of blacks in South Africa? Even without a Jaja Wachukwu at the centre stage for a 'political dialogue' with South Africa, the fear of a black South African power potential could still be sufficient to steer Nigeria on a 'Do nothing course'.[49]

2. Nigeria and the OAU

Few people today would deny that Nigeria is one of the parents of the diplomatic, economic, military and technological steps. Even if nuclear efforts were in the making, Nigeria should not admit it. It must leave room for a 'bomb in the basement' option.

The three alternative paths suggested in this section are entirely based on the premise that the Southern African problem is the cornerstone to Nigeria's African policy and that the liberation of territories still under minority settler regimes and the destruction of apartheid are of vital interest to Nigeria.

Each alternative involves significant financial commitment and costs. It means that a sizeable proportion of Nigeria's resources would be allocated to various strategic needs as they evolve. Would such a commitment command the support of the Nigerian public?

In sum, these alternatives presume that Nigeria has the economic strength, a stable political base and the military capability to pursue and implement the policies adopted. Such internal variables would greatly promote or retard the navigation of the alternative courses delineated.

(v) Do Nothing

This alternative is a major and widely contrasting path from the four features suggested earlier. It may be argued that this course would constitute an anathema to Nigeria's fundamental objectives in Southern Africa, which is basically to ensure the liberation and dignity of the blackman. But Nigeria's policy makers should not feel so secure about their ability to sustain and preserve the support of the Nigerian people— a crucial factor in determining the outcome and implementation of policies. It is possible that the future course of Nigeria's Southern Africa policy may come under scrutiny. The consensus of the course of action under the military appears to have enjoyed broad public support. But the Nigerian public is not immune to change. The Nigerian public would question the wisdom in Nigeria's decision to commit a substantial portion of the nation's energies and resources to an issue which is physically so far removed from the immediate environs of Nigeria. The public might fall under the spell of such advocacy as Jaja Wachukwu's call for a repprochement with South Africa.[48] If the public becomes disenchanted and decides to withdraw its support for the African cause, Nigeria may be forced to react to such pressures by deciding to assume a passive attitude toward the Southern African Organisation of African Unity, for it is generally conceded that Nigeria's Prime Minister, Balewa played a crucial role in reconciling the differing political persuasions in the complex and tempestous processes that led to the birth of the OAU.[50] Although the evolution of the OAU did not proceed smoothly, Balewa's gradualist, functional approach to the question of African Unity subsequently prevailed over Nkrumah's 'idealist' stance and vision of a politically integrated Africa, creating one sovereign entity out of over twenty infant sovereign states.

The idea of African unity was institutionalised in May, 1963 as the Organisation of African Unity. Since its creation, Nigeria's ardour for African unity has considerably gained impetus and support. Indeed, successive Nigerian governments have fervently supported the OAU with the conviction that Nigeria has a special responsibility to the OAU, a belief heavily influenced by its self perception as an imminent aspirant to leadership in Africa. Brigadier Joe Garba, Nigeria's External Affairs Commissioner (1975-1979) in appraising Nigeria's pre-eminent role in the organisation, stated that

> The efforts of the Balewa government and indeed of successive Nigerian governments to develop common ties between African states are part of the historical record of the Organisation of African Unity . . . the role played by Nigeria in fostering this relationship is worthy of credit.[51]

Nigeria's interest in the OAU is intensely focused. A premise consistently held by successive Nigerian administrations has been that peace and unity among African states and stability on the African continent are vital to global peace, and in particular to Nigeria's security. Consonant with this premise, Nigeria believed that the Organisation would provide machinery for the peaceful settlement of disputes. Correspondingly, Nigeria pledged to pursue an OAU policy marked by the following characteristics:

(a)   The inviolability of boundaries.
(b)   The legal equality of states.
(c)   Non-interference in the affairs of other states.
(d)   Peaceful settlement of all African disputes by negotiation, conciliation or arbitration; and
(e)   Promotion of functional unity and understanding among African states through practical steps of economic, educational, cultural, scientific and technical co-operation, as well as the expansion of diplomatic representation in Africa.[52]

Nigeria has continued to espouse the goals in the OAU Charter which was basically designed to provide both a durable and viable framework for political, economic, social and cultural co-operation among African states; provide a regular and credible forum to discuss and deal with problems arising from domestic and foreign relations; articulate Africa's vital interests and then project such interests outside the continent. More significant are the provisions of Articles II and III of the OAU Charter which inextricably committed the signatories to an unflinching commitment to the eradication of all forms of colonialism from Africa and respect for the sovereignty and territorial integrity of member states.[53]

Nigeria has found the OAU useful for various functions relevant to its foreign policy goals. In the political realm, the OAU has provided a platform for the projection and implementation of its commitment to the liberation struggle in Africa. Since the creation of the African Liberation Committee in 1963, total emancipation of the African territories still under colonial rule has been an issue area in which Nigeria has demonstrated distinct leadership. The implicit commitment of OAU Liberation Committee to armed struggle for liberation received energetic support from Nigeria. Indeed, the subscription of Nigeria to armed struggle became a crucial element (at least in proclamations) of its Southern African policy.[54] In 1971, Nigeria spearheaded the campaign at the OAU, against the Anglo-Rhodesian proposals which, according to the then Foreign Minister, Okoi Arikpo, tended to sacrifice the interests of five million Zimbabwe Africans to those of the 250,000 (minority) white settlers regime.[55]

General Gowon in 1971, played a prominent role in opposing the proposals for a 'dialogue' between African states and the illegal regime in South Africa. 'Any appeasement or accommodation with South Africa,' Gowon admonished OAU member states, 'is inconsistent with the principles of the OAU Charter'.[56] Under General Murtala Muhammed, Nigeria utilised skilfully the OAU forum on Angola. It is significant that Nigeria was able to propel the OAU member states (inspite of the split over Angola) into adopting a common stance on the recognition of the MPLA faction as the legitimate representative of the Angolan people.

In the succeeding years, particularly since the return of Nigeria to civil rule, the government's identification with the OAU as a problem solving machinery and unifying African force has not waned. It has not hesitated to take regional issues to the OAU. The dispute over the Western Sahara, for example, was one of the first OAU responsibilities that took President Shagari out of Nigeria after his inauguration. Subsequent OAU emergency meetings convened on such issues as Western Sahara, Chad, and the Horn of Africa were usually at Nigeria's instance. In addition to championing issues in Africa's interest at the OAU, Nigeria has been a major contributor, indeed, the second largest contributor to the organisation, its voluntary contribution amounting to 7.6 per cent of the total contribution.

In the economic realm Nigeria has generally subscribed to a policy of economic co-operation among OAU member states, particularly at the sub regional level. One of the reasons it vigorously supported the establishment of the African development Bank was that financial and technical assistance from the bank would provide opportunities for the more disadvantaged member states to develop their economies. Nigeria's equity participation of about 13 per cent is the highest in the bank. Nigeria's service contributions by way of skilled personnel and consultants have been substantial. Nigeria's high level of participation in the negotiations between the European Economic Community (EEC) and the developing countries of Africa, the Carribean and Pacific regions, reflected its concern for the preservation of Black African solidarity. Nigeria feared that separate African negotiations with the EEC based on ideological or past colonial ties would accentuate Africa's dependency and reflect the former pattern of European influence. Nigeria, therefore, stridently involved the OAU in the negotiations with the conviction that it was in the best political and economic welfare of Africa to present a common, united front to Europe.[57]

More recently, Nigeria's initiatives in convening and hosting the historic OAU Economic Summit was perhaps the most single demonstration of its stated goal of promoting, through co-operative action, the economic development of African states. The Economic Summit can be said to be an unprecedented collective effort by African states to channel their energies towards genuine economic co-operation to attain strength even in the face of contemporary global economic problems. The outcome of the Summit, christened *The Lagos Plan of Action,* set in specific terms the strategies for the attainment of stated economic objectives namely, the economic integration of Africa evolving into an African economic community by the year 2000.[58] These objectives remain to be implemented. Nigeria, nevertheless, has worked for the continued strengthening of the OAU through co-operation in various dimensions.

With respect to the peaceful resolution of conflicts, perhaps, the greatest threat to the unity of the OAU has stemmed not from external intervention, but primarily from an inherent lack of constitutional basis for conflict management. To ameliorate this deficiency, Nigeria has been in the forefront of nearly all peace-making efforts under the aegis of the OAU. This subject will be discussed in greater detail later to avoid an overlap in analysis. However, the vital use of the OAU as a rallying point for African issues must be underlined in any alternatives delineated. Whether African states decide to erase or retain the concept of the OAU, there seems to be no viable alternative to the African identity that the OAU represents. Akinyemi describes very well what the OAU stands for:

. . . the very existence of the OAU has concretised, has infused a more certain meaning into the concept of African identity. Because of OAU decisions and pronouncements, it is possible to talk of an African point of view . . .[59]

In the years that follow, Nigeria will probably pursue the following alternatives:

(i) Support and Participate in the OAU as Currently Organized

Nigeria's policy preference for the OAU may well be a conservative one. An attitude that tends to say, 'She is powerless of course, but thank God she is there!' Because Nigeria sees the OAU as providing strength and 'unity' in promoting issues relevant to Africa's interests, it will be less strident in attempting to disturb the status quo. This alternative assumes that there still exists a basic 'harmony' among African states illustrated by the fact of OAU's survival in almost two decades of existence. Indeed, it may be argued that it is an accomplishment in itself, for such a heterogenous regional organisation with so many divergent ideological views and interests to keep alive for so long.

It is possible that the OAU will remain the voice of Africa in spite of incessant internal rivalries. Nigeria, through the OAU, would continue to mobilise African states on a continental level to provide not only a plank, but also considerable political leverage to deal with external powers. The degree of Nigeria's involvement in the OAU is important in determining the response and co-operation of member states. If the OAU member states continue to view Nigeria as a dynamic key actor and incipient donor largely interested in the welfare of member states, it will provide a rallying point for the foundation of a strong inter-African system.

Under this alternative, Nigeria would make use of its pre-eminent position and leverage to steer member states into accepting the desirability of an inter-African security system. Working through bilateral diplomatic channels, Nigeria would emphasize the mutual security needs of member states and the ever present danger of external threats to the stability of the continent. An African High Command system may not be a perfect instrument for continental security in real terms, but if Nigeria can persuade member states of the need for co-operation given Africa's security dilemma, a deterrence purpose would have been served.

This future is particularly pertinent for Nigeria's purpose. Nigeria as Africa's leading nation has irrevocably committed itself to the liberation of Southern Africa and the eradication of the evil system of apartheid. South Africa's internal regime remains the primary enemy which unites, but threatens the entire continent. If an African security system is organised and operationalised, it can serve as a main source of aid and support to quicken the implementation of stated objectives.

(ii) Withdraw from the OAU

It has been noted that the OAU has been a vehicle for promoting Nigeria's foreign policy objectives, particularly the higher interests of Africa. In this regard, the OAU has provided a strong platform for implementing her commitment to the liberation struggle in Southern Africa. Nigeria has also used the liberation issue to encourage OAU member states to assume a common stance and thus, cohesion. It is noteworthy that since the OAU battle over the issue of 'dialogue' with South Africa was resolved in 1971-1972, there has been a visible consensus in the OAU on liberation and apartheid. The OAU has thus become a crucial rallying point for the Southern African liberation efforts.

If total liberation is achieved, and Namibia, and South Africa attain black majority rule, the cohesiveness at the OAU may be destroyed because there may be no new issues as binding as the Southern African problem. A gradual dimunition of Nigeria's influence may follow, and Nigeria would find that the basic purposes of the OAU which it has promoted at great costs would be questioned, consequently and may consider withdrawal from the OAU to pursue an inward looking policy.

The consequences of withdrawal would be grave with negative efforts. Nigeria's withdrawal would create a void which may be attractive to external forces. Encouraged by member states who have nursed fears of Nigeria's hegemonic ambitions in the continent, external powers would replace Nigeria. Consequently, Nigeria would face an eternal danger, a security threat that it had seemingly striven to avert since independence. In sum, withdrawal from the OAU will leave Nigeria dispossessed of the power it has inspired and wielded in the continent. In a broader sense, withdrawal would be detrimental to Africa's interests.

(iii) Initiate Reform of the OAU

The alternative of calling and vigorously working for a reform of the OAU would be the most significant contribution of Nigeria to the organisation in the coming years. The growing impotence of the OAU particularly in the resolution of endemic African disputes has been the major motivation for the numerous calls for a fundamental restructuring of the organisation. The present structure is criticised as lacking the constitutional bases for conflict management. The non-jurisdiction clause of the OAU Charter itself has been a major limiting factor in the effective resolution of disputes.

The primary aim of initiating reforms would be to secure the active co-operation of member states to explore unique methods which may be applied to conflict resolution to compliment the informal, voluntary process of mediation. What the OAU inefficiency in peacemaking points to, is that there is an urgent need to develop new institutional structures and procedures for conflict management in the OAU Charter.[60] This implies providing the OAU with teeth, capability and financial resources to enforce peace where peace cannot be negotiated. This point became clear in the OAU intervention in Chad. In this case, the OAU peace-keeping force, though politically acceptable to the warring factions, totally lacked coercive power to effect their mandate successfully.

What this alternative demands of Nigeria is leadership and the ability to take a bold, but decisive, rational position. If it is accepted that the OAU as constituted at present is no longer suitable for the peaceful settlement of regional disputes, Nigeria may consider adopting unilateral positive actions. Such unilateral positive actions remniscent of Nigeria's decision on Angola may be applied to the conflicts in Chad and Western Sahara in particular. The Angola decision was virtually imposed on the OAU and Nigeria's will prevailed. Such a pattern of action would trigger a two-fold reaction. It would shock the OAU member states into accepting Nigeria's leadership in unilateral decisions in the organisation, but not without resistance. Or it will enhance the desirability of a competent OAU peace-keeping force that would form the basis of collective security in the region. The latter reaction holds the key to the prospect for attempting and developing a structural reform in conflict resolution in the OAU. It will be in Nigeria's national interest to pursue this path and it might gain considerable acceptance by a public that has long clamoured for reforms in the OAU.

3. Nigeria's Mediatory Role in African Conflicts

Nigeria's chief goals in the resolution of African conflicts may be summarised as: enforcement of OAU clause of inviolability of African borders, prevention of instability on the continent, and averting the internationalisation of African disputes. But national security consi- derations also abound in Nigeria's multilateral and bilateral mediatory efforts. Nigeria perceives its security as closely linked with those of its immediate neighbours. For this reason, it is especially sensitive to the possibilities of inherent threats to its national security—threats that could be triggered by foreign intervention in protracted disputes. In the analyses that follow, it will be shown that Nigeria has consis- tently taken active measures to resolve conflicts (even on a unilateral basis) deemed vital to its security.

In general terms, the Congo crisis provided Nigeria with its first attempt at 'fire-fighting' diplomacy in the continent. Although, essen- tially a mediatory effort under the aegis of the United Nations, the Balewa government in various pronouncements attempted to underline the African dimension of the conflict. In his first official statement on the crisis at the United Nations General Assembly in October 1960, Balewa asserted his wish to see the Congo crisis resolved by African states, as he perceived the conflict as an African problem to be resolved by Africans alone. The active participation of Nigerian troops and police in the peace-keeping efforts, the government's call for a fact finding mission of African nations to the Congo to study and mediate in the conflict, and Balewa's injunction to the Nigerian troops to assume a strict neutrality in the affairs of the Congo, perhaps, illustrate Nigeria's concern for the stability of the continent.

It is important to differentiate Nigeria's mediation efforts in three categories: (a) unilateral intervention, (b) mediation under OAU auspices and (c) mediation on the basis of Nigeria's good offices, usually at the request of the belligerents. Aside from the intervention in the Republics of Benin/Togo border conflict and in the East African Community, Nigeria's conflict resolution efforts in Africa tend to be limited to (b) and (c). In the case of the East African Community, the strained relations between Uganda, Kenya and Tanzania posed a serious threat to the survival of a seemingly model African economic union. Nigeria intervened to save the union. It succeeded in effecting the withdrawal of Kenyan troops from Uganda, but it was too late to save the community.[61]

The sporadic, volatile conflicts between Togo and the Republic of Benin were alleged to be based on ideological cleavages and personality clashes between President Kerekou and Eyadema. The possibility that the conflict could spill over into Nigeria, (at least in economic terms) stimulated Nigeria's interest in peaceful resolution. Infact the incessant border closure by the belligerents posed a serious threat to Nigeria's economy. At the peak of Nigeria's port congestion in 1975, scores of trucks in Togo loaded with cement bound for Nigeria were washed away by rains as they waited for the belligerents to reopen their boundaries. Thus faced with a serious threat of economic loses, Nigeria waded into the crisis and used her good offices to obtain a peaceful settlement.

It could be argued that Nigeria intervened unilaterally in the conflict purely in self-interest. On the other hand, the spectre of a unilateral intervention would perhaps have been grave for Nigeria if it had lacked the relative economic capacity to influence or coerce both sides if they proved intransigent.

For the purposes of this book, one aspect of Nigeria's mediatory role is especially relevant—the Chadian conflict. Nigeria's interest in Chad has been constantly aroused chiefly by boundary security issues. Therefore, analysis of Nigeria's mediatory role, especially in the conflict in Chad must be guided by security and geopolitical considerations.

Nigeria shares about 98.0 kms of its North East boundary with the republic of Chad. In the Chadian lengthy civil strife, Nigeria responded to the French invitation mainly in its national interest—perhaps to avoid a spill over of the conflict into Nigeria's territory and to prevent an influx of large numbers of refugees that would of necessity impose demands on Nigeria's resources. The initial intervention was made outside the framework of the OAU—basically through the good offices of Nigeria. Throughout the initial stage, the Nigerian negotiating committee scored some successes for they were able to induce the French to acquiesce to a withdrawal of French troops from Chad in order to pave the way for the formation of a national government.

Nigeria commanded sufficient respect and influence in the negotiations. The establishment of a Council of States following the First Kano Accord (Kano I) was illustrative. To reinforce this score, the Federal military government in an attempt to legitimise its own actions and maintain peace despatched Nigerian troops to Chad. The conflict took a different turn when the French reneged on their previous agreement to withdraw from Chad. Nigeria was forced to withdraw instead. Hissen Habre, the leader of one of the contending factions in conflict, embraced the French to stabilise his position and simultaneously sought OAU legitimation of his faction. Habre's request threatened to rock the unity of the OAU as some French speaking member states were clearly supportive. At this point it was clear that Nigeria's conciliatory efforts had been seriously undermined.

Nigeria responded by instituting economic sanctions on the Habre regime. It stopped the flow of much needed oil to Chad. Habre relunctantly turned to Nigeria once more. The negotiations which followed culminated in the Lagos Accord of August, 1979, which instituted a fresh Provisional Government. Hissen Habre was forced down as Defence Minister while a new leader Goukouni Weddeye was elected by a consensus of the competing factions. The provisions of the Lagos Accord, perhaps, marked the end of Nigeria's solo mediation in Chad. But it was however, not the end of the matter. The new Provisional Government of Weddeye, even though the legitimate authority in Chad had to face not only the security void left by the withdrawal of Nigerian troops, but also the military and political challenge of Habre who turned rebel.

It was altogether natural that Weddeye should turn to any ally willing to provide a reliable even if conditional military support. Libya provided that support. The extent of both African and Western hostility to the Libyan involvement in Chad has been adequately covered by the press.[62] African states led by Nigeria, sought to involve the OAU in a peacekeeping role following the forced withdrawal of Libyan troops. Nigeria's view prevailed, but once again, the peacekeeping force was inflicted with the same lack of credibility that Nigerian troops had faced at the initial peace-keeping effort.

Nigeria's role in the conflict in Western Sahara needs a brief mention here not because it poses an immediate national security threat, but because the new civilian administration has been actively involved in the larger security interests of Africa. The conflict in Western Sahara essentially hinges on the issue of self-determination of the Polisario (The Saharawi Arab Democratic Republic) and Preservation of territorial integrity for Morocco.[63] In the African context, for Morocco to annex Western Sahara is an utter disregard of the basic principles of the OAU Charter provisions which stipulates that member states will recognise the sanctity and inviolability of borders and accept existing colonial boundaries at independence. The creation of an OAU six-member ad hoc committee in 1978 was designed to find acceptable solutions to the conflict. Nigeria and Mali constituted the sub-committee that was delegated to undertake a tour of the disputed areas. While discharging its duties as a mediator, Nigeria has studiosly avoided any political entanglements in Western Sahara—cautiously withholding recognition from the SADR (Saharawi Arab Democratic Republic) to demonstrate its avowed adherence to the principles of territorial integrity[64]

Approved by a majority of twenty six African states, the SADR was admitted into the OAU Council of Ministers meeting in Addis Ababa. The predictable public demands for a shift in Nigeria's position—to recognise the SADR were numerous. Nigeria has so far succeeded in avoiding a shift in policy in the conviction that it has been charged with the role of a neutral arbiter. Speculations on the effects of the obvious rift in the OAU (triggered by SADR's admission) on the stability and unity of the continent, raises questions about the future of Nigeria's mediatory diplomacy in Africa. Clearly a mediatory role is particularly complex and unenviable, but where the national interest is at stake, as in Chad, even the most pacific consideration should give way to some firm intervention. The following clear-cut alternatives may be considered for the future:

(i) Maintenance of Mediatory Efforts In Nigeria's National Interest

The evidence of foreign power intervention in African conflicts as in Chad, Zaire, Southern Africa, Ogaden, and Western Sahara, points to the most intractable problems posed not only for the OAU but for individual African states. Nigeria as the acknowledged leader and most vociferous in defending African interests faces the risk of additional threats. Furthermore, the proximity of some of the conflict areas (for example Chad) to Nigeria and the possibility of foreign intrusion in Nigeria via conflict areas makes the maintenance of Nigeria's active participation in conflict resolution most desirable.

However, the demands placed on Nigeria as an arbiter should not be allowed to mask objectivity. This alternative calls for Positive Activism in Nigeria's mediatory role. That implies that Nigeria should acquire the ability to take a firm, decisive stance and seek to use its leverage to obtain accelerated settlement of regional crisis rather than attempting to pacify rival factions as it did in Chad. What prevented the Nigerian government from taking a decisive action in Chad as it did in Angola? Having shown leadership in despatching Nigerian troops to keep peace in Chad in 1978, Nigeria should have avoided the trauma of a humiliation if it had maintained a firm position. The injunction to the Nigerian troops to eschew any military confrontation stripped the force of its credibility.

The salience of initiative and leadership should be emphasised in future resolution of conflicts. Firm, decisive leadership would reinforce the basis of Nigeria's leadership role in the future. It would be in the vital interests of Nigeria to avoid a semblance of weakness or vacillation in mediating. If it is not to appear weak, continuation of mediatory efforts even on a unilateral basis will appear to be the most probable desirable future.

(ii)   Benign Neglect and Passivism

Unlike the previous alternative which would require the immediate but firm attention of Nigeria in intra-African conflicts that impinge on its national interests, this new course would seek to adopt a passive approach toward the tensions between conflicting states—its primary aim being to avoid any entanglements which would commit Nigeria to peace-keeping responsibilities as was the case in Chad. To effect this, Nigeria would tacitly discourage attempts by warring factions to perceive it as a routine arbiter. Instead, Nigeria would work for and actively encourage multilateral arbitration and mediation to de-emphasize its own role. In this way, other mediators would assume some of the burdens and responsibilities imposed on Nigeria in its numerous mediatory efforts.

The problem in this alternative is that there would be a reverse danger of a steady inevitable decline in Nigeria's power and influence on the continent. While mediation in conflicts is not an easy task, the consequences of a passive posturē in African conflicts even when Nigeria's interests are actually threatened, would even be costlier in political and economic terms. The Chadian crisis presents an opportunity for Nigeria to take a longer term perspective about Nigeria's national interest in the sub-region. Perhaps, Nigeria's setbacks and loss of image in Chad provides a salutary example. The initial commitment of Nigerian troops in Chad without accomplishing desired results was economically costly. The forced withdrawal of the same troops (that paved the way for Libyan intervention) was both psychologically demoralising and even politically costlier. What seems clear, perhaps, is that the future shape of Nigeria's mediatory role will be determined by a more resolute stance: to intervene or not to intervene?

4. Nigeria, ECOWAS and the Good Neighbour Policy

In its numerous policy pronouncements, Nigeria has not only committed itself to the total political liberation and independence of the black people in Southern Africa; but has also exhibited profound interest in the economic development and social well being of African states, especially its closest neighbours of the West African sub-region. In the West African sub-region, Nigeria's foreign policy goals are closely linked to considerations of national security and development and its national perception. Indeed, to keep Nigeria's role in ECOWAS and its bilateral relations with its immediate neighbours in proper perspective one must be guided by a variety of economic, cultural, strategic, external and geopolitical considerations that have a crucial impact on its foreign policy.

The pre-eminent factor is that Nigeria looms large in any consideration of regional African relations, especially at the sub-regional level. In sub-regional proportions Nigeria occupies 35 per cent of the land area of West Africa, its 80 million inhabitants is about 56 per cent of ECOWAS countries population of 140 million and its 1977 gross national product of approximately $34.2 billion was greater than the combined total for the 14 Francophone states (approximately 21.55 billion).[65] In addition, Nigerian citizens are scattered in great numbers all over West Africa (nearly 1 million in Ivory Coast and Liberia alone) actively engaged in trade.[66]

Yet, in spite of its pivotal geopolitical and economic position, Nigeria has sought to propel its West African neighbours through co-operative strategies into recognising the great need for economic co-operation among them. More than any other West African or indeed, African country, Nigeria can unequivocally claim consistent interest in promoting the gradual integration of West African economies. Indeed, since independence, the main tenets guiding Nigeria's relations with its neighbours are its aspirations for collective African economic, social and technological development that would ensure unity and stability. Nigeria's special interest in forging good relations with its neighbours is a continuing reaffirmation of Prime Minister Balewa's resolution at independence to promote African unity. The Nigerian drive to establish a lasting framework for trade and economic co-operation with its neighbours was corroborated by the former Commissioner for External Affairs, Joe Garba, when he stated that 'the maintenance of good relations with her immediate neighbours was one of the cornerstones of Nigeria's foreign policy.'[67]

In tune with this objective successive Nigerian governments have placed high priority on economic and development matters relevant to its neighbours in its diplomatic hierarchy. Therefore, Nigeria's orientation toward future economic self-reliance and integration in the West African region was initiated primarily with its immediate neighbours. Nigeria borders on four other African nations—Benin, Niger, Chad and the Cameroons. The Lake Chad Basin Commission, Nigeria/Niger Joint Commission, the Lagos-Trans-Mombassa highway—represent Nigeria's early initiatives to develop close links with its neighbours. In addition, Nigeria's bilateral economic relationship with its immediate neighbours was in tune with its policy of heightened co-operation to reduce their vulnerability to external economic influence, perhaps thereby remotely ensuring its own security Nigeria's economic relationship with the Republic of Benin, for example, appears to be a useful mechanism for promoting the idea of self-reliance in small industries. The sugar and cement joint ventures with the Republics of Benin and Togo have been sources of foreign exchange savings for the participating countries.

Nigeria not only shares the facilities of the Kainji Dam for power generation with Niger, it also operates a joint Uranium venture in which it has 16 per cent interests. Nigeria has assisted in the construction of the Birni N'Konni Bridge in Niger, and also infused substantial aid in the country during the Sahelian drought in 1974.

In the dutiful spirit of support for a troubled and war-ravaged neighbour as Chad, Nigeria intervened and gave a special attention that was designed to secure peace. In spite of Nigeria's initial setbacks in its mediatory efforts in the Chadian conflict, the flurry of diplomatic activity which characterises Nigeria's role in Chad is significant.[68]

Nigeria's strategy has sought to lead its neighbours through co-operative means in economic development, self-reliance (where possible) and political stability. Yet its neighbours as illustrated by Chad, Benin and Cameroun, have posed a concern for Nigeria's security and a potential threat to peace and stability in the region. The conflict in Chad and its concommittant refugee problems, the alleged occupation of a Nigerian village in Sokoto state by Benin forces and the killing of five Nigerian soldiers across the Nigerian border by Camerounian gendarmes have precipitated heightened tension in Nigeria's relations with its neighbours. Tension management could infact become part of diplomatic activities with its neighbours in the future. It also raises a number of crucial questions: why has Nigeria sought to make closer relations with its immediate neighbours a main tenet of its foreign policy? What are Nigeria's ultimate goals in its relations with its neighbours? What impediments will Nigeria confront as it attempts to forge closer relations with its neighbours in the future? The answer to these questions may be found in the pronouncements of successive Nigerian leaders and the actions of Nigeria toward its African neighbours as already indicated in various sections of this essay. In addition, the futures that Nigeria will confront will serve to weaken or consolidate its position in its relations with its neighbours and in the long term in the region.

On the multilateral front, Nigeria's pre-eminence can be recognised in its unrelenting drive to help create a subregional economic community (ECOWAS). It appeared that the remarkable success of the European Economic Community (EEC) and the European Free Trade Association provided additional stimulus for revitalising Nigeria's aspirations for economic co-operation in West Africa. Thus championed by Nigeria in collaboration with Togo, the move to urge and enlist the participation of other West African states began intensively following the end of the civil war in Nigeria. Because of the traditional, almost umbilical, cultural, economic and political links between France and the Francophone states, the initial attitudes of those states toward the creation of ECOWAS were lukewarm and wary. By April 1972, however, Nigeria and Togo, (the prime movers) had set the tone by signing a treaty establishing the nucleus of ECOWAS itself in Lagos on 27 May. By 1975, 15 West African nation states, had signed the treaty with two of Nigeria's closest neighbours, Chad and Cameroun conspicuously absent.

By the terms of the treaty, a common tariff would be adopted and, most importantly, a common fund for co-operation, compensation and development would be established to serve the interests of member states who suffer losses from the liberalisation of trade. Indeed, the principal objective of the treaty was to provide a favourable atmosphere for the increase of both multilateral and bilateral co-operation among member states.

Although the basic purposes of ECOWAS serve to promote collective self-reliance within the community, the real significance of Nigeria's relations with West African nation states must be understood in the broader context of Nigeria's security interests and unacknowledged competition with France for influence in the sub-region. Nigeria's relationship with ECOWAS member states, and especially its neighbours are rendered more consequential by the fact that, the four states that border Nigeria are former French colonies. As long as France continues to maintain an economic and military presence on bordering states, Nigeria's national security will be seriously threatened; and political stability, cultural interaction and economic growth in West Africa will be greatly impeded. The stationing of French troops and French controlled military bases is an entrenched part of French diplomacy in the sub-region. Tension management in the areas of French influence has been subject to French intervention. In neighbouring areas of Benin, Chad, Cameroun, Togo and Niger, French penetration of their economic, cultural and political life is a given

Unquestionably, the French leverage in West Africa is very pronounced. Undoubtedly too, the absence of the overbearing influence of France, is crucially important to a durable regional economic arrangement. Policy makers and observers of Nigeria's foreign policy have pointed to the importance of Nigeria in the West African Community. In emphasizing the role of Nigeria, Ishaya Audu stated that;

> Our position in the organisation of African Unity and in the Economic Community of West African States (ECOWAS) is crucial. We see things objectively.[69]

Even if Nigeria were sure and confident of its leverage and the outward signs of its power (population, size, strategic location, natural resources and gross national product) the French counter leverage and influence would tend to diffuse Nigeria's efforts in the region and most probably perpetuate under-development. The problem posed for Nigeria by France was put more starkly by Mazrui when he declared that, 'the natural rival of Nigeria is France.'[70] Unless Nigeria reconciles itself to the status of a competitor with France in its own backyard, it will have to reassess its policies to counterbalance the numerous problems and dilemma that it would inevitably confront in the future.

In spite of the quest for regional collective self reliance and security, a Nigerian preference for bilateral diplomacy with its immediate neighbours should be stressed. On the bilateral level, Nigeria's avowed commitment to a good neighbour policy may require it to yield more to the demands and whims of its neighbours. The challenge for Nigeria then would be to work out how to keep its neighbours friendly without sacrificing its national interests on the altar of good neighbourliness and regional solidarity.

Acceptance of Nigeria by its neighbours, or at least the absence of hostilities, is vitally important to Nigeria's continued pre-eminent role and its security in the subregion. Furthermore, the exasperating French presence in and around Nigeria, means that, for Nigeria, bilateral relations should be pursued skillfully in order not to accentuate Anglo-French rivalry. So Nigeria's policy would foster greater economic development and political stability.

As the 1980s progress, it seems likely that Nigeria will in general terms be involved in three separate sets of relationships in its subregional diplomacy: an intensified co-operative relationship with its neighbours that would not engender fears of 'Nigerian sub-imperialism'. The second feature—that of establishing a security 'perimeter' or a sphere of influence that would depend entirely on the level of the Nigerian threat perception and the limits of its national interests or regional ambitions. Thirdly, a competitive relationship that could fuel conflict. The last probable scenario—that of conspicuously isolating itself from subregional politics to avoid over exposure, would at best be an anathema to historic Nigerian aspiration to its 'preordained' role in the region. An isolationist role for Nigeria would have no future in any analysis of Nigeria's diplomacy. Among the alternatives available are:

(i)   Intensified political, economic co-operation and flexibility with neighbours: This course involves achievement of a balanced relationship in which paternalism is almost absent.

(ii) Aid to neighbours on very generous terms.

(iii) Intensified joint development programmes, especially investments and exploitation of natural resources; and

(iv) Engaging in personal diplomacy at top official levels.

Friendship and partnership especially with its immediate neighbours based essentially on the principle of sovereign equality of countries is the keystone of this alternative. The nations that share boundaries with Nigeria are more keenly aware of, and sensitive to the intensive activities of their gigantic neighbour. Given its preponderant size, Nigeria should avoid the appearance of paternalism. The assumption is that interaction between nations are theoretically and sometimes practically one between more or less equals where reciprocity is expected.

Nigeria would therefore allay the fears of imperialism by stressing partnership and strive to promote a more favourable environment for exercising some positive influence even if remotely. But Nigeria's commitment to a 'good neighbour' policy may require it to engage in more intensified strategies to encourage economic growth, and increased participation of its neighbours in ECOWAS. The assumption is that this policy will through co-operative ventures and mutually beneficial relations with Nigeria, infuse some measure of progress and opportunities into their economies. More significantly, Nigeria's greater stake in its neighbours' economic development is best explained and illustrated by the massive influx of citizens of neighbouring states into Nigeria to participate in a relatively more prosperous economy. The major challenge to Nigeria is to adopt a preference for bilateral economic and political diplomacy that would help its neighbours while simultaneously diminishing their impact and pressure on Nigeria's domestic resources by the illegal immigration of their citizens into Nigeria. It seems perhaps inevitable that Nigeria should play a major but less domineering role in not only assisting but also encouraging the socio-economic and political development of its less developed neighbours and to itself as well. Stable, prosperous neighbours are perhaps less likely to become antagonistic toward Nigeria. More significantly, the region would in the long term provide a natural market for Nigeria's exports as its industrial base expands.

(ii) A Competitive Relationship

In the absence of mutually beneficial trade and political relations the first problem, of course, would be intense competition between Nigeria and its neighbours especially for military power. Indeed in broad terms, the aggressive Camerounian fulminations in recent times may be related to nationalist militarism fueled by French military influence in Francophone areas.[71] This means that in response, Nigeria would evolve a policy of exhibiting its preponderant position in the region. A logical extension of a competitive relationship with its neighbours would raise the future possibility of adopting the subregion as a natural sphere of influence.

(iii) A Security Perimeter or A Sphere of Influence

One challenge Nigeria will face in the 1980s and beyond is French rivalry in West Africa and its dominance of the socio-economic and political life of its Francophone satellites. In addition, France appears to have a de facto control (through military pacts) of most of Nigeria's Francophone neighbours. Without French logistical support, Nigeria's neighbours would be weaklings. The policy of establishing a security perimeter is based on the assumption that Nigeria's security boundaries are most vital to its national interests. Nigeria would therefore assume unilateral responsibilities for securing the safety of its territory and boundaries. While the probable costs of such a policy would be considerable in terms of defence spending, the consequences of leaving the nation's boundaries vulnerable to such threats as the Cameroun and Benin incursions, would be even costlier. Moreover, even if such a policy is executed in the lowest profile, it would inevitably lead Nigeria into a collison course with the French. One may well assume that even the most careful monitoring of French activities in and around Nigeria's borders may breed ill feeling between Nigeria and France. But Nigeria does have immense leverage over France (French business interests in Nigeria alone are believed to be critical to France) therefore, Nigeria with great tact may be able to force the French to reduce their military activities in the states bordering Nigeria and their over identification with ECOWAS states.

In this course, Nigeria's physical security is paramount. But the question is: how can this be effectively pursued without arousing fears of Nigerian imperialism? Nigeria's neighbours, as long as they remain within the French orbit would remain a sensitive problem for Nigerian foreign policy for a long time, even if it decides to adopt a low profile or stand aloof from regional interaction to pursue its interests independently. At the very least, Nigeria's traditional goodwill towards its West African neighbours would constitute the keystone of Nigeria's diplomacy in the subregion whether it seeks to rival the French influence through co-operation or coercion.

While Nigeria's central geo-political position and the possession of certain attributes necessary for the pursuit of a dynamic policy make it possible for one to consider these futures, it is as much the attitude of Nigeria's neighbours and ECOWAS states that will determine the future of Nigeria in the remainder of the twentieth century. Will Nigeria's neighbours accept that Nigeria plays a dominant role as supplier of foreign finance, security, or even as has been suggested the role of a 'big brother?' Is Nigeria in a position to displace the traditional capital exporting countries? Finally, what technology has Nigeria to offer? Perhaps, the factors analysed in chapter two will help to determine the probability of the futures considered in this area.

Chapter 4

Nigeria's Extra-African Multilateral Relations: Images and Self-Perceptions

. . . in all our dealings with International Organisations we are guided not by selfish national interests, but by a higher sense of responsibility and concern for countries (particularly in Africa) whose needs in some respects are greater than ours[72].

Joe Nanven Garba.

In spite of the basic constraints and limitations of its socio-economic and political system (as discussed in chapter 2), Nigeria at independence assumed the profile of an active participant in the international system. Fueled by African nationalism, Nigeria's diplomacy and participation in numerous international organisations was in turn heavily conditioned by a desire to achieve ascendancy to a better position in the inter- national arena, to further its own interests and larger African interests. Although Nigeria may have had an exaggeration of its national capa- bilities, (as exemplified by Garba's pronouncements above, it was still able to use its self-perception to project itself as a candidate for promi- nent world status and to advance its interests.

Because of its size and population of over a quarter of Africa, its rich natural resources and economic potential, it was considerably easy for Nigeria to thrust itself into a prestigious position and be accepted as a rising power in the multilateral sphere. Indeed, one· of the earliest official revelations of Nigeria's aspirations and views of itself was made by Prime Minister, Tafawa Balewa in January 1960 when he affirmed that; 'Nigeria will have a wonderful opportunity to speak for the conti- nent of Africa'.

Given its perception of its leadership role, Nigeria attempted to assert itself politically by giving a considerable degree of attention to multilateral diplomacy. The major interest areas were the United Nations and its specialized agencies, the Non-Aligned Movement and the Commonwealth. With regard to its political objectives, Nigeria sought to utilise multilateral fora to advance the goals of Pan Africanism, concern for black peoples, decolonization and elimination of apartheid. Again, a scanning of the speeches of Nigerian leaders reveals Nigeria's early attempts to use a multilateral forum (the Commonwealth for example) to effect the withdrawal of South Africa from the association.[2] Indeed, it is generally acknowledged that Nigeria played a key role in ousting South Africa from the Commonwealth.

Nigeria's active participation in multilateral organisations hightened both the international deference to Nigeria and its traditional aspiration and self perception as a major international actor. Relative to most developing nations in both Africa and Latin America, Nigeria has been successful in the political and to a lesser extent, the economic realm and appears to utilise its successes as an instrument of influence in its multilateral and bilateral relations.

National positions on international issues reflect the immense national confidence generated by its resources, accomplishments, world view and global role. Numerous pronouncements of Nigerian leaders appear to point to Nigeria's consistent articulation of the interests and aspirations of the weak nations: national self-determination, nonintervention, collective security, the peaceful settlement of disputes, the juridical sovereign equality of all nations and racial equality are salient principles and issue areas in which Nigeria has demonstrated intense persistent interest and concern.

In political matters such as the ones relating to independence for blacks and the elimination of apartheid policies in white minority regimes in Southern Africa, Nigeria has taken a persistent position that would have ensured positive results with international co-operation. In the economic realm Nigeria has pursued with intensity the position that there must be a re-ordering of the global redistribution of resources to facilitate the accelerated economic development of the disadvantaged South. Thus Nigeria took a special interest in the quest for a New International Economic Order through the United Nations and its EEC/ACP negotiations. Nigeria recognised that the mobilisation of the participating developing states would provide the disadvantaged Third World states with stronger leverage to press for better terms of trade and a greater capability to assume responsibility for the planning of their own economic development.

Nigeria's level of activity in international organisations suggests that it ardently believes in collective and juridical solutions to international problems. In this section, a cursory view of Nigeria's major interest areas in selected multilateral diplomacy will be taken and the futures delineated. Finally, the most probable future for Nigeria's multilateral interactions within the framework of a Third World solidarity will be discussed.

1. Nigeria and the Non-Aligned Movement

At independence, non-alignment was emphasized as one of the basic tenets of Nigeria's foreign policy. The rationale of a non-aligned policy was basically to preserve Nigeria's choice and freedom of action as a sovereign state. The Prime Minister, Abubakar Tafawa Balewa, had a fairly clear appreciation of the need for independence of action. In enunciating an independent foreign policy, he proceeded to elaborate on Nigeria's non-aligned posture:

> We shall not blindly follow the lead of anyone; so far as it is possible, the policy on each occasion will be selected with a proper independent objectivity in Nigeria's national interest. We consider it wrong for the Federal government to associate itself as a matter of routine with any power bloc.[3]

Balewa's statement reflected Nigeria's desire to establish a position of autonomy in its foreign relations particularly in the context of the cold-war environment that prevailed at the time of Nigeria's independence. Indeed, the non-aligned posture not only represented Nigeria's response to the bipolar character of the global system, but also a strategem for avoiding political, economic and military entanglements with any of the contending power blocs. The broad objectives, principles and doctrine of the non-aligned movement itself which included the eradication of colonialism and apartheid, promotion of global peace, sanctity of territorial integrity of new states and the solidarity of new states as a crucial force in ensuring a new international order were all entirely in harmony with Nigeria's global objectives.

Although an active participant in the non-aligned movement, Nigeria appeared to be bound by the constraints of its colonial legacy from pursuing a truly non-aligned policy and giving the principle of non-alignment a real application. While it is accurate to suggest that Nigeria did display some political independence of action—such as the championing of South Africa's expulsion from the Commonwealth the severance of diplomatic ties with France over French atomic tests in the Sahara and the refusal to join a Eurocentric Common market; its economic decisions were almost entirely Western in orientation. There existed almost entirely economic and sometimes subtle political complimentarity with the Western powers. Such scholars as Anglin have characterised the Nigerian phenomenon as 'political non-alignment and Economic alignment.[4] But this orientation is not unique to Nigeria. Laszlo describes:

> the historical process which gave the majority of the world's population sovereign and equal states, (but also) left them at the same time in a position of economic dependence, . . .[5]

In economic terms, Nigeria remained virtually a client state of the Western economic system. The decided preference for the West is explained, if not almost entirely by Nigeria's colonial legacy. Nigeria had just received its independence from Britain—a colonial overlord. Barring a revolution that would dismantle the old structure that Nigeria inherited, it would have been almost impossible to refrain from nourishing the umbilical cord that linked Nigeria to Britain; a phenomenon best explained by the fact that not less than 56 per cent of all foreign investments during the first republic were British. In addition, Nigeria inherited a service economy which consisted basically of primary agricultural products. It was perhaps logical to sustain trade with old and guaranteed partners. Against this background it may be useful to sketch a brief survey of the highlights of Nigeria's non-alignment policy since independence.

The first civilian administration lacked among other domestic constraints, the capacity to finance its development programmes. The First National Development Plan (1962-1968) for example, was financed by almost 50 per cent of private foreign investment out of a total capital expenditure of ₦2.2 billion. The search for foreign aid and investment which was largely necessitated by Nigeria's weak, predominantly agricultural economy appeared to be a viable alternative solution to the problem of economic growth. By 1964 Foreign trade investments totalled almost £400 million, most of them from Western sources.

While emphasis on trade with the West was visible, trade between Nigeria and the Eastern countries emerged only gradually, but not significantly. A Nigerian Institute of International Affairs study conducted for UNCTAD on Nigeria's trade with Eastern countries reveals that trade rose incrementally from £4,981 million in 1960 to £16,559 in 1965 and to £21,648 in 1968.[6] This represented only a minor proportion of Nigeria's total foreign trade.

Nigeria's position of economic subservience and dependence appeared to have improved with the advent of the military regime in 1966 potentially enabling the government to pursue more independent policies. It is generally conceded that Nigeria's improved oil economy was a crucial factor in strengthening its capacity to pursue a more vigorous almost aggressive policy. Furthermore, the tight bipolarity that had characterised the relations between the East and the West had virtually melted with the politics of detente in the mid-sixties. This development appeared to have eased whatever reservations Nigeria might have had about any world powers. Also the nature of the military itself and its inherent autocratic decision making processes precluded the pattern of domestic pressures which was clearly evident in the first civilian administration.

Indeed, the new operational environment in the military era is discernable in the politics that followed the internationalisation of the Nigerian civil war. France supported Biafra, so did the United States under the guise of 'neutrality' and humanitarianism. Britain's initial vacillation on deploying arms to Nigeria caused a furor. Remniscent of the 1956 Suez crisis, the Soviet Union and Britain later found themselves on the same side of a conflict. Nigeria did not hesitate to turn to the Soviet Union for desperately needed supplies of armaments when Britain initially refused to supply the arms. Perhaps non-alignment as an operative principle of Nigeria's foreign policy was best exemplified by the Angolan crisis. Nigeria's bold decisive lead in recognising the MPLA faction as the most credible and legitimate representative of the Angolan people, signalled to the world powers, particularly the United States (which had earlier attempted to solicit Nigeria's support for the ('government of national unity'), that Nigeria was not prepared to bend to the desires of any ideological group. The implication, as succintly stated by Garba was that: 'Nigeria intends to be truly non-aligned and to defend Africa's interests without equivocation.'[7]

In numerous decisions the military administration of General Obasanjo attempted to match its pronouncements on non-aligned stance with action. This situation was evidenced by Nigeria's deliberate diversification of its sources of technology. Nigerian students were sent to the Soviet Union, the United States, France, West Germany, the Socialist countries of Eastern Europe, Brazil and Italy. As Garba explained,

> our foreign and domestic policies cannot be tied down rigidly to any ideological considerations.[8]

The Foreign Affairs Commissioner emphased that Nigeria will be prepared to buy, borrow and, if necessary, steal technology from any country irrespective of ideology.

An assessment of the non-aligned posture of the Shagari administration would seem to suggest that regardless of the internal political regime, traditionally, Nigeria would see itself as a non-aligned state and would continue to espouse the principles of non-alignment as they change within the framework of an international system that seems to be constantly in a state of flux. While the dramatic and almost radical foreign policy initiatives of the post 1975 military 'republic' are not clearly discernable from the decisions of the new civilian administration, there are nevertheless, elements of continuity in Nigeria's non-aligned posture. So far, President Shagari has demonstrated this commitment in a variety of ways: his unequivocal protest to the British government to eschew the undue pressure being exerted on Zimbabwe during the Lancaster House talks, his refusal to bend to Washington's plea to boycott the Moscow games, and the condemnation of the Soviet invasion of Afghnistan, all reflect Nigeria's continuing practice of non-aligned principles.

In the coming years, Nigeria's non-aligned posture will probably be conditioned by the dynamic external environment. As non-alignment issues shift from East-West tensions to North-South politics and South-South co-operation, priorities will be guided by the national interest. There are two probable alternatives for Nigeria. for Nigeria.

(i) Positive Engagement in the Non-aligned Movement

Under this alternative, Nigeria would seek to mobilise like-minded states within the movement to spearhead attempts to effect a resolution of some of the deleterious conflicts caused by differences in orientation and perspectives and even power bloc confrontation among member states. Furthermore, Nigeria would intensify bilateral/multilateral relations within the organisation in order to reduce, at least, in part the great-power rivalry that seems to be infiltrating the movement. Nigeria will exercise a greater influence and leverage in the movement if it lobbies effectively to impress upon member states on the vital importance of sorting out their conflicts and working together to evolve common strategies. The susceptibility of the non-aligned movement to big power manipulation will exacerbate the conditions of dependence and inequity which they have long sought to overcome. Of course, a policy of intensified involvement means that Nigeria will utilise its global national interests. For example, Nigeria's desire to acquire reliable technological knowledge would be accelerated through such multilateral linkages. How successful the alternative will be depends on Nigeria's diplomatic prowess.

The accumulated success will likely preserve Nigeria's self confidence to preserve tenaciously in turn, its non-aligned policy. In a nuclear age, it seems that the most rational alternative would be to avoid entanglements with any power blocs. It is possible that this position may be misperceived as neutrality, but it would be effective in ensuring a peaceful, stable global environment so crucial for development. But the growing effort to be non-aligned may be hampered by the nature of Nigeria's political economy—a situation which will continue to fundamentally shape its relations with other countries. The intensified nationalism of the less developed countries advanced in this alternative while essential, may not be enough.

(ii) A Deliberate Policy of Alignment

Despite the fact that the non-aligned movement was designed to reduce and eventually eliminate dependency, Nigeria still has the alternative to align itself to any dominant power or group of powers to acquire at least secondary big power status. Poor economic and political management leading to a dimunition of power, influence and leverage at both the national and external levels, could compel Nigeria to shop around the global power centres. There is some possibility that Nigeria could with the swing of a pendulum seek the umbrella of a powerful ally. Most observers would expect the United States to swing swiftly to Nigeria in response.[9]

While the need for a powerful and reliable friend would always exist, the costs far outweigh the benefits; the most significant being the restriction of the freedom to criticise and especially that of determining how the country should be organised. In fact, a policy of alignment may turn out to be a comfortable and free ride without the freedom to say where you are going. There is, in addition, the possibility that alignment to established powers would render Nigeria vulnerable to an attack from opponents of Nigeria's ally. In sum, alignment may drag Nigeria into a war inspired by an ally.

2.   Nigeria and the Commonwealth of Nations

Nigeria's links with the Commonwealth were forged in colonial times and these links have never been completely severed. Indeed, Nigeria's participation in the Commonwealth organisation was heavily influenced by its British colonial heritage. A number of similarities marked the membership of the Commonwealth, among them, language, history and a shared legacy of colonial rule.

Nigeria became a member of the Commonwealth on the attainment of independence and appeared to incline toward the organisation as a strategic forum for advancing its national interests while pursuing general goals in multilateral activities. The then Prime Minister, Tafawa Balewa, elaborated on this point:

> While benefitting greatly from the free interchange of ideas and consultation between members of the Commonwealth and from their experience within the framework of the United Nations, we would have a free hand to select those policies which are considered to be most advantageous to Nigeria.[10]

A concrete example of this position was Nigeria's unflinching stance against South Africa at the Commonwealth Heads of States Summit in 1961. When the issue of apartheid came up Nigeria not only protested vehemently against the evils of apartheid and violations of Human rights in South Africa, but also demanded the expulsion of South Africa from the Commonwealth organisation. This action increased Nigeria's international image and most observers concede that Nigeria was instrumental in forcing South Africa out of the Commonwealth as well as from the Economic Commission for Africa (ECA).

By the beginning of the 1970's, however, Nigeria's interest in the Commonwealth organisation began to wane. Nothing illustrates this new attitude better than a 1971 editorial in the *New Nigerian:*

> For those member countries that are not inhabited by people of British descent, the Commonwealth is no more than an imperial junk yard bordered by strong, almost invisible, silken threads from which it will take more than the normal political courage and will power left in the breasts of the mentally emasculated and suitably educationally conditioned mind of the ex-colonial man to escape . . . It is only by deliberately deciding to leave the Commonwealth can we begin to recreate the political clan with which to move forward under our own steam.[11]

Over the years, Nigerian public disinterest in the Commonwealth has not remained constant in intensity, but has fluctuated depending upon circumstances and the mood of the nation. With the dimunition of British traditional pre-eminence in the Commonwealth and the admission of other nations from Africa and the Carribean, the organisation appears to have shifted from a paternalistic organisation of the British sphere of influence to an important or relevant forum for the exchange of technical and educational assistance and economic support for developing countries. As an advocate of multilateralism, Nigeria continues to encourage the functioning of the Commonwealth. At best, a useful measure of Nigeria's level of activity in the organisation is the important representation which it holds in the Commonwealth Secretariat through the office of the Deputy Secretary.

In spite of the general public feeling that the Commonwealth is no longer very relevant in today's diplomacy for Nigeria, the future of Nigeria's engagement in the organisation is relatively easy to ascertain. Two major options are as follows:

(i) **Positive Activism, and Intensification of Support for the Commonwealth:**

The major working assumption of this future is that an active prominent participation in the Commonwealth does not and will not constitute a liability to Nigeria. Indeed, if anything, Nigeria stands to gain by its membership in such multilateral bodies. Among the positive gains are economic and especially technical assistance through the Commonwealth Fund for Technical Co-operation (SFTC). Intensification of participation in such organisations can provide an invaluable forum for the examination of common interests and goals and provide collective solutions to problems. Even in times of dire need for political support, Nigeria would enlist the support and loyalty of member states as a collective negotiating or demanding force.[12] It was the Commonwealth, for example that successfully brought pressure to bear on the British Prime Minister, Margaret Thatcher to rescind her stance of recognising the puppet regime of Abel Muzorewa in Zimbabwe. Similarly, such pressure could be exerted to achieve independence for Namibia. If collective efforts are intensified, several multilateral purposes will be served in future.

(ii) **Selective Disengagement from the Commonwealth and the Creation of a new Institution within the Framework to serve the Interests of less Developed States:**

This choice assumes that the significance of history, language and colonial sentiments are greatly exaggerated and no longer relevant to development problems. It is plausible that in the 1980s and beyond, the federal government would be subject to domestic pressure for a complete withdrawal from the organisation. If the government encounters an organised, sustained pressure to leave the Commonwealth, it may succumb, if only to gain and preserve the support of the influential interest groups that exert pressure. The policies of the British Government on education for immigrants (most of whom are Commonwealth citizens) in recent times has tended not only to weaken Commonwealth unity but also signified the dimunition of British interest in the organisation. The introduction of prohibitive school fees in British institutions for immigrants are clearly not in tune with Commonwealth aims of co-operation for development. Nigeria has been conspicuously affected. as statistics indicate that the largest number of Commonwealth students studying in Britain after Indians are Nigerians.

Since the British attitude points to only a residual recognition of the diverse ties that bind the Commonwealth, Nigeria (in concert with other like-minded member states) has the responsibility to identify their more common interests and work toward expanding their national horizons collectively.

Even in the absence of direct and substantial interests, it seems probable that Nigeria will seek a policy of association rather than isolation, if only to augment its influence in the international arena.

3. Nigeria and OPEC

Until the discovery of oil in Nigeria in commercial quantities in the early 1960s the country's development programmes remained largely dependent on agricultural resources derived from the diverse regions and agricultural belts, and of course, from external aid. Although Nigeria's foreign dependence was still relatively high in the first decade of independence, by the early 1970s, a sharp upswing in oil prices created a boom in Nigeria's economy, decreasing greatly its dependence on foreign sources for capital development aid.[13] Consistent with the sudden boom was the cartelization of the oil industry—which found formidable strength in OPEC (The Organisation of Petroleum Exporting Countries). Nigeria is a member of this cartel. Indeed, during the mid 1970's Nigeria had consolidated its position as a crucial supplier of light quality oil to the United States second only to Saudi Arabia.[14] Nigeria's primacy in oil production and export signalled an active participation in a multilateral organisation designed to preserve the interests of the oil producing countries. Inevitably, Nigeria has been involved in OPEC negotiations for oil price agreements and has been in the vanguard of efforts to grant price concessions to disadvantaged African countries.

After almost a decade of oil boom and prosperity and subsequent dropping oil demands, OPEC found the global oil market virtually glutted, threatening to render the member states as vulnerable as did the rest of the world in 1973/74. This situation has of course, had the potential of reducing OPEC's ability to fix prices unilaterally. It is precisely in this context that producer unity has been imperative. But the question is, is it to Nigeria's advantage to remain a member of a cartel that is potentially vulnerable to an increasingly hostile Non-OPEC world?[15] At present, and in the next several years, it seems that there is only one clear choice for Nigeria, which is the continuation of membership in and support for OPEC.

Nigeria has obviously benefitted from its membership in the organisation of Petroleum Exporting Countries (OPEC) and has also used the forum to alleviate the sufferings of non-OPEC African States by granting them special concessions and contributing substantially to the African

Development Bank (ADB), and OPEC Development Fund to aid other developing states in meeting oil-related balance of payment, and development projects. The second major consideration is the technical benefit derived from OPEC association; benefits which would otherwise incur greater costs for Nigeria. In addition, OPEC pressure contributed and will continue to contribute substantial impetus to the North-South dialogue.

Although it is suffering a temporary discomfort, OPEC solidarity in the face of the global struggle toward self-sufficiency in energy will be the most crucial element of its survival. Greater dependence on oil revenue (about 95 per cent of Nigeria's total export is from oil) makes it imperative for Nigeria to cling to a formidable cartel that would guarantee consistent, profitable oil prices in the world market. This option assumes that intensification of cartelization of oil will continue to be lucrative (even if the producers cut back production) as long as alternative sources of energy have not been fully developed to displace oil. As long as oil remains a strategic resource on which nations depend, it can still be used successfully as a credible weapon, only if the exporting states act in concert, and this can best be achieved by the intensification of co-operation in areas of mutual and common interest. Nigeria has an abiding stake in helping to keep the organisation viable, to play a powerful role in international politics.[17]

The single line projection for Nigeria in OPEC is not designed to rule out plausible alternatives, such as becoming a 'non-OPEC' exporter. It is possible that Nigeria can follow the example of Mexico, Britain, or Egypt by staying outside the OPEC cartel. Indeed, their competitive prices have provided a cushion for importing countries. But the decision to withdraw from OPEC will be very political for Nigeria. Its Islamic linkages with Saudi Arabia are close and a withdrawal would be an anathema. Furthermore, the Saudis hold the key to the OPEC clout.

4. The New International Economic Order, Transfer of Technology and Trade

For sometime, Nigeria has been very active and vociferous in various international organisations engaged in the struggle for a new international order. One of Nigeria's most active and influential multilateral roles is in the North-South negotiations for a new international economic order and better conditions of trade. Being global in nature, and affecting a great majority of nation states, the issues of technology transfer, revision of uneven and unfair trade patterns were of necessity subject to multilateral negotiations and discussions.

There are two major considerations in Nigeria's position on these development and access issues.[18] First, Nigeria by virtue of its diverse and enormous natural resources ranks prominently as one of the world's largest repository of raw materials and shares an elemental interest with the developing world in finding answers to imperialist exploitation. Because of the desperate need of the developed industrialised states for raw materials and the accompanying exploitation of the raw material producing states, Nigeria has a stake in participating in the efforts to alter that pattern of exploitation.

The second major consideration is the overwhelming dependence on foreign trade, and advanced sophisticated technology. The stakes for Nigeria and developing countries would be to attain a balanced, more equitable exchange between the raw material exporters and the industrialised states, and better prices for its commodities.

The international order is essentially based on power relationships. It was not surprising then that the success of the OPEC cartel in 1973/74 in cutting production, raising oil prices and imposing embargoes on political antagonists contributed immensely to the search for a new International Economic Order. One of the responses to the OPEC action was the establishment at the Sixth Special Session of the United Nations General Assembly in May, 1974, of a framework for reordering the global economic patterns. Since Nigeria as a member of OPEC also shares with the rest of the developing world the problem of economic underdevelopment and exploitation, it sent a high-level delegation to the General Assembly, and pushed for 'fair and just' trade agreements on less developed countries' raw materials.

The successes scored at the UN Special Session subsequently led to the Non-Aligned Conference on a Third World Strategy on Raw-Materials and Economic Development in 1975. The essence of the Third World Strategy is to effect a global negotiation on raw materials including petroleum. Over the years, the developing and the industrialised countries have established permanent negotiating bodies to achieve at least a mutual working relationship, but the status quo appears increasingly difficult to change. Indeed, it appears that the developing countries are losing this initiative to the industrialised countries.

Among the most serious problems that Nigeria has confronted in its development in the past and will continue to face in the forseeable future, none is as crucial as its need for modern technology. Throughout this study, it has been noted, at least implicitly, that Nigeria has enduring aspirations to middle power position. In the achievement of a middle power status, the acquisition and indigenous maintenance and direction of research in advanced technology is essential. Perhaps an awareness of its deficiency in the area of technology has propelled Nigeria into an active participation in such negotiating UN agencies as UNCTAD, the Group of '77' and GATT.

Nigeria has emphasized the acquisition of technology as a long-term investment and as a means of reducing and eliminating dependence on external sources. This is why Nigeria has pursued parallel paths of instituting indigenisation policies while opening its doors to multinational enterprises capable of working with Nigerians to establish a national technology. What is disturbing as a *Nigerian Standard* editorial points out is that:

> even the technical experts right here in our country have refused to impart essential know how, higher skills and formulae to their Nigerian subordinates.[19]

One of the factors responsible for the Nigerian predicament as has been rightly observed, is the unco-operative and exploitative attitude of the multinationals and the inertia of other foreign investors operating in Nigeria.[20] With very rare exceptions, the industrialisation process has centred on assembly plants and little effort has been made to effect real transfer of technology. The solution to the problems of Nigeria's technology dilemma, therefore, lies not only in evolving an indigenous technology to aid production under local conditions, but also in obtaining international co-operation in form of research, international code of technology transfer, and training. This underlies the importance of participating actively in such bodies as UNCTAD. Indeed such organisation allows more effective collective negotiations and potential progress in securing effective agreements more favourable to the developing countries.

The establishment of steel industries in various locations in Nigeria through bilateral agreements with the Soviet Union and the Federal Republic of Germany is illustrative of the urgency of industrial development and growth in Nigeria. What is significant in the establishment of the steel industry is that it will greatly reduce Nigeria's dependence on the generosity of the industrialised countries for a resource so critical to development and growth. What seems clear from the very brief discussion on the salient access issues critical to the future of Nigeria, is that the most feasible alternative to accelerated development is collective self reliance, designed to make it serve a sensible dual role of an exporter of technology as well as raw materials. This strategy should not, of course, be divorced from national self reliance for that would form the basis of other collective efforts. In the face of the inevitable obstacles to the achievement of a more equitable and balanced world order by the North, it is likely that in the years ahead, there will be an increasing tendency and consolidation of Third World Coalition or a South-South co-operation.[21] This implies a visible show of concern by Nigeria over the political and economic rights of developing countries, maintaining a visible profile in its diplomacy, and working assiduously within the framework of a Third World or South-South solidarity to promote both bilateral and multilateral economic, political and cultural linkages.

The concept of a South-South solidarity would alter fundamentally the basic structure of the international system. Indeed, it may turn out to be as Buchan envisioned, a 'revival of the spirit of internationalism',[22] which is constantly shrinking with the impotence of the UN—a revival that is glaringly indicative of the Third World's readiness to share in the responsibility for global management and to recognise their efforts to enlarge their own prospects for development. Nigeria in its quest for development and genuine independence, will find in the South-South co-operation a collective strategy to progressively achieve economic self determination. The process has already gained momentum in the collective African strategy for achieving the New International Economic Order. At the First OAU economic Summit in Lagos in April, 1980, a continental plan for the total emancipation of black peoples was charted[23] involving strategies that would tackle poverty at the global, regional and sub-regional and national levels. Furthermore, the idea of dividing Africa into four economic zones is to achieve the goal of accelerated self sustenance, through the concept of a South-South co-operation which if effectively organised would move beyond the sentiments of the traditional so-called Third World politics. It would offer a uniquely effective catalyst for increased trade interaction and the sharing of technology. Ties of inter-dependence between developing nations and between nations that share not only similar development problems, but also a heritage of colonialism and under development would be strengthened. This form of relationship has vital 'built in' advantages over relations with the great powers. The reasons are not hard to find: first the 'dominance complex' that pervades the traditional relationship with the established powers would be almost totally absent in Third World interactions. Second, the disparity in resources and development is not as conspicuous. Consequently, the costs of technological co-operation would not be as astronomically prohibitive as those from the industrialised countries. Further, technical co-operation between developing countries would be unsophisticated, more adaptable to developing environments than the 'push botton' technology of the developed countries.

5. Nigeria and the United Nations

Nigeria's interest in the United Nations is clear cut. Successive Nigerian regimes have placed a high premium on the efficacy of the organisation as a forum in which it can press overriding concerns of Africa's diverse endemic problems. Nigeria's principal source of hope was the benevolent provisions in the United Nations Charter for dependent territories. The Charter appeared to reflect on an abiding concern regarding 'non-self governing Territories' stating that:

> Members of the United Nations which have or assume responsibilities for the administration of territories whose peoples have not yet attained a full measure of self government recognise the principle that the interests of the inhabitants of these territories are paramount, and accept as a sacred trust the obligation to promote to the utmost, within the system of international peace and security established by the present Charter, the well-being of the inhabitants of these territories, and, to this end: to develop self-government, to take due account of the political aspirations of the peoples, and to assist them in progressive development of their free political institutions, according to the particular circumstances of each territory and its peoples and their varying degrees of advancement.[24]

This provision was an implicit recognition of the rights of colonies to self-determination, reinforcing the basic principles of the Atlantic Charter of 1941.[25] The distinctive nature of Nigeria's identification and belief in the efficacy of the UN is explained by the special United Nations policy enunciated by Prime Minister, Abubakar Tafawa Balewa, at independence. The aims of Nigeria's United Nations diplomacy, he proclaimed, were:

(i) Respect for political independence and territorial integrity of all states;

(ii) Total liquidation of all forms of colonialism and imperialism including white minority regimes in Southern Africa;

(iii) Respect for fundamental human rights;

(iv) Promotion of international peace and security as well as measures aimed at reducing world tensions;

(v) Reunification of all divided lands through peaceful negotiations;

(vi) General and complete disarmament and

(vii) The establishment and strengthening of the UN agencies concerned with multilateral economic aid and equitable trade terms.[26]

It was clear at the time that Nigeria's expectations of the UN for the solution of international problems (especially those relating to Africa) were quite high. These aims were most clearly demonstrated in Nigeria's active participation and vociferous demands on issues of decolonization, disputes over sanctions against Rhodesia and South Africa, new international economic order, finance matters and disarmament. In the United Nations, Nigeria is observed to take one of the hardest stands against colonialism and racism, each time voting in favour of total diplomatic and trade sanctions on the white minority regimes of Southern Africa and other perpetrators of the abominable system of apartheid.[27] Since its admission to the UN, Nigeria's diplomatic representation has been consistently at high level—maintaining a permanent delegation to the UN as one of its consular postings. The permanent high level delegation also reflects its political interests in using the UN forum to foster its national interests and the higher interests of Africa.

One of the most significant measures of Nigeria's diplomatic, political interest and activity in the United Nations is its high scores as one of the most active in the UN committees. Because of its interest and commitment to the issue of decolonization and racism, Nigeria, since the mid-seventies has been consistently elected to the chair of the Special Committee on Apartheid. The most significant of the committee's achievements is that it has on numerous occasions with varying degrees of success sought to induce various organs of the United Nations to isolate South Africa and to scrutinize more closely the inhuman policies of the white minority regime. In May 1976, a programme of action against apartheid was formulated by the committee in Havana. The programme which was subsequently endorsed by the United Nations General Assembly led to a World Conference for Action Against Apartheid in Lagos on August 22, 1977. Under lining the significance of the conference to Nigeria, Lt. General Oba sanjo, the Head of the Federal Military Government asserted:

> We in Nigeria do not regard this Conference as just another
> United Nations meeting taking place in Lagos. For us this is a gathering of men and women of conscience from all corners of the globe who have come to Lagos to harmonise views and work out programme of ACTION of all nations and peoples of the world to effect complete liberation of Southern Africa without delay and without undue suffering and to bring about the eradication of the inhuman policy of apartheid in South Africa.[28]

A similar conference was held in Paris in 1981 by the United Nations, with the co-operation of the OAU, and Nigeria featured prominently.

Nigeria was elected to a non-permanent seat on the Security Council in 1978-79, a position that she perceived would greatly enhance her ability to push issues vital to her national interests, especially the Southern African issues and participate prominently in debates and decision making. Nigeria has also provided unflinching support for UN peacekeeping efforts. Nigerian contigents have provided invaluable support for UN peace keeping forces in the Congo, Kashmir, and Lebanon. At the same time Nigeria has demonstrated profound interest in disarmament issues, insisting that there must be disarmamemt to release resources for development.

Nigeria's membership and level of participation in UN agencies reflect the degree of significance it attributes to the organisation as a problem solving body. Nigeria is one of the twenty developing countries which shares membership of almost all the UN Specialised Agencies. Although these organisations vary in the degree of relevance to its foreign policy, participation appears to give Nigeria great prominence. Nigerian nationals have featured prominently on high level executive appointments in UN agencies and the UN itself. Two of such significant appointments are the elevation of Professor Lambo as the President of WHO and Mr. Shuaib Yola as a deputy Under Secretary General to the UN.

In the economic sphere Nigeria has participated actively in the struggle of the developing nations to achieve a more equitable world order, a transfer of technology and better terms of trade. Its participation in the Economic Commission for Africa (ECA) has enabled it to pursue its national goals and the economic objectives of Africa. While it contributes to the continued viability of the UN, Nigeria in spite of its relative level of development has also continued to be a prominent beneficiary of important UN functional assistance programmes. Chief among the aid programmes operating in Nigeria are WHO, UNESCO, FAO, UNICEF and UNDP. According to a United Nations Year Book Report, Nigeria ranked fourth in 1978 after India, Indonesia and Brazil in technical assistance granted by UNESCO.[29]

In sum, after thirteen years of military rule, the first top level elaboration of the UN policy of the second civilian republic was made by President Shehu Shagari in a statement at the 35th United Nations General Assembly in 1980. Quite rightly Nigeria called on the General Assembly to 'launch a decade of reparation and restitution for Africa as a master plan for the economic recovery of Africa.'[30] Following the path established by his predecessors, President Shagari expressed an avowed commitment to liberation efforts and global solutions to international problems. If the declared objective of the Shagari administration is to join other nation states in looking to the UN for answers to global problems, then a more closely related and probable future would be to mobilise the resources of like-minded states within the UN framework to make the organisation an instrument for harmonising views and solving problems. There are two major choices for Nigeria.

(i) **Make Greater Use of the UN and Press for a Permanent Seat on the Security Council**

It seems apparent from the 1980 landmark pronouncement of President Shagari at the UN, that the new administration, treading the path of its predecessors supports the UN because the Charter expresses not only its fundamental aims in the world, but also promises global solutions to international problems. But not only has the idea been tested and belied by the inability of the UN to bring sufficient pressure to bear on nations flouting sanctions imposed on the illegal regime of South Africa, the ability of that regime itself to maintain and sustain the explicit support of the established powers (who were the founders of the UN) beclouds the usefulness of the UN. Yet, Nigeria and other developing nations seem to believe that the UN grouping is so universal and the purposes and principles of the organisation so collectively oriented that near effective solutions will be found to international conflicts through collective action.

The belief in multilateral diplomacy as a means to collective action explicitly suggests that Nigeria must emphasize its UN role in the future as a ruse to achieve its greater national objectives. This implies that Nigeria would increase its initiatives to harness UN resources for more effective implementation of decisions and resolutions taken within the organisation. Nigeria would increasingly seek to mobilise the active support of powerful lobbies and inter-Governmental organisations within the UN to attain, at least, some dependable cohesiveness on common problems.

This alternative recognises that in today's world the ability of nations to achieve national objectives in isolation or outside the framework of multilateral diplomacy is increasingly becoming limited. The effective promotion of national interests, therefore, would depend largely on sustained efforts to interact with and mobilise the support of other states. The UN would continue to serve as one of the most important institutional settings for the discussion of global problems.

Consonant with the intensification of Nigeria's multilateral diplomacy in the UN would be a parallel intensification of efforts to push for a permanent representation of Africa on the Security Council. The objective would be to ensure that Africa and other developing nations are routinely represented and visibly participating in the crucial decision-making organ of the UN. Enhancement of the interests of developing nations requires a direct participation and full engagement in the Security Council. This advantage is particularly relevant to Africa because there are vital issues (examined in this study) lined up in the United Nations waiting for urgent solutions. The task of decolonization, for example, must be accomplished. The incessant obstruction of the process by the great powers, sometimes with the exercise of the veto powers illustrates vividly that they have rhetorically accepted decolonization only on their own terms. The participation of lesser powers on the Security Council would diffuse great power dominance of the United Nations.

In sum, the major line of reasoning in support of this alternative is that about fifty independent African countries through their membership form a substantial numerical political bloc in an organisation of one hundred and fifty seven nations. Therefore, any allocation of permanent Security Council responsibilities should take Africa into consideration. Nigeria's level of activity in global politics appears to confer on it the responsibility to work assiduously toward ensuring a continuing voice for Africa and other developing states in the strategic areas of the United Nations.

(ii) Withdraw From the United Nations

It is difficult to exclude altogether the plausibility of this next alternative, namely, withdrawal from the United Nations. The idea of disengagement would naturally seem a radical approach, yet there are cogent and compelling reasons to support such a line of action. Firstly, the idea of the United Nations as the best instrument for the achievement of a viable global peace and the *deus ex machina* of international diplomacy appears to have gradually eroded with the seeming impotence of the organisation.

Nigeria has taken a special interest in the organisation, placed its limited resources at its disposal to help the collective objectives of the UN as a conflict management machinery. Indeed, Nigeria's worldview has been UN centric. As an advocate of decolonization, Nigeria has acted in concert with other nations to achieve UN decolonization objectives. But recent records show that the UN has proved incapable of exerting pressure on member states to implement decisions especially those relevant to self determination in Southern Africa.

Secondly, the UN impotence in the face of international anarchy is illustrated by the number of major conflicts settled outside the framework of the Organisation. The Vietnam war, the Arab-Israeli confrontation in 1967 and 1973, the Pakistani war of 1971, and more recently the Camp David Accord between Israel and Egypt and the successful transition from white minority to black majority rule in Zimbabwe are all illustrative of settlements achieved outside the UN. The question arises whether Nigeria should continue to expend much needed resources (human and material) on an organisation that is growing increasingly weaker, almost discredited and ignored by its member states. The implication is that the UN has ceased to be accepted as the major peace-keeping organ and nations have increasingly sought to preserve their own national interests rather than utilise the UN as an umbrella or a bridge.

Thirdly, perhaps a complete disengagement option will be justified if the old structure of power continues to be nourished and sustained. The UN Charter in establishing the Security Council, guaranteed a privileged position for the foundation members. Ramphal described it as 'members for life'. Its five permanent members have ensured a continuous exercise of their veto powers over the decisions of the rest of the world. Would a withdrawal policy be in the best interest of Nigeria and the rest of mankind? Or should Nigeria stay and fight the abuse and usurpation of power by the Security Council?

If the aims of Nigeria's multilateral diplomacy continue to be political and functional as it has been most clearly discerned from its participation in various agencies of the United Nations; the Security Council and the General Assembly, it has a primary responsibility to remain in the UN and actively seek a basic restructuring of the Security Council and reform of the UN itself to assure a meaningful representation of other less developed countries. A withdrawal policy would not only be self defeating, but would also increase Nigeria's isolation from global matters and slow down its ascendancy to international prestige and power status.

Chapter 5

Nigeria and the Great Powers

Power in the world is no longer confined to the small directorate of five . . . power is now more dispersed, the reality of power anyway—military power, economic power, political power.[1]
Shridith S. Ramphal

Although it is being widely accepted that the old structure of a rigid bipolar world has shifted remarkably to a multipolar world, the attributes of power still constitute a major area of disagreement among analysts. Spiegel's study over a decade ago appears to be the most internationally accepted ranking of world powers. The multipolar world that developed in the 1970s have been categorised as the superpowers—the United States and the USSR. In second position are Japan, the Federal Republic of Germany, China, France and Great Britain. The third category of middle powers are seventeen in number including Nigeria.[2] But it is a combination of the second level of 'great powers' that is relevant to the purpose of this essay.

The great powers have been accepted as one of the inescapable realities of the modern global system. No less real are their enormous capacity to condition the behaviour of other lesser states on a global level. The overiding factors conditioning Nigeria's relations with the great powers are its basic vulnerabilities as a dependent nation in dire need of development assistance, such as technology and ability to dictate and sustain the price for its raw materials. This feeling basically accounts for the posture of restraint and caution that observers of Nigeria's foreign policy have aptly described as 'economic alignment and political non-alignment'.[3] Nigeria had exhibited a tendency at

123

independence to lean economically on the Western powers while attempting to avoid political entanglements especially in super power conflict. In spite of a deliberate policy of cautious diplomacy with the dominant powers, Nigeria's pro-Western leaning was easily discernable. Heavily dependent on trade and aid (in form of loans) on Great Britain and its Western allies, Nigeria was almost nationally crippled by such potential impediments to its national freedom of action. Yet, for all the limitations of its economic dependence, Nigeria was actively and constructively engaged in such professed non-partisan organisations as the non-aligned movement. Historically, Nigeria has given great deference to Britain. The close relationship between Nigeria and Great Britain has remained, but with sporadic threats to its severance as in the cases of Britain's vacillation on arms shipment solicited to aid Nigeria's civil war efforts, or the strong allegation of British duplicity in the coup of February 13, 1975.[4]

Perhaps, alert to possible repercussions of continued dependence on one ally, Nigeria by the end of the 1960s became convinced of the necessity to diversify its relationships. Thus, it sought to cultivate more extensive relations with East European countries, Japan, the USSR and the Federal Republic of Germany as a way of accelerating and multiplying its options particularly in trade matters and technology transfer. It has been frequently expressed, however, that the Nigerian opening to increased areas in the international environment has brought with it unprecedented dependence on foreign trade, foreign technology and foreign capital. Such arguments, partly erroneous and largely correct, have been used throughout the discussions in this book to verify government policies.

It is virtually impossible to discuss in any detail the bilateral relationships of Nigeria and the seven great powers delineated above. It may be possible, however, to draw conclusions on the common tendencies of the great powers toward Nigeria and the long term political pressures that Nigeria may face in its relations with the great powers.

In its relations with the two most prominent great powers—the Super powers, the United States has increasingly assumed some salience. Although this salience is of relatively recent origin, the United States appears to have now assumed a position of influence in Nigeria's policy (more implicitly) far greater than anyone would have envisaged when Nigeria gained its independence from Britain. The United States had always regarded Africa of which Nigeria is a unit, as the exclusive preserve and responsibility of the European powers. Consequently, there were negligible direct bilateral links at Nigeria's independence.

Nigeria's first real impact on the United States was economic. The 1973-74 Arab oil embargo had reverberations on the US economy and it naturally turned to Nigeria for oil supplies. This development propelled Nigeria into a position of vital economic importance to the United States. In 1976 Nigeria became a significant if not a principal producer of oil, supplying approximately 48 per cent of total oil exports. By 1977, Nigeria's oil exports to the United States had reached a peak of 90 per cent, elevating it to the position of the second major supplier of petroleum after Saudi Arabia.[5] These statistics are not meant to imply a one sided relationship. The petroleum trade has had an equivalent impact on Nigeria's economy. Oil accounts for approximately 90 per cent of Nigeria's total foreign exchange earnings. Therefore, the United States, demand for a substantial portion of Nigeria's petroleum in turn made the United States a prime supplier of much needed foreign exchange. Further to Nigeria's advantage was the enormous deficit in the bilateral trade. By 1980, the United States was over $8 billion dollars in deficit in its trade with Nigeria.[6]

Nigeria has also become politically important to the United States in recent times. Its importance is a direct result of Nigeria's almost messianic mission in Africa and United States strategic, political, economic interests and competition with the Soviet Union in Africa. Political interest in Nigeria was sharpened during the Angola crisis, which brought the United States to the sudden realization that Nigeria by virtue of its new dynamism and influence in African affairs, held the key to the solution of the crisis. The Ford administration sought to use Nigerian as a leverage to influence the legitimization of UNITA and the FNLA as a means of ending the crisis. Under the leadership of General Murtala Muhammed, the political relationship between Nigeria and the United States—(representing the great powers) began to be shaped. The General's historic address to the OAU Extra-ordinary Session debating the Angolan issue is illustrative of the shift in posture:

> . . . Africa has come of age. It is no longer under the orbit of any extra continental power. It should no longer take orders from any country, however powerful. The fortunes of Africa are ours to make or mar. For too long we have kicked around; for too long we have been treated like adolescents who cannot discern their interests and act accordingly. For too long it has presumed that the African needs outside 'experts' to tell him who are his

friends and his enemies. The time has come when we should make it clear that we can decide for ourselves; that we know our own interests and how to protect those interests; that we are capable of resolving African problems without presumptuous lessons in ideological dangers, which more often than not have no relevance for us nor for the problems at hand.[7]

Despite Nigeria's position stated above, there is evidence that the United States still has the opportunity to influence or at least, remain visible in Nigerian politics. Firstly, there are powerful interests in Nigeria which have sought to develop greater ties with the US especially those educated in the US. Secondly, Nigeria changed its constitution in 1979 to a Presidential federal one very much akin to the United States model. Naturally, this emphasizes the American belief in its 'democratic' constitutional paradigm. It has established an ideological affinity or linkage from which Nigeria may find hard to extricate itself. In addition to what Mazrui aptly described as 'fuel and federalism,' the Nigerian-American linkage will be further reinforced by the binding ethnic identification of Nigeria with over twenty five million Black Americans of African descent, who constitute a potential foreign policy resource for Nigeria. In his address at Howard University during a historic state visit to the United States in 1977, General Obasanjo observed that:

'the greatest weakness in the foreign policy of African countries is that although the United States has one of the largest concentration of blacks in the world, this political power has not before now been used to influence its African policy.[8]

Similarly, in pursuit of its objectives in Southern Africa, Nigeria has recognised the United States and its European allies as the key to the solution of the problems, a perception very dominant during the discussions on the Anglo-American proposal for Zimbabwe's independence.

All these developments form the nucleus of the mutual Nigerian-American relationship, a relationship which is focused on mutual economic, political, cultural and US strategic, military and ideological objectives.

The Soviet Union has always been generally perceived as the counter force to American global supremacy, whose goals, perceptions, strategies and general interests incessantly, conflict with parallel American interests.

In the wave of African nationalist movements, the Soviet Union was confident of its ability to outdo the Western imperialist system. It therefore anticipated, quite rightly that large countries like Nigeria, would reach for other systems as soon as they attained independence. The formula of the Soviet policy was a simple one: to radicalise African nationalist leaders through domestic socialism and interaction with the Communist world community, and propel them into discarding English imperialism. While the revolutionary fever caught on in Nkrumah's Ghana and later in Sekou Toure's Guinea in 1958, it failed in Nigeria. Evidence of failure could be discerned from the constant concern of the Balewa administration over the involvement of its citizens with Communist countries. Communist literature was prohibited, the Kuti case indeed became a test of government attempt to virtually 'demonize' communism.[9] Although the Soviet Union maintained a diplomatic presence in Lagos, bilateral involvement was minimal.

A demonstrable shift in relations was seen in 1968 with the Soviet involvement in the Nigerian civil war. The Soviet Union supplied desperately needed arms and counsel to the Federal government of Nigeria and is believed to have been instrumental in recruiting Egyptian pilots for the Nigerian Air Force.[10] Soviet aid to Nigeria in the face of British vacillation and American neutrality had helped to establish (particularly for the Soviet Union) a *modus vivendi* for closer co-operation in the future. But bilateral relations did not flourish as would have been expected. It is not an exaggeration to say that the Soviet Union has been a strong and most reliable supporter of the African cause, notably on issues of decolonization, eradication of apartheid and better terms of trade. Despite the low level of political relations with the Soviet Union, Nigeria has benefitted greatly from their technical assistance. The heavy Soviet involvement in the Ajaokuta Steel Manufacturing project is illustrative.

Nigeria's relations with France has in recent times as in the past, been marked by a 'love-hate' attitude and of course competition. The following indicators reflect this phenomena. Nigeria is bound on its Western, Northern and Eastern territory by the former French speaking colonies—the Republic of Benin, Niger, Chad and the Cameroun. The 'father-son' relationship nurtured between France and Nigeria's neighbours has necessitated a heavy French military, economic and political presence.

Nigeria's policy, in so far as it placed a great emphasis on African unity, economic co-operation and good neighbourliness, needed the co-operation of its four French neighbours. Today, it is difficult to discern why the Republics of Cameroun and Chad excluded themselves from ECOWAS—a subregional economic community designed to achieve accelerated economic development and collective self reliance. What is, perhaps less difficult to observe is that the overbearing French presence contributed not only to a protracted negotiation for the establishment of ECOWAS, but has continued to provide obstruction to the consumation of the subregional economic-cultural and scientific experiment.[11]

On the regional level, France has continued to thwart Nigeria's foreign policy efforts to attain stability in Africa. Indeed, France has become a thorn in Nigeria's side. What makes French policy so objectionable to the Nigerian people is not only its delusive self perception as an extraordinary power capable of containing aggression against its satellites, but its innate impudent use of power to establish and operate *cordone sanitere* bases all over Africa. French activities in Shaba, the Central African Republic, its role in the Chadian conflict, or its attempt to consolidate a French army in Africa under the ruse of a Pan African Security Force, all point to the various tensions in Nigerian-Franco relations.

In spite of the serious threat posed by the French presence at Nigeria's door step, they have successfully sought to penetrate Nigeria's economy. The fact that many of the largest European firms—both in the manufacture of automobile and oil exploration and production are 'safe' and turning out huge profits, is indicative of the general impression that likens France to a 'naughty boy' who gets away with misbehaviour. In other words, French interests in Nigeria have grown steadily, although without publicity. French interests have conflicted with Nigeria's, but without retributions. The French support for the Biafran cause during the Nigerian civil war, though perceived by the French to have been strictly on principles, may indeed have been a strategy of containment of Nigeria's power and influence in Africa. What is easily discernable is that the French political, economic and strategic stakes in Africa are incompatible and indeed, on a collision course with Nigeria's. Mazrui succinctly restated the problem. According to him, 'France is the natural rival of Nigeria'.[12] Mazrui's thesis is based on the assumption that France is potentially poised to defend European interests which may conflict with Nigeria's defence of Africa's interests.

Whether real or imagined, the French pressure in Nigeria and on its security perimeter is a potent force that should not be ignored.

The other great powers, Japan, the Federal Republic of Germany and China have sought investment arrangements with Nigeria, beyond the alleged involvement of West Germany through economic activities in the continued survival of the racist Pretoria regime, it has studiously avoided political entanglements with Nigeria. Instead, they have like Japan, sought to provide technological support which the greater Western powers like the US and Britain had been reluctant to supply.[13] Japan consistently suffers a shortage of raw materials. The large deposits of raw materials in Nigeria and the large market which it provides for finished Japanese products will be a great incentive to maintain friendly relations with Nigeria.

Nigeria's abstinence from the crucial voting on the admission of Mainland China to the United Nations marked a weak beginning in bilateral relations between the two countries.[14] However, China's non-aligned posture and identification with the Third World are ideal qualifications for establishing genuine, constructive relations for mutual benefits.

In spite of the military, economic and political powers that have emerged in the contemporary world scene, power equation is still militarily bipolar. The stability of the world is still largely determined by the power equilibrium between the two super powers and their allies are expected to fall in line. Further, in spite of detente and the Soviet professed principle of peaceful co-existence; the ideologies and interests of the super powers remain incompatible. Their operative formula is to take advantage of local conflicts to project and maximise their own interests. It is also relevant to add that once they are involved in a conflict, they inevitably become a factor in the process and resolutions. The United States having blatantly established its support for the survival of minority illegal regimes in Southern Africa, did set in motion a situation of competition with the Soviet Union and its allies. Today, the solution to the Namibian problem is predicated on preconditions set by the United States and its allies and a continuation of Soviet backed military support to Angola. The foremost task of future Nigerian policy toward these extra continental powers is to diagnose astutely the complexities of big power politics and apply its relative power prudently to acquire their technical knowledge and political experience, while being constantly aware of their disruptive influences. In the remainder of the 20th century,

Nigeria in its relationship with the great powers should seek the following:

(i) Intensified, but Cautious Relationship with the Great Powers

Nigeria seems to have little choice regarding its relations with this group of powers. But it can, with great caution and tact direct its dealings with them toward the achievement of national objectives. This alternative is based on the assumption that the technology and the expertise of these powers are profoundly needed to attain the scientific-technological transformation so crucial to the development of Nigeria.

The United States, the Soviet Union, Japan and the great European powers still control a substantial amount of investment and advanced technologies throughout the world. Achieving a closer and long-term relationship with them will help toward achieving self-sufficiency. At the same time Nigeria must give the great powers the option to demonstrate, through concrete actions a desire for strengthened ties. To this end, Nigeria in turn will eschew ideological considerations in its policy decisions. However, the power and flexibility of Nigeria vis-a-vis the great powers will depend to a great extent on Nigeria's economic role and continued viability in the international system. There is no doubt that Nigeria's reduced export earnings in oil will provide a stimulant for the revival of traditional exports which had been the primary source of revenue prior to the oil boom. By the end of the 1980s, Nigeria would have attained self-sufficiency in food production and even become a major exporter of food. Self-sufficiency in steel production by the end of 1990 would have decreased Nigeria's dependence on external sources. Even the minimum pursuit of these vital goals would serve to remove some of the great power myths that Nigeria is, a 'sleeping giant', a less serious nation.

(ii) An Assertive Policy Toward the Great Powers

It is tempting to feel that Nigeria in the future would be compelled to adopt a subservient posture toward the great powers as a result of the crisis created by declining oil export revenue and recession. While it may be logical to assume that income from the sale of petroleum is the base for Nigeria's ability to play an international role, it may be stated that despite the reduction of petroleum income, Nigeria's political influence and/or leverage is still potent. The big powers have placed Nigeria foremost in their considerations in conflict management. In other words, there is an innate responsibility ascribed to Nigeria in the global policies of the big powers that could neither be defined nor limited in terms of economic buoyancy. Nigeria can use the overwhelming influence and power which it enjoys to exert pressure on the big powers to adhere to the cause of African countries which Nigeria advances.

In the future, Nigeria will still suffer some major vulnerability in national and sub-regional affairs with an increasingly visible French presence. An assertive foreign policy would be a natural response based on the concern for national independence, sovereignty and territorial integrity. The option of carving out a defence perimeter (discussed in detail in Chapter 4) is reiterated here. Should Nigeria's foreign policy objectives and security be thwarted by big power intervention such that it appears to be fated to remain a dependent giant, a bold nationalistic policy should be evolved which would automatically declare Nigeria and its immediate environs prohibited from neo-colonial hegemony. The strength and effectiveness of Nigeria's military capability may be brought to test in this option, but the real factor that will work in Nigeria's favour is the climate that would be created by the mutual suspicion and continued rivalry between the U.S. and the Soviet Union. Their conflictive mutual global interests would serve as a mutual restraining factor and leave Nigeria the option of asserting its own rights.

(iii) Diversification of Relations

The assumption underlying this alternative is that a solid and bold foreign policy is predicated on a genuine reduction of dependence (especially economic) on routine partners. A policy of diversification of its relations reinforced by a sound viable economy will convert Nigeria into an even more significant force in global politics.

There is a growing demand for natural resources and raw materials and Nigeria is a significant repository. Also, most great powers are now embarking on finding new markets for their products. Nigeria satisfies the pre-requisites of supplier and market. It follows that both Nigeria and the Nigerian market will become increasingly important to the established powers in the coming years. The increasing influence, leverage and freedom of action for Nigeria would stem from the competition to which the big powers will be subjected vis-a-vis Nigeria. This will be an appropriate scenario for Nigeria to exercise its political will, completely independent of any uncooperative powers.

A new dynamic and diversification policy would involve significant modification in the source of armaments supplies, technical manpower training, military training and technological aid. The danger inherent in special relationship with great powers is described by Akinyemi:

> . . . The economy of a super power, its ability to seek and get alternatives, its ability to withstand economic and political shock and its ability to inflict punishment are enormous.[15]

In sum, Nigeria should in future be wary of the generosity of the major powers. This alternative stresses a move towards new but cautious relationships towards the middle powers like India, Eastern European countries, Sweden, Venezuela, Brazil and Mexico, with a parallel reduction or the absence of any kind of special relationship with the big powers. The idea of cultivating more extensive and diverse relations with countries that are industrialised, but politically low-keyed, will be a way of multiplying Nigeria's international options in vital areas of development—technology and trade. The idea is also designed to enable Nigeria influence the great powers through third parties, especially in times of crises.

Footnotes

PREFACE

1. See for example, the 'Independence Issue' of *New Nigerian*, Saturday, 30 September, 1978 which contained several articles on the future directions of Nigeria's foreign policy. The various attempts to postulate a new philosophy of foreign policy for Nigeria include Ray Ofoegbu, *The Nigerian Foreign Policy*, Star Printing and Publishing Co. Ltd., Enugu, 1979. For example, Ofoegbu urged an abandonment of Nigeria's non-aligned posture. See also, Chuba Okadigbo's 'Pan-Africanism As New Nigerian Foreign Policy' in *New Nigerian*. Op. Cit. VII and XII.
   in *New Nigerian*. Op. Cit. VII and XII.

2. For a succinct and provoking article, See Tunde Adeniran, 'Coping With External Affairs' *Sunday Times*, August 1982, p. 11. 'Evolving a Defence Policy' *New Nigerian* (Editorial) 28 February 1982, p. 3. A cursory look at the opinions expressed in numerous Nigerian newspapers reveals a tendency to question 'where Nigeria is going.'

3. Ronald Steel; *Headline Series*, No. 193, (February 1969), pp. 21-36.

CHAPTER I

1. Rajni Kothari, *Footsteps into the Future: Diagnosis of the Present World and a Design for an Alternative* (The Free Press, New York, 1973).
2. See 'A Short History of Futuristics' in a catalogue published by the World Future Society (Washington D.C.) 1980.
3. See Uma Eleazu, 'African Studies and Studies of the Future,' *Issue,* Vol. IV, No. 4, pp. 3–8.
4. It may be noted that the philosophical assumption underlying the studies of the future is that man is capable of controlling and shaping his own destiny. The thought of the future itself is designed to help us engage in self analysis, clarify our values, and develop long-range planning for alternatives.
5. For a more expanded perception of the thrust of futures study, see Herman Kahn and Anthony, Weiner, *The Year 2000: A Framework for Speculation on the Next Twenty Years.* (New York, The Macmillan, 1967) especially chapters 1 and 2.
6. See *Economic Growth in the Future,* published by Edison Electric Institute (Mc Graw-Hill. N.Y. 1976). See also Wassily Leontief et al, *Future of the World Economy: A United Nations Study* (Oxford University Press, 1977), Robert U. Ayres *Uncertain Futures: Challenges for Decision Makers.* (John Wiley and Sons
7. The Driving force of authors on futuristics and future oriented organisations like the Club of Rome, Delphi Studies or World Future Society is to explore desirable futures in the hopes of building a better world.
8. See Editor's introduction: 'Prediction and Forecasting in Foreign Policy,' in *Co-operation and Conflict,* Nordic Journal of International Studies (Sweden XVI, 1981), pp. 1.
9. Rajni Kathari *Ibid,* pp. 2.
10. See Lars-Goran Stenelo, 'Prediction and Foreign Policy Heritage,' in *Co-operation and Conflict* op. cit. pp. 3-17.
11. Stenelo, *Ibid.*
12. *Ibid.* This hypothesis is further elaborated in another study by Stenelo. In his *Foreign Policy Predictions* (Lund 1980), he tackles this point by means of conceptual and empirical analysis to bolster his arguments.
13. *Ibid.* pp. 80-109.
14. In empirical terms, Stenelo lucidly and persuasively demonstrates

that 'Doctrines' as in the case of the 'Domino Theory' or the 'Communist Aggressor' in American foreign policy became a heritage and basis for analogy for future foreign policy.

15. Cited in Editor's Introduction, *Co-operation and Conflict op. cit.*
16. Joseph Frankel, *Contemporary International Theory and the Behaviour of States,* (Oxford University Press, New York: The Macmillan, 1967), pp. 398.
17. Kothari, *Op. Cit.* p. 118.
18. Uma Eleazu, *Op. Cit.* p. 56.
19. Christer Jossen, Editorial in Co-operation and Conflict. *Op Cit.*
20. There is a significant risk in speculating about the future even when 'scientific' criteria and methodologies are employed. The uncertainty is exemplified by concepts, used in predictions such as 'forecasts', 'conjectures', 'peering', 'prophecies', all of which point to the tendency to guess. Fortunately recent serious studies on the future have attempted to base predictions on empirical analysis.
21. Stenelo, *Op. Cit.* p. 100. Stenelo is quite perceptive in his conclusion that credibility is a crucial methological problem for the predictor.
22. Kothari, *Op. Cit.*
23. *See Martin Dent*, 'Nigeria, Ghana and the World,' *Venture,* Vol. 21, No. 2, February 1976. pp. 1-12.
24. The national interest as perceived by successive administrations can be gleaned from the doctrines they tried to enunciate, especially from major policy pronouncements.
25. Read Vernon Van Dyke; *International Politics* (Meredith Corporation, N.Y. 1972) Chap. 1. Dyke like other political scientists have wrestled with the concept of 'national interest' and discovered that it is essentially a short hand expression of the sum total of the objectives and goals of a nation state.
26. See Joseph Frankel, *Op. Cit.* p. 76.
27. Frankel, p. 77.
28. Frankel p. 80.
29. See especially Gordon J. Idang, *Nigeria: Internal Politics and Foreign Policy (1960-1966)* Ibadan University Press, 1973, pp. 5-19.
30. Quoted in Sam Oyovbaire, 'The National Interest and Nigerian Foreign Policy in the 80s'. Text of a presidential address delivered at the annual meeting of the Nigerian Society of International

Affairs, Lagos.

31. The first top level elaboration of Nigeria's foreign policy objectives often referred to as the 'Dodan Declaration'. Dodan is the name of the military barracks where the military heads of state resided. Various national newspapers and media published this broadcast, among them, the *Daily Times,* 30 July 1976.

32. Olajide Aluko's criticism of the Dodan Declaration as quoted in the text was fully elaborated at a lecture which he delivered at the Nigerian Institute of International Affairs in March 1979.

33. Olajide Aluko, *Ibid.*

34. See for example, General Mohammed's address to the OAU. General Obasanjo's address to various black communities on his historic visit to the United States in 1977. Ministry of information releases.

35. The Presidency in Nigeria, 'Continuing Nigeria's preoccupation with African Problems.' Office of the President, Department of Information.

36. Donald E. Nuechterlein, *National Interests and Presidential Leadership* (Colorado, Westview Press, 1978), especially chapters 2 and 3. Nuechterlein's analysis is perhaps the most useful for identifying the intensity of the national interest.

37. The mood of the nation, especially as presented by the news media has been lucidly analysed by Stanley Macebuh in the *Nigerian Forum:* (September/October, 1981), pp. 293-301.

38. *Nuechterlein, National Interests and Presidential Leadership Op. Cit.* For a consonant view see, Coplin, William D. *Introduction to International Politics: a Theoretical Overview* (Chicago, Marham Publishers 1971)

39. Stenelo, Lars-Goran, in *Conflict and Co-operation Op. Cit.*

40. See Mark W. Delancy, 'Nigeria: Foreign Policy Alternatives', Paper presented at the University of Nsukka, Nigeria 1979.

41. Claude S. Phillips, Jr. *The Development of Nigerian Foreign Policy* (Evanston: North western University Press 1964) pp. 60-82; J. Isawa Elaigwu, 'Nigeria and Non-alignment: Rhetoric and Performance in Foreign Policy.' Paper presented at the International Conference on Non-alignment Jan. 23-26, 1980. Nigerian Institute of International Affairs, Lagos.

42. Douglas G. Anglin, 'Nigeria: Political Non-Alignment and Economic Alignment,' *Journal of Modern African Studies* Vol. 2, (July 1964), pp. 247-263. Anglin persuasively argues that Nigeria deli-

berately pursued a policy of economic alignment out of self-interest.

43. See Stenelo. 'Predictions and Foreign Policy Heritage', *Op. Cit.* pp. 3-17.

44. A. Bolaji Akinyemi and Margaret Vogt, *'Nigeria and Southern Africa: The Policy Options'* Edited by Douglas Anglin, Timothy M. Shaw and Carl G. Widstrand. (University Press of America 1978) pp. 151-168.

45. A careful study of the foreign policy pronouncements of successive Nigerian leaders points to the irresistable tendency to view Nigeria's role especially in African affairs as divine. It is suggested here that the early efforts at independence to assert this role even in rhetoric, may have formed the embryonic stage of Nigeria's African policy.

46. The selected speeches of Generals Ironsi, Murtala Muhammed, Gowon and President Shagari have to date not been compiled. But a cursory look at Nigerian Newspapers would help indicate this line of perception.

47. It would perhaps, be interesting to conduct a systematic study on Nigeria's posture in the realm of morality. Is Nigeria's concept of morality and moral principles conducive to the traditional character of the international system in which the coercive weight of power is pre-eminent?

48. As analysed by R. A. Akindele, in the *Nigerian Forum*, (March 1981) pp. 29-35.

49. See Sam Epelle Nigeria Speaks—Speeches by *Alhaji Tafawa Balewa* (Longmans of Nigeria) 1964, p. 73.

50. *Ibid.* p. 91.

51. Olajide Aluko, 'Nigerian Foreign Policy,' in *The Foreign Policies of African States,* (Hodder and Stoughton, Kent, 1977) p. 170.

52. See Keesing's Contemporary Archives, March, 1971.

53. This was clearly visible in General Murtala Muhammed's landmark address at the Extraordinary Summit Conference of the OAU held in Addis Ababa, Jan. 11, 1976. See Federal Ministry of Information Press Release, Lagos, Jan. 12, 1976. The United States' reaction was a Veto of Angola's application for membership to the United Nations.

54. President Shehu Shagari, Address at the United Nations General Assembly. See *Concord* (Nigeria). 11 October 1980, pp. 8 and 9.

55. *Ibid.*

56. President Shehu Shagari's first annual dinner address to the members and staff of the Nigerian Institute of International Affairs, 1980.

CHAPTER II

1. F. S. Northedge, (Ed.) *The Foreign Policies of the Powers*, (London: February, 1968) p. 15.

2. A.B. Akinyemi, *Foreign Policy and Federalism: The Nigerian Experience*, (Ibadan University Press, 1974) especially Chapter 2 on 'The Political System'.

3. *Ibid*. p. 29.

4. *Ibid*. p. 29.

5. See Uma Eleazu, *Federalism and Nation Building: The Nigerian Experience* 1954-1964 (Arthur H. Stockwell Ltd., Devon 1979) Eleazu offers a succint and refreshing perspective of federalism in Nigeria. The question posed in the text is the major thrust of Eleazu's treatise. See also, Awa, E. *Issues in Federalism* (Benin, Ethiope Publishing, 1977). A.B. Akinyemi, P.D. Cole and W. Ofonagoro, (Eds.) *Readings on Federalism*. Nigerian Institute of International Affairs, Lagos 1979.

6. Eleazu *Ibid*. p. 7.

7. Eleazu *Ibid*. p. 102.

8. Raph Uwechue, *Reflections on the Nigerian Civil War: Facing the Future* (Jeune Afrique Paris 1968) p. 155.

9. The conflicting policy pronouncements of the regional governments often glaringly illustrated the deep divisions in the Nigerian policy. Indeed Nigeria's lack of cohesion in foreign policy in the first republic has never escaped the attention of analysts.

10. Intense ethnic divisions contributed immensely (and may yet contribute) to the failure of Nigerian Federalism. It is true that ethnicity is a significant problem in Nigeria, but then ethnicity is not unique to Nigeria. Scholars like Uma O. Eleazu, Raph Uwechue and Bolaji Akinyemi, have in their various discourses attempted to tackle the problem of Nigerian Federalism. For a more scientific study of Federal systems in the world see Temple University Centre publications for the study of Federalism, Pennsylvania, especially their journal *Publius*.

11. Quoted in Eleazu, *Op. cit*. p. 254.

12. Raph Uwechue, *Reflections on the Nigerian Civil war, op. cit*. Note especially the qualification 'this time, — after careful consideration . . .' which appears to suggest differences in the policy process in the Gowon and Murtala Muhammed regimes. In other words, the sudden fragmentation of the regional centres from four

to twelve in 1967 was not necessarily the result of a rational or consultative decision making, but a reaction to the threat of secession. Whereas, the further division of the country into nineteen states was made after due consultations. Indeed, this could provide a basis for study of *decision making* in the Nigerian policy.

13. See especially R.A. Akindele, Nigerian Parliament and Foreign Policy, 1960-1966, *Quarterly Journal of Administration, 7 (3) (1973), pp. 279-291.*

14. See especially 'An Elastic Federal Union' in Raph Uwechue, *Op. cit.,* pp. 150-172. Also Uma Eleazu, *Federalism and Nation Building Op. cit.* especially chapter 9—'Federalism and the Future of Nigeria'. pp. 249-268.

15. *Ibid.*

16. The 'New Nigerian Foreign Policy' based on the celebrated 'Adedeji Report'. A policy review body was re-echoed in the foreign policy provisions of the New Nigerian constitution.

17. Section 14 of the *Report of the Constitution Drafting Committee containing the Draft Constitution.* Now section 19 of the *Constitution of Federal Republic of Nigeria.*

18. *Ibid.* See also A.B. Akinyemi (Ed.), *Foreign Policy and the New Constitution* (Nigerian Institute of International Affairs Monograph Series, No. 4).

19. F. Chidozie Ogene, 'Foreign Policy Position: An Assessment of the First Year of Shagari's Administration', in *Daily Times* (Wednesday, 1 October, 1980) p. 9.

20. See Schedule 2, Part 1, Item 19. Article 2 paragraph 3, Article 5 paragraph 3(a) Article 12, sections 1, 2, 3 sections 136, 2 (a) 139, 140. Item 3 in schedule (a) part 1. *Constitution of the Federal Republic of Nigeria.*

21. See *Financial Times* Supplement (Tuesday, 29 August, 1978) pp. 16, 19, and 21.

22. A.B. Akinyemi in an address to the Nigerian Senate on 'The Presidential System and International Affairs', Lagos, 1980.

23. *Ibid.* p. 8.

24. The Constitution of the Federal Republic of Nigeria, Article 53(b)

25. Akinyemi, A. Bolaji, *Op. cit.*

26. See, F. Chidozie Ogene, in *New Nigerian* 30 Sept., 1978.

27. The prerequisites of power as elaborated by Osita Eze in a proposal presented to the Research Department of the Nigerian Institute of International Affairs. The crucial elements of power, Eze

argues, include a reasonable degree of autonomy in the decision-making process, the resources available in the country and the political philosophy underlying the nation's strategy for economic development.

28. Implicit in this observation is the possibility that even the most rationally formulated foreign policy may be marred by ineffectiveness in the execution stage—i.e. in relations with other states.

29. Olajide Aluko, Essays on Nigerian Foreign Policy, (George Allen & Unwin Ltd. London, 1981) pp. 162-163.

30. *Ibid.* Professor Aluko has played a leading role in providing insightful analysis into the role of the foreign policy bureaucracy in Nigerian foreign relations.

31. Douglas G. Anglin, *Op. cit.* Indeed, the perception of the leadership of the path to Nigeria's development derived essentially from Nigeria's colonial heritage. Perhaps, only a radical reversal of policy could have changed the trend.

32. See Federation of Nigeria, *National Development Plan 1962-1968* (Lagos, Ministry of Economic Development 1962).

33. Okwudiba Nnoli, 'Nigerian Policy Towards Southern Africa,' in *Nigerian Journal of International Affairs,* Vol. 2 Nos. 1 and 2 1976), pp. 26-29.

34. Nigerian Scholars like Claude Ake and Osita Eze have written a number of provocative books and articles on Africa's political economy. In the studies referred to in the text, they have consistently viewed the deplorable state of Africa's and specifically Nigeria's political economy as the tragedy of neocolonial dependence exacerbated by the attitudes of the ruling class.

35. See *Africa,* Monthly Magazine, London No. 58.

36. Report of the *Second National Development Plan,* 1970-1974, pp. 86-87. See also *Third National Development Plan, 1975-1980 (Lagos Ministry of Economic Development, 1975).*

37. Olajide Aluko, "Nigeria and the Superpowers" in *Essays in Nigerian Foreign Policy,* Op. Cit. p. 138.

38. Nigeria: Bulletin on Foreign Affairs Vol. 9, No. 11 (November 1979) Also cited in *New Nigerian* (Wednesday 1 Oct., 1980) p. 9.

40. See Isaac Aluko-Olokun, 'The Nigerian Economy in Crisis', *Nigerian Forum* (June 1982) pp. 573-585. See especially *Central Bank Report.*

41. *Ibid.*

42. The fall in oil prices is a combination of factors. It is believed that by the late 1980s, more than one third of the world oil supply from outside North America and the communist bloc would come fron Non-OPEC nations. In addition, the emphasis on, and acceleration of efforts to create alternative sources of energy would exacerbate an 'oil glut' situation.

43. President Shehu Shagari's broadcast to the nation in April, 1982, announcing stringent economic measures to contain the decline of foreign exchange earnings and economic growth. Reported in all the Nigerian daily newspapers—*Daily Times,* 22 April, 1982, pp. 1-3.

44. See *The Statesman,* 22 April, 1982, pp. 5-6.

45. *Ibid.* An implicit admission that Nigeria's economic strength and effectiveness inevitably depends on the external environment.

46. The major and lesser industrial countries depend on petroleum for a substantial proportion of their energy needs. It is naturally in their interest to protect the economic growth of their nations from being endangered by a seeming impenetrable OPEC solidarity.

47. National security and defence are highly important issues in a nation's policy. These were elements of Nigeria's foreign policy interests, but their attainment has been largely hampered by internal pressures.

48. This matter is reasonably well covered by Gordon J. Idang, *Op. cit.* Olajide Aluko, *Essays on Nigerian Foreign Policy. Op. cit.*

49. *See the Military Balance 1977-1978* (London: The Institute for Strategic Studies) pp. 45. This is an estimated figure. The number varies with the source of information.

50. Cited in O.S. Kamanu, 'Nigeria: Reflections on the Defence Posture for the 1980s'. Research Department. Nigerian Institute of International Affairs, Lagos.

51. *The Punch,* (Nigeria) Saturday, 10 April, 1982, p. 12.

52. See A. Bolaji Akinyemi, 'Confrontation and Dialogue: Essence of a Leading Role for Nigeria', *Venture,* vol. 24, no. 1 1972. The concept of 'Middle Power' has been used to denote those developing countries which possess relatively superior components of power necessary for ascendancy to great power status. See for example, Stephen Spiegel, *Dominance and Diversity: The International Hierarchy* (Boston: Little Brown, 1972), pp. 93-105.

53. Consult Max G. Manwarring, 'Brazilian Military Powers: A capa-

bility Analysis, in Wayne A. Selcher (Ed.) *Brazil in the International System: The Rise of a Middle Power.* (Westview Press Boulder, Colorado 1981), pp. 65-98. Manwarring has painstakingly organised a scientific study of military capability—a crucial factor in assessing the relative position of any nation vis-a-vis the other states.

54. The estimated figure for 1980-81, a drastic reduction from the civil war armed forces strength of over 250,000.

55. There are diverse comments and assessment of combat capabilities of Nigeria in comparison to other 'middle powers'. A systematic study needs to be conducted on this.

56. Margaret A. Vogt, 'Nigeria's Defence: An Assessment', *Nigerian Forum,* (April 1981), pp. 73-87.

57. Max G. Manwarring, *Op. cit.* See also Riordan Roett, 'Brazil Ascendant: International Relations and Geopolitics in the late 20th century', *Journal of International Affairs,* Vol. 29, No. 2, 1975.

58. See Max G. Warring, *Op. cit.*

59. Consonant with Osita Eze's indices of national power are the crucial elements of military capability which are listed in the text. Most basic texts on international relations address this problem. For further reading, see especially Ray S. Cline, *World Power Assessment: A Calculus of Strategic Drift,* (Washington, D.C.: Georgetown University Center for Strategic Studies, 1975): Klaus Knorr, *Military Power and Potential* (Lexington, Mass, D.C. Health and Co, 1970).

60. See *New Nigerian,* (August 18, 1975).

61. Kamanu, O.S. 'Nigeria: Reflections on the Defence Posture for the 1980s'. *Op. Cit; Financial Times Survey* (London) (29 and 30 August, 1978).

62. *New Nigerian,* (28 February, 1982), p. 3.

63. There is a near consensus of the strategic view that Nigeria will continue to feel a climate of uneasiness with the French threat, especially along its borders. Ali Mazrui put it succintly, 'the enemy of Nigeria is France, not South Africa'.

64. David Easton, *A Systems Analysis of Political Life* (New York: Wiley, 1965) pp. 37-237.

65. William D. Coplin, *Introduction to International Politics* (Rand McNally College Publishers 1974), p. 69.

66. *Ibid.*

67. Discussed in James N. Rosenau, *Domestic Sources of Foreign Policy* (New York: Free Press, 1967). Although Rosenau focuses primarily on American Foreign policy, some of his typologies are applicable to the Nigerian situation. For more general reading, see Gabriel A. Almond and G. Bingham Powell, Jr; *Comparative Politics: A Developmental Approach* (Boston: Little, Brown, 1966), especially chapter 5.

68. See Olajide Aluko, Mark W. De Lancy, *Op. Cit.*

69. A.B. Akinyemi, *Foreign Policy and Federalism Op. Cit.*, pp. 2-3.

70. *Ibid.* pp. 4, 69.

71. *Ibid.*

72. *Ibid.*

73. *Ibid.*, p. 104.

74. Gordon Idang, *Op. Cit.*

75. The military as a consequence of its acceptance of incorporating the civil service bureaucracy in decision-making as a most effective means of effecting a smooth administration, over-relied on the administrators and created instead 'Super Permanent Secretaries.' See Alaba Ogunsanwo, *The Nigerian Military and Foreign Policy 1975-1979: Processes, Principles and Performance and Contradictions*, (Princeton: Center for International Studies, University of Princeton 1981).

76. J.N. Garba, 'Nigerian Foreign Policy and the National Interest', Address to the Students of Ahmadu Bello University, Zaria, 10 February, 1978.

77. While the Nigerian Chamber of Commerce and other financial interests have become significant in recent times, their role in shaping foreign policy has not been determined. They will in the future exercise some leverage over government if they continue to support (as they have in the past four years) government economic foreign policy.

78. Very rewarding insights on Nigeria's political parties, their interests and conflicts has been provided in Walter Ofonagoro's study.

79. *Nigerian Tribune* (Editorial) 18 March, 1981.

80. *Daily Times* (Opinion), 18 March, 1981.

81. The most significant analysis of the Nigerian public reaction to the Camerounian assault on Nigeria is presented by Stanley Macebuh in *Nigerian Forum*, (September/October 1981) pp. 301-306.

82. A.B. Akinyemi, 'Presidential System and International Relations'. An address to the Nigerian Senate. (Unpublished). The psychological dimension of the decision maker is starkly presented by Akinyemi. Care should be taken not to exaggerate the role of the leadership or underemphasize it. See James N. Rosenau, 'Pretheories and Theories of Foreign Policy', in R. Barry Farrell cited below.

83. James N. Rosenau, 'Pre-Theories and Theories of Foreign Policy', in R. Barry Farrell, (Ed.) *Approaches to International and Comparative Politics.* (Evanston, North Western Press, 1966, pp. 27-92.

84. Gordon J. Idang, *Op. Cit.* pp. 51-55, provides an insightful analysis of Balewa's idiosyncracies.

85. *Ibid.*

86. A.B. Akinyemi, *Federalism and Foreign Policy*, p. 106.

87. See Colin Legum, *Observer*, (London) 3 August, 1975. See also, Olajide Aluko, *Essays in Nigerian Foreign Policy Op. Cit.* p. 105. He presents the Nixonian view of Gowon as 'magnanimous' which is almost reflective of Colin Legume's Christian perception of Gowon.

88. Olajide Aluko, *Ibid.*, especially Chapter 1. 'Nigeria's Initiative in Economic Community of West African States', pp. 11-20. For additional reading, see U. Joy Ogwu, 'Nigeria's Role in ECOWAS', Text of a lecture delivered at the Command and Staff College, Jaji. Kaduna (Unpublished), Onwuka, and Oscar Benson Ede, 'Nigeria-Cameroon Border Problems: Causes and Some Suggestions'. Seminar paper delivered at the Research Department of the Nigerian Institute of International Affairs, Lagos. June 16, 1981.

89. Oscar Ede, *Op. Cit.* p. 14.

90. Speech delivered by General Murtala Muhammed at the Extraordinary Session of the Organisation of African Unity in Addis Ababa in January 1976, quoted in an address by J.N. Garba, Commissioner for External Affairs, at the University of Ife on 'The New Nigerian Foreign Policy'. *Nigeria. Bulletin on Foreign Affairs*, (Vol. 6 No. 12, December 1976) p. 4.

91. Basil Davidson, 'Africa Finds a New Power', *Daily Times*, (Friday 3 November, 1978), p. 3.

92. Lt. General Olusegun Obasanjo at the 15th Ordinary Session of the OAU Assembly of Heads of States and Government in Khartoum. *Federal Ministry of Information Release* (No. 992

and 993, Lagos. 19 July, 1978). Implicit in General Obasanjo's address was the recognition of the Cuban role in the liberation struggle.

93. Olusegun Obasanjo, *Op. Cit.* In the same breath, he admonished the Cubans against exchanging one form of imperialism and oppression for another.

94. In a comparative foreign policy study, such conclusions can easily be reached by looking at a given set of foreign policies and pronouncements, and looking back to the processes from which the policies emanated. It is possible to identify the various inputs to policy, their relative influence on one another, and the resultant cohesion.

95. One is inclined to view the Balewa/Wachukwu relationship in the first civilian republic in less sympathetic terms. Their vulnerability lay in their lack of coordination and cohesion.

96. Colin Legum *Observer* (London) 15 March, 1981.

97. *Ibid.* Colin Legum.

98. For President Shehu Shagari's world view of international politics, see *The Nigerian Forum*, (March 1981).

99. F. Chidozie Ogene, *Daily Times*, (Wednesday, 1 Oct., 1980) p. 9.

CHAPTER III

1. The struggle between the United States and the Soviet Union soon after WW II became an all-engulfing contest, both powers employing political, ideological, military, economic means to undermine each other. As the cold war intensified, the antagonists, each sought to spread its influence. American presence was represented by the western colonial powers, consequently, their conflicts enveloped the weaker African states. For a brief but insightful analysis, see Gerald J. Bender and Richard L. Skiar, 'Africa and the Super powers' *World Issues,* (October/November, 1978), pp. 3-10.

2. See U. Joy Ogwu 'La Co-operation Sur-Sur: Problemas, Posibilidades y Perspectivas en Una Relacion Emergente' in *Nueva Sociedad* (May-June, 1982), pp. 27-39.

3. The 'Concentric Circle' typology is employed especially by Olajide Aluko in his *Essays on Nigerian Foreign Policy. Op. cit.*

4. This assumption that a successful policy in the ECOWAS sub-region which is Nigeria's immediate environment is the key to Nigeria's political future in the international arena.

5. Joe Nanven Garba, Nigeria's Commissioner for External Affairs (1975-1979) in an address to the Nigerian Diplomatic Corps, (June 21, 1976).

6. *Daily Times* (January 2, 1960) cited in A.B. Akinyemi, *Foreign Policy and Federalism* Op. cit.

7. Gordon J. Idang, *Nigeria's Internal Politics and Foreign Policy, 1960-1966* (Ibadan: Ibadan University Press, 1975) p. 120.

8. Specifically since 1975, successive Nigerian governments have consistently sounded a keynote in their external relations which has been defined as 'protection of the dignity of black peoples' wherever they may be. This moral commitment manifests itself especially in Nigeria's support for the oppressed blacks in Southern Africa. For key presidential pronouncements on this doctrine, see reports on General Obasanjo's United States visit, 'The Presidency in Nigeria' Office of the President, Department of Information, p. 12.

9. *Nigeria Speaks—Speeches by Sir Abubakar Tafawa Balewa:* Introduced by Sam Ekpelle (Longmans of Nigeria, 1964), p. 91.

10. Okwudiba Nnoli, 'Nigerian Policy Towards Southern Africa', *Nigerian Journal of International Affairs,* Vol. 2, Nos. 1 and 2,

(1976), p. 15. See also A.B. Akinyemi, Foreign Policy and Federalism Op. cit. p. 107.

11. *Ibid.*

12. See Olajide Aluko, *The Foreign Policy of African states,* Op. cit. p. 170.

13. *Ibid.* p. 172.

14. *New Nigeria* (Editorial) 9 June, 1971, p. 1.

15. *Morning Post* (Nigeria) 9 June, 1971, p. 4.

16. See Ian Mackler, *Pattern for Profit in Southern Africa,* (New York: Atheneum 1975), p. 19.

17. This has been suggested by A. Bolaji Akinyemi and Margaret Vogt, 'Nigeria and Southern Africa: The Policy Options,' in *Conflict and Change in Southern Africa: Papers from a Scandinavian Conference* Edited by: Douglas Anglin, Timothy Shaw, and Carl Widstrand. See also, Okwudiba Nnoli *Op. Cit.*

18. That public consensus and support is a crucial ingredient for the success of government policy has been glaringly demonstrated by the Nigerian public support for Nigeria's Southern African policy.

19. A. Bolaji Akinyemi and Margaret Vogt, *Op. Cit.* p. 150.

20. Ian Mackler, *Pattern For Profit in Southern Africa* p. 27 for his succint definition of the system of apartheid.

21. George A. Obiozor, *Nigerian Participation At The United Nations* (Doctoral Dissertation (Columbia University, New York), pp. 11-19.

22. The nationalisation of companies which disregarded Nigeria's sanctions against South Africa amply demonstrated at the time, Nigeria's determination to utilise its economic leverage to enforce sanctions.

23. The decision of the federal military government to turn down Henry Kissinger's request to visit Nigeria early in 1976, can be viewed as one of those political pressures which Nigeria attempted to exert on the United States for America's response, see Peter Enahoro, 'Carter Woos Africa,' *Africa Magazine* No. 76 (December, 1977).

24. *See Africa Report* (November-December, 1976) pp. 2-3 for Brigadier Garba's response to the Kissinger's visit in an interview with Anthony Hughes.

25. Nigeria's earlier stance on the Anglo-American Peace Proposal had been one of support for a constitutional settlement. See *Africa Report Op. Cit.* p. 3.

26. Lecture delivered by the Nigerian Vice-President, Alex Ekwueme at the International Conference on Movement Against Apartheid. Ministry of Information Press Release, No. 415, Lagos, March 15, 1982.

27. *National Concord* (Nigeria) 20 June, 1981, pp. 1-16.

28. This implies that the doctrine was not conceived in a vacuum. Rather it was formulated as the result of the practical conception of the Nigerian national interest (cited in A. Bolaji Akinyemi and U. Joy Ogwu, 'Nigeria and Overseas Africans': *The limits of National Interest.* (Forthcoming).

29. *Ibid.*

30. *Press Release,* No. 2300, *(21 November, 1980) Department of* Information, Executive Office of the President, Lagos.

31. Ian Macler, Pattern For Profit in Southern Africa, especially chapter.

32. See *Africa* No. 58, June 1976, p. 14.

33. A comprehensive treatment of the issue of a high command for Africa has been provided by Akinyemi and Vogt.

34. See U. Joy Ogwu, 'Nigerian and Brazil: Perspectives on a Dialogue'. *Nigerian Forum* (July 1981) pp. 167-172.

35. See Speech delivered by General Obasanjo at the World Conference Against Apartheid held in Lagos, Jan., 1978.

36. *Investment in Apartheid,* compiled by International Confederation of Free Trade Union, and published at the request of the Special Committee against Apartheid. Department of Political and Security Affairs, United Nations, (June 1978) pp. 1-28. See also, Sean Gervasi, 'What Arms Embargo?' *Southern Africa,* Vol. X, No. 6 (August 1977, p. 6).

37. Dependency and its complexities elaborated by Susan Strange, 'What is Economic Power and Who Has It?' *International Journal* 30 (Spring 1975): 207-224.

38. Osita Eze, 'Multinationals in Southern Africa' (Unpublished).

39. *Ibid.*

40. See Ogwu, J. 'Report of a Nigerian/Brazilian Dialogue on Foreign Policy' Published by the Nigerian Institute of International Affairs Lagos, 1982.

41. *Daily Times,* (Nigeria) Saturday, 5 September, 1981) p. 5.

42. *See African Development,* (November 1976), p 1085.

43. See Ogwu, J. 'Shaping US African Policy: What Role For Black America?' in *Nigerian Journal of International Affairs.* (Vol. 5,

Nos. 1 and 2, 1979) pp. 1-21. See also A.B. Akinyemi and U. Joy Ogwu 'Nigeria and Overseas Africans' Op. cit.

44. Reported in *Newsweek* (5 November, 1979) See also 'The Nuclear Threat From South Africa,' Special Report in AFRICA, (No. 113, January, 1981) pp. 45-47.

45. Views expressed by the members of the Diploma Class of 1979/80 (Nigerian Institute of International Affairs.)

46. Ali Mazrui 'Africa's Nuclear Future', in the 1979 Reith Lectures on BBC. *Survival,* (March-April, 1980), p. 79. See also 'The Global Race for Nuclear Arms' in *Newsweek,* (15 September, 1980), pp. 20-25. A growing number of Third World countries are poised to build potentially deadly atomic arsenals.

47. Wolfgang J. Koschnick 'Return of The German Menace' *World View,* (January/February 1977), pp. 19-25. For a more scholarly, comprehensive analysis of Brazilian/German nuclear cooperation. See Wolf Grabendorff, 'Brazil and West Germany' in Wayne A. Selcher (Ed.) *Brazil in The International System: The Rise of a Middle Power* (Westview Press, Inc. 1981) pp. 181-200.

48. It may be noted that Jaja Wachukwu's call for the reopening of a dialogue with South Africa was perceived by most people as a threat to the public consensus that Nigeria's Southern African policy had enjoyed over the years.

49. Osita Eze in his project proposal on 'Nigeria's Role in Africa', persuasively argues that because of the high level of the development of their resources, Angola, Zimbabwe and especially a Black South Africa are likely to pose the greatest threat to Nigeria's aspiration to leadership role in Black Africa.

50. Okoi Arikpo 'Nigeria and the OAU', in *Nigerian Journal of International Affairs,* Vol. 1, No. 1 (July, 1975), pp. 1-11. Nigeria's pioneering role in continental organisations has been generally acclaimed by political observers. See also Gordon J. Idang, p. 120.

51. Joe N. Garba, An address to the Diplomatic Corps in Lagos. *Federal Ministry of Information Release,* No. 88, 21 January, 1976.

52. Quoted in Gordon J. Idang, Op. cit. pp. 120-121.

53. A. Bolaji Akinyemi, *Angola and Nigeria: A study in the National Interest.* Graduate Institute of International Studies, Geneva 1978) pp. 5-6. See also, Arikpo, Op. cit. pp. 3-11.

54. *Ibid.*

55. Okoi Arikpo *Ibid.* p. 5.

56 Yakubu Gowon, Address at the OAU General Assembly, Addis Ababa, June, 1971 (Lagos Ministry of External Affairs Official Record, p. 15). Cited in Ibrahim Gambari, 'Nigeria and the World: A Growing Internal Stability, Wealth, and External Influence' *Journal of International Affairs* (Vol. 29, No. 2, 1975).

57. See Wenike Briggs 'Negotiations between the Enlarged European Economic Community and the African, Carribbean and Pacific (ACP) countries in. *Nigerian Journal of International Affairs*, Vol. 1 No. 1 (July 1975) pp. 12-32.

58. Ambassador Ijewere. Text of 'a brief' on Foreign Policy at the Nigerian Institute of International Affairs.

59. See Stanley Macebuh, Editorial in the *Nigerian Forum.* (May 1981).

60. U. Joy Ogwu, 'The OAU and Intra-Regional Conflict Management: The Special Role of a New Machinery for Peacekeeping' in *Nigerian Forum, Ibid.* pp. 103-110. See especially *Peacekeeping* a monograph summarising papers presented at a national seminar on *Nigeria and Peacekeeping in Africa,* Nigerian Institute of International Affairs 1979.

61. Information derived from a Special Briefing on Nigerian Foreign Policy held in Kaduna in July 1978.

62. An examination of the Daily newspaper clippings available at the press library of the Nigerian Institute of International Affairs, reveals a near consensus of both the press and public of a general uneasiness about the Libyan presence in Chad.

63. Nigeria appears to tread cautiously on the issue of recognition of Polisario. This stance or lack of it is potentially dangerous. A definite Nigerian position is likely to swing the majority opinion in the OAU as it did in the case of Angola. See *New Nigerian* (Monday, 29 September, 1980) p. 5.

64. The concept or principle of 'territorial integrity' in African conflicts has grown to become an immensely thorny problem. The incessant quest for self-determination within existing nation states appears to nullify both the principle and a previously held consensus (among OAU member states) that existing boundaries will be respected.

65. The Military Balance 1979-1980, The International Institute for Strategic Studies. (London) pp. 48-59.

66. *Daily Times,* 27 July, 1980, p. 5.

67. Joe N. Garba in interview with Anthony Hughes, *Africa Report,*

    Op. cit. The Shagari administration has reiterated this posture in numerous policy pronouncements.

68. Information derived from a *Special Briefing. On Chad, organised by the Nigerian Institute of International Affairs in Lagos 1981.*

69. *Prof. Ishaya Audu*, quoted in the *Guardian* (London) Monday, 11 August, 1980, p. 14.

70. Ali Mazrui, 'Nigeria in the Nuclear Age', lecture delivered at the Nigerian Institute of International Affairs, Lagos, 1981.

71. See Okechukwu Mbonu 'Nigerian Neighbours' Aggressiveness', in *Daily Times* (Nigeria) (11 January, 1982) p. 3.

CHAPTER IV

1. Joseph N. Garba (Nigeria's External Affairs Commissioner (1975-1979) in an address to the students of the University of Ife, on 'The New Nigerian Policy'. For the full text see, *Nigeria: Bulletin on Foreign Affairs,* Vol. 6 No. 12 (December 1976) pp. 3-12.

2. See especially, *Balewa Speaks . . .* Op. Cit. *Nigeria: Bulletin on Foreign Affairs.* Ibid pp. 6-8. It is acclaimed that Nigeria played a leading role in hounding the illegal government of South Africa out of the Commonwealth of Nations.

3. House of Representatives Debates, (Lagos, 20 August, 1960) Column 2670.

4. Douglas G. Anglin, *Op. Cit.*

5. See Ervin Laszlo, 'Introduction: the objectives of the New International Economic Order in historical and global perspective' in Ervia Laszlo et al, *The Objectives of the New International Economic Order* (New York: Pergamon for UNITAR, 1978).

6. *Prospects for Trade and Economic Cooperation between Nigeria and the Socialist Countries of Eastern Europe.* Study of UNCTAD Secretariat UN, 1979. TD/B/748.

7. See address by Brigadier J.N. Garba to students of Ahmadu Bello University, Zaria, on 'Nigeria's Foreign Policy and the National Interest', *Federal Ministry of Information Release.* (Lagos, 11 February, 1978).

8. Ibid.

9. It may be noted that one of the recurrent features of American global policy is to win as many countries as possible to its ideological camp—to save the free world from other ideological groups. What Ali Mazrui terms a 'compact' between Nigeria and the United States may indeed be real. See for further reading, Ali Mazrui. 'Fuel and Federalism in Relations Between Nigeria and the United States' Lecture delivered at the Nigerian Institute of International Affairs, (Lagos, 23 February, 1981).

10. Balewa Speaks *Op. Cit.*

11. *The New Nigerian* (Editorial) 8 January, 1971, p. 1.

12. *The Round Table* (Editorial) Issue 282, (April 1981) p. 100. The editor argues that the 80s promise striking changes in the strength of the Commonwealth, especially in the face of seeming UN impotence. See also Shridith Ramphal, *Ibid.,* pp. 164-170.

13. See R. Scott and Sandra C. Pearson 'Oil Boom Reshapes Nigeria's

Future' *Africa Report,* (February 1971) pp. 14-23. See also, C. Fred Bergsten, 'The Response to the Third World', *Foreign Policy* No. 14 (Spring 1974), pp. 3-34. Ian Seymour, *OPEC: Instrument of Change* (The Macmillan Press Ltd., 1980).

14. *Time,* (August 25, 1980), p. 43. Highlights Nigeria's lucrative commercial ties with the United States.

15. It is possible that the political ramifications of membership in OPEC vis-a-vis the industrial countries may be disadvantageous. OPEC was primarily designed to protect oil producing nations from foreign companies and their countries. With the productions of more oil and less demand in the coming years, OPEC members may become vulnerable, whereas, non OPEC oil producing countries may have more leverage.

16. This option assumes that the current market oil glut will go away and OPEC will regain the upper hand that it had in the 1970s, the kind of leverage and power which humbled the Western economies and forced them to the negotiating table. This thesis is further developed in C. Fred Bergsten 'Response to the Third World' *Foreign Policy,* No. 14 (Spring 1974) pp. 3-33.

17. The considerations discussed by Bergsten all came into play in Nigeria's march to primacy.

18. Nigeria possesses a significant resource base. But the basic issue is the transfer of technology for the achievement of development without mortgaging the nation to multinational companies. See O.S. Kamanu, 'Nigeria and the Multinationals: Challenge and Response' paper presented at the Conference on the New International Economic Order, Lagos, October, 1977.

19. *Nigerian Standard* (Opinion), 22 September, 1980, p. 3.

20. O.S. Kamanu, 'Nigeria and the Multinationals . . .' *Op. Cit.*

21. Consult Robert A. Mortimer, *The Third World Coalition in International Politics.* (N.Y.: Praeger Publishers, 1980. See also special issue on 'South-South Cooperation in *Nueva Sociedad* (Venezuela) No. 60 May/June 1982.

22. Alistair Buchan, cited in Shridith S. Ramphal, 'The Commonwealth in the 1980s: an era of Negotiations', *The Round Table* 282, (April, 1981) pp. 170-178.

23. The OAU Economic Summit held in April, 1980 as analysed by G. O. Ijewere in a paper presented at the Nigerian Institute of International Affairs. (17 October, 1980).

24. United Nations Charter quoted in Vernon Van Dyke, *International*

Politics, Op. Cit. pp. 503-525.

25. Declaration of Principles known as the *Atlantic Charter,* 14 August, 1941 concluded between the United States and Great Britain. The relevant clause 3 states that they respect the rights of all peoples to choose the form of government under which they will live, and they wish to see sovereign rights and self-government restored to those who have been forcibly deprived of them. Source: J.A.S. Greenville. *The major International Treaties 1914-1973* Methuen and Co. Ltd. (London 1974) pp. 198-199.

26. These were essentially the principles that guided Nigeria's United Nations policy. See Gordon Idang. *Op. Cit.* p. 131. These principles were reaffirmed by the military government in 1976. See J.N. Garba, 'The New Nigerian Foreign Policy' Federal Ministry of Information News Release, No. 1538, 1 December, 1976).

27. George A. Obiozor, Nigerian Participation at the United Nations—1960-1977 (Unpublished). Content analysis of Nigeria's participation at the United Nations.

28. Lt. General Olusegun Obasanjo. An address to the delegates at the World Conference for Action Against Apartheid, in Lagos, 22 August, 1977. Reported in *Daily Times,* (26 August, 1977), pp. 5 and 9.

29. United Nations Year Book 1978-1979 pp. 664.

30. Shehu Shagari, An address to the General Assembly of the United Nations. Reported in *National Concord,* (11 October, 1980), pp. 8 & 9.

CHAPTER V

1. Shridith S. Ramphal, the Commonwealth Secretary General in *The Round Table,* Op. Cit. p. 171. A provocative and passionate speech perceiving great promise for the Commonwealth in the 1980s.

2. See Steven Spiegel's *Dominance and Diversity: The International Hierarchy* (Boston: Little Brown, 1972). Spiegel's classification shows two super powers, five secondary powers (Japan, Federal Republic of Germany, China, France, UK) and seventeen middle powers among them, India, Brazil, Mexico, Argentina and Nigeria. His analysis is skillfully complemented by Ray S. Cline in World Power Assessment *Op. Cit.* written three years later.

3. Douglas G. Anglin, *Op. Cit.*

4. A very lucid analysis of Nigerian/British relationship in the post Gowon era is provided by Olajide Aluko in *Essays on Nigerian Foreign Policy,* Chapter 4.

5. *Time,* (25 August, 1980), p. 43.

6. The figures vary according to source. Ali Mazrui in 'Nigeria, Western Economies and the Black World', puts the figure in excess of 10 billion dolars.

7. General Murtala Muhammed in an address at the Extraordinary Session of the Organisation of African Unity in Addis Ababa, Ministry of Information Release No. 1538, 1 December, 1976.

8. Lt. General Obasanjo's address at Howard University, Washington D.C., U.S.A., October, 1977. The potential value of mutual relationships with Blacks all over the world should not be underscored. These black communities may be seen as potential power bases for wielding political power capable of influencing their various governments for policies favourable to Nigeria.

9. For Prime Minister Balewa's defence for his government's decision prohibiting Mrs. Ransome-Kuti from travelling to the Soviet Union, see *Balewa Speaks. Op. Cit.*

10. For a succint analysis of the Soviet involvement with Nigerian within the context of broader Soviet policy in Africa, see Arthur Jay Klinghoffer, 'The Soviet Union and Africa', in Roger E. Kanet (Ed.). *The Soviet Union and the Developing Nations.* (The Johns Hopkins University Press, Baltimore and London 1974), p. 51-78.

11. There is a near consensus at least among Nigerian scholars that France poses not only a security threat, but more significantly the

greatest impediment to the security of Nigeria's political, social and cultural aspirations and interests in the African region. On 27 May, 1981 a seminar on 'French Policy in Africa' was held under the auspices of the Nigerian Institute of International Affairs. The papers presented reinforced the French subtle menace.

12. Ali Mazrui, 'Nigeria in the Nuclear Age' *Op. Cit.*

13. Information derived from a special brief on Nigeria and Steel development by the former Hon. Minister for Steel, Dr. Paul Unongo at the Nigerian Institute of International Affairs, Lagos 26 July, 1980. In spite of the German or Japanese cooperation, technology must be viewed as a means for greater future independence from those benevolent supplier states.

14. See George Obiozor. *Op. Cit.*

15. A.B. Akinyemi 'Nigeria and the Superpowers: Equality, Not Uniformity of Relations'. Lecture delivered at the University of Ilorin, 14 Jan., 1978 (Unpublished).

Bibliographic Essay

Future Studies

It has been noted in Chapter one of this essay that fascination with the future is not a novelty in the history of man. Futures study received immense attention in the classic Utopian writings of *Plato's Republic* or Sir Thomas Moore's *Utopia* written in 1516. Although these were earlier attempts to think in the future tense, they tended to stretch the imagination beyond its natural elasticity. The result was that they envisioned a future which was idealist and implausible rather than pragmatic and scientific. According to Mumford, these writings were essentially escape oriented.[1]

In recent times, however, modern futuristics has shifted from idealism to more scientific forecasting. Writers on the future attempt to examine in more systematic ways the variables in the global system, a nation state, or indeed any subject that can influence the future. It is the interaction of these variables that projections or prognostications are based. Other writers like Lars-Goran Stenelo have attempted theoretical formulation of the relationship between the past, the present and the future—examining the dimensions and implications of the past to better comprehend the future.[2]

In the past, the study of the future was more readily acceptable in the natural sciences and economics and defence studies, perhaps because of the high degree of predictability. Economic forecasters and scientists could with a certain degree of precision (based on scientific methodology) predict future trends and long range planning and achieve credibility. But in the social sciences the problem of precise predictions and loss of credibility was a deterrent. The success and prominence of the Delphi Studies in the 1980s appeared to have paved the way for the acceptability of future studies in the social sciences.[3]

Futurology is a newcomer to the field of foreign policy. Utilising various approaches, scholars in Sweden in particular have attempted to focus on decision makers and the decision making process in a particular policy.[4]

Thomas Horberg in his study argues that the decision theory demonstrates how analysts can develop a programme of action to take account of alternative futures. Others have based their predictions on foreign policy doctrines.[5]

Except for Aluko's study, it must be noted that there is remarkably little preoccupation with the future of Nigeria's foreign policy.[6] This deficiency indeed calls for closer attention to future oriented studies, perhaps, not only in foreign policy, but also in other spheres. This study has employed existing theoretical concepts in futures research especially the predictive models which enables us to delineate the likely consequences of alternative choices.

Notes

1. See Lewis Mumford, *The Story of Utopias* (New York: The Viking Press, 1962).
2. Lars-Goran Stenelo, 'Prediction and Foreign Policy Heritage' Op. Cit. Also by the same author. *Foreign Policy Predictions.* (Student llitteratur, Lund 1980).
3. Delphi Studies established in the early 1960s. One of its significant successes is the evolution of the *Delphi technique*—a method of obtaining information in field research to arrive at a conclusion concerning future happenings.
4. Thomas Horberg: 'Studying Foreign Policy Prediction: Methodological Notes', in *Cooperation and Conflict.* Op. Cit.
5. Stenelo, Horberg, Mouritzen, *Ibid.*
6. Olajide Aluko in *Essays on Nigerian Foreign Policy.* Op. Cit. Ch. 17.

In addition to the authors cited above, there is a plethora in recent times of futures study in almost every subject that it would be impracticable even to make the briefest listing here. However, in the first chapter of this study, frequent reference has been made to Herman Kahn, one of the most perceptive and prolific writers in forecasting. Throughout the world, various organisations with a future orientation have been commissioned to do some scientific forecasting. Nothing explains the need for a better world and better societies more convincingly. A brief listing is as follows:

World Future Society
4916 Street, Elmo Avenue
Washington D.C. 20014, U.S.A.

The Club of Rome
Swedish Secretariat for Future Studies, Sweden.

The Institute of World Order, New York,
engaged in World Order Models Project (WOMP)
World Order Models Project.

Among its most prolific writers are Richard A. Falk, Rajni Kothari, Ali Mazrui, Johan Galtung, Saul H. Mendlovitz. This organization is transnational, embracing other systems, transcending ideological and state boundaries. Their objective is to evolve a comprehensive framework for global reform. See their scholarly journal, *Alternatives*.

Appendix

Nigeria's Foreign Relations: A Select Bibliography

Edited by
R. T. Okotore

Compilers

L.E. Odinika
Senior Librarian (Documentation)

S. A. Dada
Senior Librarian (Readers and Bibliographic Services)

Dupe Irele
Librarian I (Documentation)

GENERAL

Adam, Mohammed Mlamali. The honest broker finds new reserves of energy. *AFRISCOPE,* May 1981: 65. Nigeria's former low profile foreign policy now changes with her continental leadership.

Akindele, R.A. Nigerian parliament and foreign policy 1960-1966. *Quarterly Journal of Administration,* 9 (3), April, 1975: 279-291. Examined the role of Nigerian Parliament in the formulation, implementation and control of Nigerian Foreign Policy.

Akinyemi, A. Bolaji. Africa—challenges and responses: a foreign policy perspective. *Deadalus* Spring 1982: 243-254. The author is the Director-General of the Nigerian Institute of International Affairs, Lagos.

———— Foreign policy and military rule. In: Oyediran, O. (ed.) *Nigerian Government and politics under military rule, 1966-1979.* London: Macmillan, 1979: 124-149.

———— Introduction *In* Akinyemi, A.B. (ed.) *Nigeria and the world: readings in Nigerian foreign policy.* Lagos: OUP for NIIA, 1978.

———— Nigerian foreign policy in 1975: national interest redefined. In: Oyediran, O. (ed.) *Survey of Nigerian Affairs, 1975,* Ibadan: OUP for NIIA, 1978: 106-114.

———— Religion and Foreign Affairs: Press attitudes towards the Nigerian Civil War. *The Jerusalem Journal of International Relations,* 4 (3), 1980. Evaluates and analyses factors which determine the foreign policy stance of a country.

Aluko, Olajide. Britain, Nigeria and Zimbabwe. *African Affairs,* January 1979: 91-102. Analyses Nigeria-American rapprochment within the context of changing U.S. strategy in Southern Africa.

Aluko, Olajide. *Essays in Nigerian Foreign Policy.* London: Allen & Unwin, 1981. The Nigerian Foreign Policy towards West African Countries, and other powers and the Country's foreign policy options in the 80's were examined.

———— The 'New' Nigerian Foreign Policy: developments since the down fall of General Gowon. *Round Table,* October 1976: 405-414.

———— Nigeria and the Superpowers. *Millenium: Journal of International Studies,* S (2), Autumn 1976: 127-141.

———— Nigeria. The United States and Southern Africa. *African Affairs,* 78 (310), January 1979: 91-102.

———— Nigerian Foreign Policy. *In:* Aluko, O. *(ed) The Foreign Policy of African States,* London: Greenwood Press 1977: 163-195. The author stresses Nigeria's relations with African States and its non-alignment policy.

_____ Oil at concessionary prices for Africa: a case study in Nigerian decision-making. *African Affairs,* 75 (301), October 1976: 425-443.

Amupitan, Ola.: Checking Aliens. *National Concord,* 20 July, 1982: 2. The paper contends that there is need to control influx of Aliens into Nigeria. See also: *National Concord,* 21 July, 1982 (Editorial Opinion).

Anda, Michael: Ordeal with Super Powers. *Daily Times,* 7 July, 1982: 8. Analyses the collaboration of super powers in the exploitation of the Third World, using boundary disputes between Uganda and Tanzania and Nigeria's experience regarding Foreign intervention in her internal affairs during the Civil War as case studies.

Balabkins, Nicholas W.: Indigenisation: the Nigerian experience. *Africa Insight,* 10 (1) 1980: 21-26. The author, explains the process of indigenisation that swept through African States after independence, paying more attention to Nigeria.

Big-Egba, Nathan: Nigeria's Foreign Policy, options and considerations. *Nigerian Tide,* 15 July, 1982: 15. The article focuses on the main components of Nigeria's Foreign Policy namely—policy towards her neighbours, the rest of Africa and the policy of Non-Alignment.

Bissel, Ricard E.: African Power in International Resource Organisation. *Journal of Modern African Studies,* March 1979: 1-13. Contends that Africa's role in the International Economic Order during the last five years has been changing for the worse, in spite of the leading role played by Nigeria in International forum and that the situation is symptomatic of the weakness of African States.

Gabric, Miodrag, M.A.: Non-alignment and International Economic relations. *Reviews of International Affairs,* 33 (770) 5 May, 1982: 6-8. A call on Non-aligned nations to face up to the stark reality prevailing in international economic relations.

Cocoa Producers Alliance: Minimum prices set. *Africa Research Bulletin: Economic, Financial and Technical Series.* 30 April, 1980: 5480-81. Reports on the agreement reached by Ghana, Nigeria, Togo, Gabon and Cameroun at the Heads of Summit meeting held in Ivory Coast.

Coleman, J.S.: The Foreign policy of Nigeria. In Black, J.E. & Thompson, K.W. (eds) *Foreign Policies in a World Change,* New York: Harper and Row, 1963.

Davis, M. (ed.): The politics of International Relief Processes in Large Civil Wars: An Editorial Comment *Journal of Developing Areas,* 6 (4) July, 1972: 487-92. The experience of International Relief efforts during the Nigerian Civil War are lessons in the political problems involved in such operations.

Faduigba, Nick: Nigeria: Shagari Lay it on the Line. *Africa,* November 1980: 30-32. Examines U.S.-Nigeria relations based on trip by Nigerian President Shehu Shagari to confer with President Carter. Economic relations and Southern Africa are cited.

Fajana, O.: Nigeria inter-African economic relations: trends; problems and prospects. *Nigeria and the World.* Lagos: Oxford University Press for NIIA. 1978: 17-29.

Fashehun, Orobola: Nigeria and the issue of an African High Command. *Afrika Spectrum.* 80 (3) 1981: 301-61.

_____ Selected bibliography on the foreign policy of Nigeria, 1970-77 *A Current Bibliography on African Affairs,* 12 (2) 1979-80: 166-169.

Feustel, S.: Nigeria: Leadership in Africa. *Africa Report,* May-June 1977: 48-50.

Gambari, Ibrahim Agboola: *The domestic politics of major foreign policy issues in Nigeria.* London: University of London, 1979. Investigates the interplay of domestic issues and foreign policy making in Nigeria from independence to the end of Civil War.

_____ Nigeria and the world: a growing internal stability, wealth and external influence. *Journal of International Affairs,* 29 (2), Fall 1975: 155-69. Examines the internal and external factors responsible for the political and economic transformation of Nigeria since independence, the likely political and diplomatic manifestations of its new economic standing in Africa.

Garba, J. N.: The New Nigerian Foreign Policy *Quarterly Journal of Administration,* 11 (3) April 1977: 135-46. A description of Nigeria's foreign policy under the military Government of General Obasanjo.

_____ Statement by ...... concerning the problem of detente, arms embargo, severing of diplomatic relations with South Africa. New York: United Nations, 1976. Also U.N. Centre against Apartheid: Notes and Documents paper presented at the International Seminar on the eradication of apartheid and in support of the struggle for the Liberation in South Africa, Havana, 1976.

_____ Towards a dynamic foreign policy. *Nigeria Bulletin on Foreign Affairs,* 6 (1), January 1976: 14-20.

Gerken, K.J. et al.: Understanding foreign assistance through Public opinion. *Yearbook of World Affairs,* 28, 1974: 125-149. Analyses aid data from 12 countries, Kenya, Nigeria, Senegal inclusve and African Students (in Germany) reactions that aid appeared to be influenced by the image of the donor.

Herskovits, Jean: Africa's new power. *Foreign Affairs,* 53 (2), January 1975: 314-333.

Herskovits, Jean: Dateline Nigeria: a Black Power. *Foreign Policy,* 29, Winter 1977/78: 167-88. Describes domestic & International Politics of Nigeria.

_____ One Nigeria: Foreign Affairs, 51(2), January 1973: 392-407. Optimistic appraisal of political developments in post civil war Nigeria.

Ihhangani, R.C.: Aliens and Immigration laws in Nigeria. *Nigerian Forum,* 2 (3) March 1982: 506-518. Important provisions of the Immigration Act of 1963 revisited and offering how the influx of aliens can be controlled.

Ijewere, G.O.: Nigeria in International relations. *Review of International Affairs,* 32 (738), 5 January, 1981: 26-30. Examines the role of Nigeria in world politics.

Imodibie, Kress A.: How dynamic is Nigeria's foreign policy? *The Nigerian Standard,* 23 July, 1982: 6. Argues that Nigeria needs to change its strategy in Africa and abroad if she is to play her proper role as the leader in Africa and the world.

Isong, C.: Nigeria's external finance. *Nigerian Journal of International Affairs,* 1 (1) July 1975: 47-59.

Kadzai, I.: Nigeria global strategy. *Lagos: Nigerian Institute of International Affairs, 1976.*

Mayall, James: Oil and Nigerian foreign policy. *African Affairs,* 75 (300), July 1976: 317-30. Analyses oil boom and its effects on the country's external relations.

Mike, Atumba: Nigeria's foreign policy before & now. *New Nigerian,* 8 March, 1980: 5. Focuses on the political, economic, ideological and other strategic interests of Nigeria which determine her relationship with other countries.

Nigeria: Africa's Radical Tribune: *Foreign Report.* 12 July, 1978:

5-6. Covers Nigeria's reaction to the Shaba Invasion, Soviet and Cuban involvement in Africa, Relations with South Africa and recent agreement with Romania and Poland.

Nigeria: In *Africa Contemporary Record Annual Survey and Documents 1980-81,* Special Report: New York, African Publications, 1981: 566-591. Contents include: Foreign Affairs, African Relations, aids to African Countries, Middle East Relations, Relations with U.S. and Britain etc.

Nigeria pledges cash aid to International Programme for Development of Communication (IPDC). *Daily Times,* 10 June, 1982: 5.

Nigeria Trade Summary, December 1971. Lagos: Goverment Printer: 6 and 9. Summarises the value of Nigeria's exports and imports to and from Egypt in 1971.

North-South Summit on Economic Relations. 22-23, October, 1981, Mexico. At the preparatory meeting in Vienna in March 13-14, 1981, it was agreed that Algeria, Nigeria, Australia, Brazil, China, France, India, Japan, Sweden, Saudi Arabia, U.K., U.S., West Germany should be invited. Issues discussed included raw materials, energy and international trade financing.

Nunn, Grady M.: Nigerian Foreign Relations In: Blitz, L.F. (ed.) The Politics and Administration of Nigerian Government. New York: Praeger. 1965: 249-64. Factors affecting Nigerian Foreign Policy were discussed.

Nzimiro, Ikenna: The political and social implications of International Corporations in Nigeria. In: Carl Widstrand, (ed.). *Multinational Firms in Africa.* Stockholm: Scandinavian Institute of Africa Studies 1975: 210-43.

———— Nigerian Foreign Policy. *Enugu: Enugu Star Printing, 1979.*

Ofoegbu, Mazi Ray: *Nigerian Government and politics under Military rule 1966-79.* London: Macmillan, 1979: 124-149.

———— Towards a New Philosophy of Foreign Policy for Nigeria In: Akinyemi, A.B. (ed.) *Nigeria and the World,* Ibadan, Oxford University Press, 1978: 116-37. A new era of detente demands more positive action by Nigeria and greater involvement in world affairs.

Ogene, Francis: The Foreign Service the Nation deserves. *Nigerian Forum,* 1 (4) 1981: 151-159. The author examined the Nigerian Foreign Service, identified its problems and suggested changes that may be necessary in order to bring the service in line with the need of our times.

Olofin, S.: Ultra-Import-biased taste in Nigeria's External Trade Relations In: Akinyemi, A.B. (ed.). *Nigeria and the World,* Ibadan, Oxford University Press for NIIA. 1978: 32-44. Expresses fear that the economic benefits of the oil boom may be neutralised by the country's preference for imported goods.

Ogunbadejo, Oye: Foreign Policy under Nigeria's Presidential System. *Round Table,* Oct. 1980: 401-408. Examines Shagari's Foreign Policy under the country's new pluralistic political system

_____ General Gowon's African policy (Foreign and domestic policy, 1967-1970). *International Studies,* 16, Jan/March 1977: 35-50. Description of Nigerian Foreign Policy in the continent of Africa.

_____ Nigeria and the Great Powers: the impact of the Civil War on Nigerian Foreign Relations. *African Affairs,* 75 (2) Jan. 1976: 14-32. Assesses Nigerian relations with the Western Powers, the Soviet Union & China and reviewed the new Non-alignment policy. Confirms his initial thesis that Nigeria's stance is far from being truly independent.

_____ The Presidential System and Foreign Policy: Problems and prospects in Nigeria. *Australian Outlook:* 34 (3) Dec. 1980: 325-337. Assesses Nigeria's new system of government, that no new foreign policy directions have been established and asserts that the present foreign policy which is militant on African issues and positive non-alignment in the world affairs is a continuation of the Military regimes foreign policy.

_____ Nigeria and the New International Economic Order. *Rivista Internationale di Science Economiche e Commerciali,* Jan. 1980: 64-84. Discusses the ramifications of the call for NIEO and Nigeria's position in the world Economy.

Ogunsanwo, Alaba: Nigeria's foreign relations 1970-75. *Nigerian Journal of International Affairs,* 4 (1 & 2), 1978: 35-59. Examines the content and conduct of Nigeria's external relations from 1970 to 1975.

Oil War: Nigeria Gets the Flax. *Africa,* (129), May, 1982: 12-20. These articles by special correspondents examine Nigeria's precarious position and President Shagari's austerity measures'.

Ojedokun, Olasupo: The changing pattern of Nigeria's International Economic Relations: The decline of the Colonial Nexus 1960-1966. *Journal of Developing Areas,* 6 (4) July 1972: 535-553. Analyses factors, economic and political, domestic and foreign which shaped the character of the country's International economic ties.

Ojo, Latunde John: *Nigeria's foreign policy 1960-1966: Politics, Eco-*

nomic and the struggle for African leadership: Ann Arbour, Michigan Univ. Microfilms, 1975.
and her stance on continental and regional issues.

Okorie, Emma: Why Aliens invade Nigeria. *Times International* 3 (14) 21-27 Dec., 1981: 10. Outlines reasons for the influx of Aliens to Nigeria and the possible national security problems.

Otojareri, O.: The Pope advises Nigerians. *Times International* 3 (23) 22 Feb., 1982: 8 Reports about the Pope John Paul II and his evangelical visit to Nigeria.

Oyebode, Akindele B.: Towards a New Policy on Decolonization. In: Akinyemi, A.B. (ed.) *Nigeria and The World,* Ibadan: Oxford University Press, 1978: 97-115. Focused attention on the present stage of the national liberation process and attempted to draw the parameters of what should be a new Nigerian Policy.

Prain, Ronald: Metals and Africa: Economic Power in an International Setting. *African Affairs.* 77 (307) April 1978: 236-46. First analysis of. Africa's mineral wealth, second, the importance of Africa to the rest of the world as a supplier of minerals and metals, third, Africa's potential for political and economic influence.

Schwarz, Freerich: *Nigeria: The Tribe, the Nation or The Race.* Cambridge: M.I.T. Press, 1965: 2332. Contends that since independence the Federal Government policy is to avoid a Foreign policy stance that might cause social and political strife at home.

Shagari, Shehu Usman Aliyu: Annual Foreign policy address. *Nigerian Forum,* 1 (6) Aug., 1981: 203-206. Text of the Address by Alhaji Shehu Shagari, President of the Federal Republic of Nigeria, delivered at the annual patron's dinner of the Nigerian Institute of International Affairs.

Shaw, Timothy et al: Nigeria in the World System: alternative approaches, explanations and projections. *Journal of Modern African Studies,* 18 (4) December, 1980: 551-573. An attempt to find alternative approaches to Nigerian foreign policy.

Simmons, Michael et al (eds.): *Nigerian Handbook 1982-83.* London: 25-33. Topics include foreign relations, Nigeria and the wider world, relations with the first world, The British connection.

Tella, Liad: Akinyemi's strategic doctrine. *Daily Times,* 11 March 1981: 8. A second strategic proposal put forward by Akinyemi is Brazil-Nigeria-Angola Axis to secure the South Atlantic against incursions by the Super Powers.

_____ Nigeria's Foreign Policy—Akinyemi Balls for New Strategy.

Daily Times, 7 March, 1981: 10. The Director General of NIIA proposed the need for Nigeria to increase her military force and capability to the level of a European Middle power. He further advocated for a Nigeria-Brazil-Angola Treaty to secure South Atlantic against incursions by big powers.

Ukpong, Ignatius: The impact of Foreign Aid on Electricity Development in Nigeria. *Journal of African Studies,* 2 (2) Summer 1975: 275-86. Analyses energy development, energy consumption and the impact of Foreign aid on energy production and distribution.

Uwechue, Ralph: Development aid should reflect co-operation not charity. *Africa,* Sept. 1979: 44-46. An Interview with Sweden's Prime Minister, Ola Ullsteri.

Wright, Stephen: Nigeria: The politics of Sports: a channel for conflict and a vehicle for national self-expression. *Round Table,* 272, Oct. 1978: 362-267. The author looks at Sports as Nigeria's Foreign policy vehicle to further the goal of Liberation of Southern Africa. Africa boycotted the Olympic Games of 1976 and the Commonwealth Games of 1978.

———— Limits of Nigeria's Power Overseas. *West Africa.* No. 3339 27 July, 1981: 1685-1687.

World Bank approves ₦98.5 million loan for Nigeria. *Nigerian Statesman,* 24, 1982: 20.

AFRICA

Achebe, Chinua: Why Afro-European Dialogue Fails. *West Africa,* 25 Feb., 1980 341-343. Analyses the impediments to a true cultural exchange between Europe & Africa.

Adelaja, Kola. (ed.): Perspectives on African Foreign Policy: *Proceedings of the Inaugural Conference of Nigerian Society of International Affairs,* held at the University of Ife, 1973.

Africa-China: Moves to strengthen relations. **Africa Research Bulletin:** *Political, Social and Cultural Series,* 15 May, 1980: 5656-5657. Discusses renewed Chinese diplomatic overtures to African States including Tanzania, Zaire, Zambia, Zimbabwe, as well as some North and West African States particularly Nigeria.

Africa-U.S. Trade. *Africa,* June 1980: 81-91. U.S. African Policy under Carter and ties with Key African States including Nigeria are examined.

Ajala, A.: The origin of African Economic Development. *Nigerian Forum*, 1 (7 & 8), Sept-Oct., 1981: 243-250. The origin of African boundaries and the Post-Independence conflicts over boundaries are discussed.

Ajibola, W.A.: Some trends in Nigeria's African policy. In: Akinyemi, A.B. ed. *Nigeria and the World*. Lagos: Oxford University Press for N.I.I.A. 1978.

Akinyemi, A.B.: Confrontation and dialogue. *Venture*, 24 (1), Jan. 1972: 17-20. Contrasts the views of moderates and radicals on how to confront apartheid and suggests a leading role for Nigeria.

Anene, J.C.: *The International Boundaries of Nigeria, 1885-1960: The framework of an Emergent African Nation:* London: Longmans, 1970. Documentary sources, oral history and ethnographic materials are the sources for this study.

Aniagolu, E.: Hosni Mubarak: A continuation of the Sadat's legacy. *Nigerian Forum*, 2 (3), March 1982: 494-499. A critical examination of Hosni Mubarak's policies. Do they represent a continuation or departure from Sadat's policies?

Dada, Akinremi: Nigeria in Inter-African Politics 1960-1970: A linkage analysis. (Ph.D. Thesis) Washington D.C.: The American University, 1975. A study of the underlying factors affecting external behaviour of Nigeria in the continent.

Bassey, Bassey Ekpo: Nigeria's African Policy and the truth about international politics. *Sunday Call*, 12 Sept., 1982: 5. Nigeria's African policy and International politics is a catalogue of failures, shifts and reverses.

Bennet, Douglas J.J. et al: Political and Economic Interests in Africa *U.S. Department of State Bulletin*, April 1980: 26-30. Discuss the challenges facing Africa, the importance of *Nigeria's* development to U.S. interests, the U.S. initiatives, human concerns and transition in U.S. policies.

Davis, M. (ed.): *Civil Wars and the Politics of International Relief: Africa, Soutn Asia, and the Caribbean*. New York: Praeger 1975. Contains essays by Warren Weinstein on Burundi and Alvin G. Edgell on Nigeria Biafra.

The Debate on International Involvement on Africa. *Africa Currents*, No. 12/13, 1978/79: 2-24. Includes speeches by political leaders and leading editorial comments on Angola, Zambia, Senegal, Nigeria Sudan, Mozambique, Guinea, Kenya and Tanzania.

Ekpenyong, J.L.: Nigeria's unguarded boundaries. *Nigerian Forum*,

1 (7 & 8), Sept.-Oct., 1981: 270-282. This paper points out some of the main problems Nigeria faces in guarding our borders and establishing border posts and patrols.

Fasheun, Orobola: Nigeria and the issue of African High Command: Towards a Regional and/or Continental Defence System? *Afrika Spectrum* 25, 1980: 309-16. Analysis of the positions taken by the various Nigerian governments, civil and military on the controversial issue of an African Security Organisation formally titled African High Command.

Feustell, Sandy: Nigeria leadership in Africa. *Africa Report,* May-June, 1977: 48-50.

_____ Foreign Policy: It's Africa all the way. *New African,* Jan. 1982, 172: 90. Defends the contention that Africa is the centre-piece of Nigeria's foreign policy and correlates this by her assistance (financial, and technical) to newly independent African States.

Herskovits, Jean (Ed.): Subsaharan Africa. In: Schlesinger, A.M. Jr. (ed.) *The Dynamics of World Power: A Documentary History of United States Foreign Policy, 1945-73.* Vol. 5. New York: Chelsea House Publishers 1973: 539-1231. An extensive collection of speeches and editorials on U.S. Africa relations including Nigeria.

Ikoku, Chimere: Africa: The obstacles to total freedom: *The Nigerian Standard,* 25 June, 1982: 8. Deals with objectives and strategic interests of various outside powers in Southern Africa and considering racist South Africa's fast developing nuclear capability and ever expanding arms arsenal and militarisation, Nigeria would be her ultimate target.

Mbonu, Okechukwu: Demarcating Nigeria's Borders. *Times International,* 3 (5), 19-25 Oct., 1981: 10-11. Looks at the crucial issues affecting Nigeria's International borders and the provisions of the International Law.

Namibia's Independence: Ekwueme States Nigeria's stand. New Nigerian, 15 March, 1982: 12. A review of the International aspects of the Namibian situation and Nigeria's positive stand.

Nigeria: Africa's New Political and Economic giant. *To the Point International,* 5 (1), 9 Jan., 1978: 15-18. Discusses the emergence of Nigeria as the Key to U.S. Policy in Africa and Southern Africa under the Carter Administration and examines possible contradictions.

Nigeria: Emergent Giant. *Bulletin of the African Institute of S. Africa,* 11 (2) 1973: 56-60. While acknowledging Nigeria's political and economic ascendancy in Africa, lack of freedom and liberty in Nigeria and Gowon's increasing attention to Southern Africa are criticized.

Ogunsanwo, Alaba: China's policy in Africa, 1952-1971. *New York: Cambridge University Press 1974.* From the peripheral status it occupied in the middle fifties, China's policy in Africa rapidly achieved a self propelling and compulsive momentum.

Omotoso, Kole: Egypt-Israeli Treaty: What Next Black Africa? *Africa,* May 1979: 34-35. Raises questions about how Africa particularly OAU will respond to the controversy over the Egyptian-Israeli peace treaty in a way that reflects African interests as opposed to those other interests—Arab, Soviet or Western.

Olatunde, J.B.: Commercial representation in Nigeria's overseas missions: its nature, functions and problems. *Nigerian Journal of International Affairs,* 2 (1/2) 1976: 50-66.

Olofin, S.: Ultra-Import-biased taste in Nigeria's external Trade Relations In: Akinyemi, A.B. ed. *Nigeria and the World.* Ibadan: Oxford University Press for NIIA. 1978: 32-44. The economic benefits to Nigeria of the oil boom may be affected by the Country's ultra-import biased taste.

Ologe, K.O.: The economic and Strategic Significance of the Atlantic and Indian Oceans for African States. *Nigerian Journal of Political Science,* 1 (1) June 1979: 63-76. Discussed interconnectedness of World Oceans, providing Africa's share of their use and resources and finally, the implications for Africa of the emerging ownership system.

Onitiri, H.M.A.: Nigeria's International Economic Relations: a survey. *Nigerian Journal of Economics,* Nov. 1960: 13-38. An examination of the principles which should underline Nigeria's foreign economic relations.

Onwuka, R.I.: Oil Politics and Nigerian Petroleum Policy. *Afriscope,* 11 (9) Sept., 1981: 32-33. Describes Nigeria's precarious position and contends that diplomatic activities should be intensified in search of buyers for her oil among the non-aligned and the Eastern Countries.

Osagie, E.: The ideological element for Nigeria's relations with African States. *In:* Akinyemi, A.B. ed. *Nigeria and the World,* Ibadan: Oxford University Press for NIIA, 1978. 1-12

Osuntokun, Jide: Nigeria-Fernandopo: relations from colonial times to the present. In: Akinyemi, A.B. ed. *Nigeria and the World,*

Ibadan: Oxford University Press for NIIA, 1978.

＿＿＿＿＿ Recent changes in Africa's investment climate: Studies of Nigeria, Kenya, Ivory Coast, Zambia, Liberia, Sudan, Cameroun, Ghana. *Africa Business and Economic Review,* 1 (1980). Examines investment incentives, tax laws, foreign exchange allocations, profit repatriation and past experiences of investors.

＿＿＿＿＿ Revolution Summit: Lagos and Africa's Economic Destiny. *Africa,* June 1980: 13-19. Contents: Blue prints for Survival, –The Road to Lagos, – The Hurdles Ahead.

Rivkin, Arnold: Nigeria: A Unique Nation. *Current History,* 45 (268), Dec. 1963: 329-334. Focuses on Nigeria's role in African Inter-State relations.

Rondos, Alex: Twenty years after Independence: Dominant Neighbour in West Africa. *West Africa,* No. 3297, Sept. 29, 1891-1894. An assessment of Nigeria's real significance to her neighbours–Benin, Niger, Chad and Cameroun.

Shuttle Diplomacy by Adefope. *Africa Diary: Weekly Record of Events in Africa,* 19 (3) 15-21 Oct., 1979: 9353. The Commissioner for External Affairs visited various African Heads of State and Governments to discuss Southern African problems.

S.I.F.I.D.A.: (Societe Internationale Financiere pour les Investissements et le Development en Afrique), 60 African Projects have Received Finance over the past ten years. *Telex Africa,* 193, 29 June, 1982: 33. Gives a geographical distribution of S.I.F.I.D.A's African Investments with NIGERIA as one of the beneficiaries.

Usman, Y.B.: Debate on Libya warms up. *West Africa,* No. 3318, 2 March, 1981: 421-423. Highlights the danger for the Nigerian government to allow itself to be drawn into conflict with Libya on the side of France.

Zartman, William: The foreign policy dynamics of countries great and small in Africa and the South African issue. *International Affairs Bulletin,* 4 (3), 1980: 18-25. Investigates the structure of African countries foreign relations and looks into their policy settings and interests.

AFRICA, CENTRAL

Chad

Air pact signed. *Daily Sketch,* 15 June, 1978: 1. An agreement has been signed by the two countries, there will be flight to and from both countries, twice a week.

Chad and Nigeria's Aid. *Daily Times,* 18 Oct., 1982: 1. Asserts that as a demonstration of Nigeria's commitment to the peace, political stability and progress of Chad, Chadian requests for assistance is being considered realistically.

See also: *Nigerian Standard,* 16 Oct., 1982: 3.

Chad leaders sign peace treaty: Parties agree on National Union Government. *Daily Times,.* 17 March, 1979: 1. Kano Accord allows warring Chadian leaders to work out the modalities for a Ceasefire and setting up of neutral forces to be provided by Nigeria.

Chad: New Njamena-Lagos Relations. *Times International,* 4 Oct., 1979: 4. This paper is an attempt by the countries involved to unravel some of the knotty boundary problems existing between them via the creation of a Lake Chad Basin Development Authority.

Chad Peace Talks can't hold. *The Punch,* 8 March, 1979: 16. Reports that the Kano confab on Chadian reconciliation could not start because of the absence of two key figures—President Felix Malloun and Prime Minister Habre.

Chadian leaders call on Head of State. *Federal Ministry of Information, Press Release,* No. 421, 16 March, 1979. Leaders of the various Delegations who took part in the Chad reconciliation conference in Kano paid a courtesy call and talked about the success of the conference.

Chadian leaders urged to work for peace. *New Nigerian,* 12 March, 1979: 1. Addressing the opening session of the Kano conference, Lt. General Obasanjo urges participants to find a lasting solution to the Chadian problem.

Dahmani, A.: Tchad: reconstruire Sur des rivines. *Jeune Afrique,* 9 Janvier, 1980: 32-33. Economic and political analysis of Chad after the peace agreement signed in Lagos on 21 August, 1979.

Fact finding panel for Chad. *Nigerian Herald,* 12 April, 1979: 1. A fact finding Commission has been set up to verify the position and relative importance of the Chadian factions would be signatories at the Kano Accord.

Federal Government assures Chad of full support—to make her abandon proposed merger with Libya. *Nigerian Standard,* 29 Jan., 1981: 1. The Foreign Minister announced that Nigeria was prepared to give Chad the support to make her abandon plans for a merger with Libya.

Federal Government approves ₦1 million for Chadian refugees. *Nigerian Standard,* 6 May, 1980: 13. One million Naira approved for the maintenance of Chadian refugees in Borno State.

General Gowon given a rousing welcome in Chad. Nigeria: *Federal Ministry of Information Press Release,* No. 1435, 7 Dec., 1972.

General N'Gakoutou Bey-Ndi on a two-day working visit to Nigeria, *Federal Ministry of Information, Press Release,* No. 816. 13 June, 1978. Discusses security within African countries and improving economic and social co-operation between Chad and Nigeria.

Kanu, Chijioke: Nigeria and the Chadian Strife. *Sunday Chronicle,* 11 March, 1979: 2. Considers mediatory efforts by Nigeria in the Chadian conflict as being in consonance with her fundamental foreign policy objectives.

Menace by Chadian soldiers to stop now. *New Nigerian,* 11 Oct., 1980: 3. The invasion and killings of Nigerian citizens by fleeing soldiers has been stopped.

Messages to Chad from France and Nigeria. *West Africa,* No. 3346 14 Sept., 1981: 2099-2100. A correspondents analyses the importance of talks between Chadian, French and Nigerian leaders.

Nigeria, Chad work out peace formula. *Nigeria: Bulletin on Foreign Affairs,* 6 (9) Sept., 1976: 19-20.

See also: *Daily Times, 21 Sept., 1976: 40.*

Nigeria-Chad may exchange teachers. *New Nigerian,* 26 March, 1968: 9.

Nigeria completes troop withdrawal from Chad. *The Nigerian Standard,* 26 June, 1982: 1. Announcement of withdrawal of Nigerian troops by the Commandant of the OAU Peace-Keeping Force, Major-General Emmanuel O. Ejiga. See also: *Daily Times,* 29 June, 1982: 10. See also: *New Nigerian,* 12 June, 1982: 1.

NIGERIA: Relations with Chadian Elements. *In: Thompson, Virginia and Adloff, Richard. Conflict in Chad,* London: Hurst, 1981: 76, 92, 93, 94, 100, 107, 112-116. Reflects on the perseverance shown by successive Nigerian leaders in exerting their influence on Chad's evolution. A measure of their concern to contain the strife there within Chad's old frontiers and also to find a solution that would ward off intervention by France or by the Arab States.

Nigerian soldiers ordered out of Chad. *Daily Times,* 6 June, 1979: 1. The transitional government of Hissene Habre and Goukouni Weddye has ordered out the Nigerian Peace-Keeping Force there.

Nigerian troops back from Chad Republic. *Nigerian Tide,* 8 June,

1979: 16. The neutral Nigerian troops in Chad have been withdrawn.

Nigeria's commitment to Chad. *Daily Times,* 23 Jan., 1982: 11. Nigeria and OAU member countries contributing the Peace-Keeping Forces in Chad may not succeed in finding lasting peace.

Obasanjo appeals to Chadian leaders. *New Nigerian,* 20 August, 1979: 28. At the meeting to ratify the agreement reached by leaders of Chad, the Head of State, General Obasanjo sues for peace in Chad.

₦101 million Contingency Fund is for Chad. *The Punch,* 2 April, 1982: 1. Emergency votes of Shagari by ₦101 million in the 1982 Budget was to help fulfil Nigeria's commitment to Chad.

Shagari urged to allow Assembly to examine Libya/Chad issue. *New Nigerian,* 2 Feb., 1981: 2. A call has been made to the President to ask the National Assembly to study the implications of the proposed Libya/Chad merger.

The situation in Chad. *Daily Times,* 7 June, 1979: 14. Federal Government's Statement on Chad in response to former French Foreign Minister who requested Nigeria's assistance in the search for peace, stability, and reconciliation in Chad.

The tragedy of Chad. *West Africa,* No. 3367, 15 Feb., 1982: 421-422. A correspondent reports that 80 percent of the Chadian refugees in Borno State, Nigeria suffer from two or more debilitating diseases.

Twelve Chadian soldiers held in Nigeria. *Daily Times,* 9 June, 1981: 1. Twelve Chadian soldiers were arrested and were helping to solve the problem of five Nigerians killed.

Weddeye flies in. *The Punch,* 16 Jan., 1981: 1. President Weddeye flies into Nigeria with two armed soldiers on an undisclosed mission.

AFRICA, WEST

Cameroon

Ahidjo visits Nigeria. *West Africa,* No. 3364, 25 January, 1982: 218-9. Visit seen as a normalisation of relations between the two countries after the border incident in May 1981, in which five Nigerian soldiers were killed.

Okoli, E.J.: Ahidjo's visit likely to defuse expected Nigeria-Cameroon border-clash escalation, *New African* No. 174, March 1981: 19 Gives the background to a delicate situation, the 1980 border clash which will require diplomatic handling.

Ede, Oscar Oyene B.: The Nigerian-Cameroon boundaries. *Nigerian Forum* 1 (7 & 8) Sept.-Oct., 1981: 292-300. The author argues that among Nigeria's five International boundaries, the one with Cameroon posed the greatest problem.

Macebuh, S.: Public opinion and Nigeria/Cameroon crisis. Nigerian *Forum*, 1 (7 & 8), Sept./Oct., 1981: 301-306. Looks at public opinion to the issue of Nigeria-Cameroon boundary crisis.

_____ Nigeria-Cameroon border clash: War, War Fever. *Afriscope*, 11 (5) May 1981: 6-7. Argued that diplomatic move within African organisation to effect peace is ideal, but lamented that the performance of OAU's Mediation Committee was not inspiring.

Weladji, C.: The Cameroon-Nigeria border. *Abbia*, June 27/28, 1974: 157-72, June 29/30, 1975: 163-95, map: 31/32/33, Feb., 1978, 173-93. Mainly documents with some interpretations.

GHANA

Akinyemi, A. Bolaji: Ghana-Nigeria relations: from sports to politics. *Afriscope* 4 (10) Oct., 1974. The author assessed Nigeria-Ghana relations since independence, revealed the rivalry between them and suggested ways to normalise relations.

Aluko, Olajide: *Ghana and Nigeria 1957-60; a study in Inter-African Discord.* New York: Barnes and Noble, 1976. An observer might assume that Ghana and Nigeria would cooperate in African affairs, but very little co-operation did really take place between the two countries between March 1957-70.

Bisi, Lawrence: The Lagos-Accra Sports Axis. *Afriscope*, 4 (7) July 1974: 54-5. Provides a historical overview of sporting links between Nigeria and Ghana and gives credence to the argument that their inherent rivalry in sports continue to plague the cordial relations that should exist between them.

Egbochuku, Stanley: Nigeria lifts oil embargo on Ghana. *Business Times*, 17 May, 1982: 32. The author reflects on the resumption of oil supply to Ghana.

Elema, E.O.: Normalising relations with Ghana. *Nigerian Tide*, 16 Oct., 1982: 7. Persistent search for closer ties with Nigeria, as manifested by repeated Ghanaian delegations to Nigeria, is indicative of the fact that Ghana's fragile friendship with Libya and Iran have not solved her deep rooted economic problems.

_____ Long shadow over Ghana and Nigeria: the Rawlings equation. *Afriscope* 12 (3) March 1982: 13-15. Discusses the history of the relationship between Ghana and Nigeria under the different regimes which have ruled the two countries.

AFRICA, EAST

Angola

Akinyemi, A. Bolaji: *Angola and Nigeria: a study in the national interest.* Geneva: Graduate Institute of International Studies, 1978.

Aluko, Olajide: African response to external intervention in Africa since Angola. *African Affairs*, 80 (319) April 1981: 159-179. The author argues that since the Angolan war of 1975-76 the question of external military interventions in Africa has come to dominate International debates on African Affairs. It looks critically at factors that make the post 1975 external interventions significant.

Delancey, Mark W.: Nigerian views of the Angolan conflict. *Bulletin of the Southern Association of Africanists*, 4 (2) Summer 1976: 39-54. Analysis of various comments by Nigerians on the Angolan civil war.

Ekpebu, L.B.: *Conference on Nigeria and the world. 27-30 January, 1976:* Angola—the development of a new Nigerian policy on decolonisation in Africa. Lagos: Nigerian Institute of International Affairs, 1976. The paper discusses the future of decolonisation efforts in general and on the fate of Angola in particular and sees the new Nigerian policy towards decolonisation as the greatest threat to the neo-colonial exploiters and racists in their determination to frustrate Africa's march to full independence.

Elaigwu, J. Isawa: The Nigerian Civil War and the Angolan Civil War: Linkages between domestic tensions and international alignments. *Journal of Asian and African Studies*, 12: 1-4, Jan.-Oct., 1977: 215-35. States that great power involvement in domestic conflicts has become a major factor increasing the intensity of such conflicts.

Federal Military Government takes new stand on Angolan situation: Neto's government recognised. *New Nigerian*, 26 Nov., 1975: 1. Looks at the Federal Military Government's recognition of MPLA as a feat of international relations after the abundant evidence of direct involvement of racist South Africa's troops in the conflict. See also: *The Nigerian Observer*, 27 Nov., 1975: 3. *Daily Sketch*, 27 Nov., 1975: 3.

Jose, Babatunde: Angola: New phase in diplomacy. *Times International*, 6 Nov., 1978: 4. Focuses on the Angola's current diplomatic offensive and notes her tendency to move closer to the West confirmed by recent improvement of relations between Paris and Luanda with less emphasis on Angola's Marxist orientation and more emphasis on Angola's non-aligned policy which could allow her go with any country of her choice.

Nigeria: the oxygen of MPLA offensive. *Times International,* 19 Jan., 1976: 4. Defends Nigeria's recognition of MPLA as the legitimate government of Angola and condemns South Africa's and America's role in Angola.

Nigeria to co-operate with Angola. *West Africa,* 25 Aug., 1980: 1625. An update on Angola-Nigeria joint commission charged with promoting and co-ordinating economic, technical and cultural co-operation between the two countries.

Nwuneli, O.E. and Dare, O.: The Nigerian Press and the Civil War in Angola. *A Current Bibliography on African Affairs,* 9, 4, 1976/ 1977, 302-16. Analysis of press coverage of the war and its effects culminating on a major shift in Nigerian Foreign Policy. Includes important evidence of the Nigeria's dependence on her own press.

Ogunbadejo, Oye: Angola: ideology and pragmatism in foreign policy. *International Affairs,* 52 (2) Spring 1981: 254-269. Discusses how ideology and pragmatism have blended to provide the basis for Angola's external relations between the support received from the Soviets and Cuba for its liberation and the dictates of economic development.

Ogunmade-Davis, Akin: Why we must back to the last. *Sunday Punch,* 18 Jan., 1976: 13 & 15. Analyses Angola's strategic posture, sees her as the only viable buffer state between Nigeria and South Africa and strategically as the key country to the final liberation of Namibia, Zimbabwe and South Africa. That NATO members realise the geopolitical importance of Angola in the liberation of South Africa.

Sobowale, Dayo: Angolan-Nigerian relations—talking of barking and biting. *Daily Times,* 8 August, 1979: 9. Comments on Thatcher's new diplomatic attempt and her pro-racist policy which is at variance with Nigeria's expectations, warned that African nations particularly Nigeria could take action against Britain if she sanctioned Muzorewa's Administration.

We greet Dr. Neto. *Daily Star,* 16 Jan., 1978: 3. This editorial opinion analyses the collaboration between Nigeria and Angola in their liberation efforts in Southern Africa to keep the colonialists in check.

ZIMBABWE

Nigeria: Africa's Pace-Setter on the Rhodesian sanction issue. *African Index*, 1-15 June, 1979: 39-40. Outlines Nigeria's interest in the sanctions against Rhodesia and her options with Western multi-nationals and the Commonwealth.

₦1.281 million aid pledged to Zimbabwe. *New Nigerian*, 28 March, 1981: 13. Demonstrates Nigeria's commitment to Mugabe's government.

A Zimbabwean Government-in-Exile? *Foreign Report*, 6 June, 1979: 1-3. Describes efforts by Nigeria to encourage the Patriotic Front to establish a government-in-Exile, as a sign of progress and on effort to strengthen its political and diplomatic position internationally.

SOUTH AFRICA

Adebisi, Busari: Nigeria's relations with South Africa, 1960-75. *Africa Quarterly*, 16 (3) Jan., 1977: 67-89. Argues that Nigeria's political leadership in the post independence period failed to grasp the full implications of institutionalised racism in South Africa, and that it is easy for South Africa to circumvent trade restrictions which Nigeria attempted to implement.

Akinyemi, A.B. & Margaret Vogt: Nigeria and Southern Africa: the policy options. *Conflict and Change in Africa,* 1979: 151-68. Evaluates the rationale behind Nigeria's decision to commit so much of the national resources to problems which after all affects an area which is nowhere close to her borders. Also stated opinions of Nigerian scholars on Nigeria's role in Southern Africa.

Akpan, M.E.: African goals and strategies towards Southern Africa. *African Studies Review,* 14 (2) Sept., 1971: 243-63. Emphasises that African goals have not been reached in spite of various strategies employed.

Arnold, Guy: Which way in Southern Africa? *Africa Report:* July/ August, 1980: 40-44. Assesses the impact of Robert Mugabe's election victory in Zimbabwe, the Lusaka economic summit, Zimbabwe's independence and OAU Summit in Lagos.

Hveen, H.: Afrika i Verdes Konomien: Utvikliigog under–Utvikling. *International Politikk,* 1976: 729-46.

Mbadinuju, C. Chinwoke: The ideological framework of African opposition to South Africa's Apartheid Policy. *Third World Review,* 1 (1) Fall 1974: 52-8.

Nigeria's campaign against South Africa. *Foreign Report,* No. 1518 11 Jan., 1978: 8. Brief comment on the more militant stance towards Southern Africa taken by the Nigeria's new Foreign Minister.

Nwoli, O.: Nigerian policy towards Southern Africa. *Nigerian Journal of International Affairs,* 2 (1-2) 1976: 14-34. Policies of the Balewa, Gowon and post Gowon regimes towards Southern Africa were examined.

No going back on Africa's Freedom. *Daily Sketch,* 8 June, 1976: 16. Discusses recent developments in Nigerian Foreign Policy, and their possible impact' upon the Liberation Struggles in Southern Africa.

Ogbu, Edwin Ogebe: The International Trade Union Movement and Apartheid South Africa. *Objective Justice,* 5 (4) Oct.-Dec., 1973: 26-30.

_____ No compromise with Apartheid: *Unit on Aparthied Notes and Documents,* 5/74, 1974. Focuses on sports contracts with South Africa and the proposal for independence for Bantustans of Transkei.

Oil to South Africa. *Africa Diary: Weekly Record of Events in Africa,* 19 (15) 9-15 April, 1979: 9461; 9219. The Federal Military Government ordered an investigation into the alleged shipment of Nigerian oil to Apartheid South Africa.

Polhemus, James H.: Nigeria and Southern Africa: Interest, policy and means. *Canadian Journal of African Studies,* 11 (1) 1977. Analysis of Nigeria-South Africa strained relationship.

EUROPE, EAST

Mandeley, John: Nigeria's growing trade with Eastern Europe. *West Africa,* 24 Dec., 1979: 2383-85. Discusses a Report by the UNCTAD Secretariat, published in 1979.

Soviet Union

Economic co-operation between Nigeria and the USSR. *Times International,* 3 (7) 2-8 Nov., 1981: 18. Records the willingness of both to co-operate in economic and technical developments of their respective countries through exchange of specialists.

Legvoid, R.: *Soviet Policy in West Africa,* Cambridge: Harvard Univer-

sity, 1970. Guinea, Ghana, Ivory Coast, Mali, Nigeria and Senegal analysed because they represent countries the Soviet Union has dealth with in Black Africa.

New Document on Soviet-African ties. *Daily Times,* 21 July, 1982: 9. Successful development of the Soviet Union's friendly relation with African countries discussed. Also highlighted were the flow of trade, texts of agreements between USSR and African countries.

New Step in Soviet-Nigerian relations. *Times International,* 3 (7) 28 Nov., 1981: 16. The visit of Soviet MP's marked a new step in Soviet-Nigeria relations.

Nigerian Senators visit the USSR. *Times International,* 3 (1) 21-27 Sept., 1981: 11. Outlines purpose of the visit—to familiarise Senators with the USSR's experience in solving a number of social problems.

Ogunbadejo, O.: Ideology and pragmatism: the Soviet role in Nigeria, 1960-77. *Orbis,* 21 (4), Winter 1978: 803-830.

Ojo, J.B.: Nigerian-Soviet relations: retrospect and prospect. *African Studies Review,* 19 (3), December, 1976: 43-63.

Rotibi, Bayo: Ajaokuta Steel—Dredging goes on to tender. *African Economic Digest,* 24 Oct., 1980: 2-3. Reports resumption of work on Nigeria's Ajaokuta iron and steel industry following patch-up in Soviet-Nigerian dispute over Soviet assistance.

Stevens, Christopher: Africa and the Soviet Union. *International Relations,* 3 (12), Nov. 1971: 1014-25. A general review with some emphasis on Soviet relations with Ghana and Nigeria.

——— *The Soviet Union and Black Africa:* New York, Holmes and Meinar, 1976. A study of USSR's political economic and military relations from 1953 to 1972. Ghana, Guinea, Mali, Nigeria and Kenya.

Survey of Soviet African Trade. *Africa Business and Economic Revision,* 1 Jan., 1980: 67-72. Much of Soviet Economic aid and trade efforts are concentrated along Africa's eastern and western coastlines, embracing such countries, as Tanzania, Congo, Equatorial Guinea and Guinea. A table of Import-Export figures for Soviet trade with Ghana, Nigeria, Ethiopia, Ivory Coast and Guinea is provided.

Vodinsky, A.: Economic co-operation between the Soviet Union and Nigeria. *Foreign Trade,* No. 11, 1980: 19-21. Economic and technical co-operation between Nigeria and the Soviet Union increased.

Yugoslavia

Nigeria-Yugoslavian relations. *Nigerian Statesman,* 31 March, 1982: 3. The editorial comment on the growing cordial relations between Nigeria and Yugoslavia.

EUROPE, WEST

Jean-Baptiste, E.N.L.: Swiss backdoor trade with Nigeria. *Afriscope,* 1 (9) Sept., 1981. It explained, how inspite of the Nigerian Government's ban on the import of Swiss textiles, the trade goes on as vigorously as before.

Cervenka, Zdenek: West Germany and Africa: the time for change is now. *Africa,* June 1978: 80-86. The visit to Nigeria and Zambia by Chancellor Helmut Schmidt should be appropriate time to clear the air on West Germany's relations with the racist regime in South Africa.

Traile, Susan: Belgium looks for new trading Partners. *African Economic Digest,* 26 Sept., 1980: 5. Describes diversification of Belgium's trade in Africa to include such countries as Nigeria and Zaire.

Great Britain

Aluko, Olajide: Nigeria and Britain since Gowon. *African Affairs,* 76 (304) July 1977: 303-320.

Carim Enver: Blue circle boosts cement production. *AED,* 7 Nov., 1980: Describes the work of Britain's Blue Circle Industries in cement works in Nigeria.

Lord Carrington's visit. *Afriscope,* 11 (2) Feb. 1981: Examines Lord Carrington's visit to Nigeria—its impact on Angola-Nigerian relations and world peace. Discussed many issues of mutual interest and international importance—ranging from Namibia to apartheid in Southern Africa.

Morris-Jones H. et al (ed.): Decolonisation after the British and French experience. *Studies in Commonwealth Politics and History No. 7,* 1980: 193-221. Contents include the military relations between Great Britain and the African members of the Commonwealth.

Okoli, E.J.: Mending Anglo-Nigerian fences. *West Africa,* No. 3288, 28 July, 1980: 1373-1375.

Rotibi, Bayo and Karan Thapar: United Kingdom fetes Nigerian Leader. *African Economic Digest*, 2 (12) 20-26 March, 1981: 2-5. Extensive report on President Shehu Shagari's visit to Britain. British-Nigerian economic and political relations, including statistics of Britain's trade in Africa and list of British Companies with contracts in Nigeria are also provided.

Shagari traces our commercial and economic ties with Britain. *New Nigerian*, 29 March, 1981: 19. Reviews the history of Britain's commercial and economic relations with Nigeria.

France

Alima, Jos-Blaise: Lagos and Paris. *Africa*, June 1973: 32-33. Describes attempt to improve diplomatic relations between Nigeria and France inspite of a history of strained Franco-Nigerian relations.

Bachi, Daniel: Le General de Gaule et la guere au Nigeria. *Canadian Journal of African Studies*, 14 (2) 1980: 259-72. Analyses France's position in the face of Biafra's secession, Biafra highlighting background to her involvement in the war.

Bini, Obi: France's Imperial Role in Africa. *Guardian*, 21 Jan., 1981: 15. In the wake of recent Franco-Libyan diplomatic confrontation over the later's intervention in Chad, French influence is more dominant; her economic, political and military influence in West and Central Africa is examined.

Economic relations between France and Nigeria in 1980. *National Concord*, 14 July, 1981: 5. Focuses on the accelerated growth of the Franco-Nigerian economic ties in the 1980's.

Egbochukwu, Stanley: Nigeria's trade with France expands. *Business Times*, 8 (24) 15 March, 1982: 40. Assesses the growth and volume of trade between Nigeria and France.

France and Nigeria-creating a pro-federal island. *West Africa*, No. 2708, 26 April, 1969: 484.

French Economic Mission in Nigeria: French Businessmen on tour of Nigeria. *Daily Times*, 24 January, 1973: 18. The mission—to strengthen trade relations between Nigeria and France. Diplomatic problems with France was also discussed.

French interests in Biafra. *Africa Confidential*, No. 25, 22 Dec., 1967. The author explains France's pro-Biafran sentiments. France's political and oil interest in Biafra were considered.

French Trade Mission arrives. *The Nigerian Chronicle*, 16 May, 1977: 3. How important is France to Nigeria as an Economic Partner.

Nigerian Observer, 14 July, 1972: 8. Reflects on the importance of France to Nigeria as a trading partner.

Jeantelot, Charles B.: Relations Commerciales Franco-Nigeriannes. *Nigeria Demain,* 52, May-June 1978: 5-8. Franco-Nigerian commercial relations examined.

Nigeria/France now clear old prejudices. *Sunday Times,* 4 Feb., 1973: 2. Prejudices and misgivings that hindered mutual understanding and co-operation between Nigeria and France were examined.

Nigeria: Garba's warning to the West. *West Africa,* 5 June, 1978: 1090-1091. Nigeria is worried about a proposal made at the recent Franco-African Summit in Paris that a Pan-African defense force be set to help secure Africa's national boundaries against outside forces.

Nigerian-French relations resumed. *West Africa,* No. 2526, 30 Oct., 1965: 1235-36. Examines Nigeria's increasing ties with France.

Nweke, G.A.: External intervention in African conflicts: France and French-speaking West Africa in the Nigerian Civil War, 1967-1970. Boston: Boston University *African Studies Centre,* 1976.

Oloruntimehin, Olatunji B.: Africa in France's International Relations: new perspectives under President Francois Mitterrand. *Nigerian Forum,* 1 (6) Aug. 1981: 218-226. The author sees Nigeria as a major target of France as well as other major powers.

Role of French Firms in Nigeria. *Daily Times,* 14 July, 1969: 14. The correspondent assesses the scope and influence of French firms in Nigeria.

Rondos, Alex: Mitterand and Africa. *West Africa,* No. 3329, 18 May, 1981: 1074-1077.

Sampio, M.: France hits the Nigerian jackpot. *African Business,* No. 30, Feb., 1981: 13.

Why France and Nigeria should strengthen economic co-operation. *Nigerian Tribune,* 24 May, 1972: 4. Discusses ways to strengthen the links between Nigeria and French industrialists in order to improve economic relations between the two countries.

MIDDLE EAST, ASIA & THE PACIFIC

Bukarambe, B.: The Middle East: an overview. *Nigerian Forum,* 2 (3) March 1982: 481-493. The paper is devoted to the long enduring problem of the Arab-Israeli conflict, highlighting the factors responsible for the conflict.

Israel

Adedipe, Sina: The flaws in Dr. Akinyemi's letter to legislators. *Sunday Concord,* 6 June, 1982: 3. Looks critically at Akinyemi's submissions, highlighted what he considered to be reasons for the diplomatic break and emphasised that re-establishing diplomatic ties with priorities rather than by an OAU decision.
See also: *Nigerian Statesman,* 18 May, 1982.

Agbatekwe, Aaron: Nothing should now hold us back from Israel. *Daily Times,* 24 June, 1982: 15. Analyses Nigeria-Israeli Relations and the need for a review now since circumstances which led to the imposition of diplomatic boycott are no longer tenable.

Akinsanya, A.: On Lagos decision to break diplomatic relations with Israel *International Problem* 17 Spring 1978: 65-79.

Akinyemi, A. Bolaji: Nigerian-Israeli Relations. *Nigerian Herald,* 1 June, 1982: 10-11. An update on progress of Nigeria-Israeli relations, adducing reasons why Nigeria should not reopen diplomatic relations with Israel.

Aluko, Olajide: Israel and Nigeria: continuity and change in their relationship. *African Reviews: A Journal of African Politics Development and International Affairs,* 4 (1) 1974: 34-50. Examines Nigerian-Israeli relations when interjected with a new variable, namely the Arab-Israeli conflict.

———— As diplomatic offensive hots up: Israelis and Arabs scramble for Nigeria. *Weekly Focus,* 6-12 April, 1981: 1. Evidence of protracted diplomatic offensive by some Middle Eastern States to woo Nigeria's sympathy.

Edet, Asuquo: Should Nigeria review relations with Israel? (Rejoinder). *Sunday New Nigeria,* 30 May, 1982: 3. Defends the resumption of diplomatic ties with Israel and points out the misconceptions in Gausu Ahmed's invocation of the Kissingerian concept of the linkage.

Ekwonna, Chris: Let's renew ties with Israel. *Daily Sketch,* 14 June, 1982: 7. The author stresses the need to renew diplomatic relations with Israel and dismisses the concept of 'Africa being the corner stone of Nigeria's Foreign Policy' as meaningless and lacking in focus.

Gambari, Ibrahim Agboola: Nigeria's Policy on Israel. *Nigerian Herald,* 10 June, 1982: 6. Argues that Nigeria needs to re-establish diplomatic ties with Israel.

Israel's intrigues in Africa. *New Nigerian,* 21 February, 1972. The anti-Israeli articles carried by the New Nigerian on the eve of Israeli

Ambassadors visit to Kaduna and Sokoto States.

Nigeria debates the Israeli link. *Foreign Report*, 5 March, 1980: 8. Nigeria was considering re-establishing diplomatic links with Israel, but this cooled down after report leaked out that Israel was involved in the explosion of a Nuclear device off the South African Coast.

Nigeria-Israel Relations. *Nigerian Statesman*, 18 May, 1982: 3. A plea for the re-opening of diplomatic links with the Israelis as Nigeria would stand to gain from Israel's technical and agricultural know-how.

Nigeria-Israeli Relations—international commentary. *Financial Punch*, 31 May, 1982: 13. Argues that Nigeria stands to gain from Israeli technonological know-how.

See also: *Sunday New Nigerian*, 9 May, 1982: 3.

Recognise Israel now. (Editorial) *Daily Star*, 7 June, 1982. Analyses the origin of the break up of diplomatic relations with Israel and urges the resumption of diplomatic links with same.

Synge, Richard: 'BADEA Backs Lagos Plan of Action' *African Economic Digest*, 25 July, 1980: 2-3. Describes Arab Bank canvassing for development projects agreed to at the OAU Economic Summit in Lagos, Nigeria.

Ugorji, M.C.: Need for a change: Nigeria's relationship with Israel. *The Nigerian Standard*, 17 Jan., 1978: 6. The author contends that Egypt sees no usefulness in continuing hostilities with Israel, why Nigeria?

UNIBEN Students want normal relation with Israel. *Sunday Observer*, 8 June, 1982: 3. Presents factors responsible for Israeli Egyptian disagreement; that the situation having changed, Nigeria should reconcile with Israel.

See also: *Nigerian Tribune*, 1 June, 1982: 11.

Uranga, Emmanuel: Nigeria and Middle-of-The-Road Foreign Policy. *Daily Times*, 31 May, 1981: 5, 7, 27. Analysis of factors which determined Nigeria's relations with Israel, from the Nigerian Civil War to the period when Arab-Israeli conflict began, and the Egypt-Israeli disagreement that led to diplomatic break with Israel.

We must be friendly with all nations *Daily Sketch*, 4 May, 1972: 7. Statement by Chief Akin Deko at a symposium organised at Ibadan by the Nigeria-Israeli Friends Association urging Federal Government to maintain cordial relations with all nations in the Middle East in order to foster World peace.

Why Nigeria should recognise Israel. *Sunday Statesman*, 23 March,

1980: 13. Points out that Egypt has re-opened diplomatic relations with Israel, despite the fact that the OAU member states boycotted Israel because of Egypt. Nigeria is urged to resume ties with Israel.

BRAZIL

Brazil seeks Nigerian markets. *African Business*, No. 29, Jan. 1981: 27. Looks at Brazil's growing trade relations with Nigeria.

Brazil's offensive in Africa. *Times International*, 2 (11), 1980: 17. Looks at the Brazilian plan to relaunch trade relations with Africa.

Nigeria-Angola-Brazil axis: *Seminar held at the Nigerian Institute of International Affairs*, Lagos, 13 April, 1976. Unpublished. Possibility of joint defence effort to ward off possible super powers' aggression were discussed.

Nigeria, Brazil sign Co-operation Agreement. *Nigerian Standard* 31 March, 1981: 9. Nigeria's Brazilian policies are examined.

Nigerian-Brazilian dialogue on foreign policy—a report of a Nigerian-Brazilian dialogue, Sao Paulo, Brazil, 29 July—1 August, 1980. Lagos: Nigerian Institute of International Affairs, 1982. The dialogue examined the Nigerian-Brazil relations pointing out that relations should not be restricted to commercial interests alone.

Ogwu, Joy U.: Nigeria and Brazil: a model for the emergent South-South Relation In Carlson Jerke (ed.) *South-South Relations in a Changing World Order* Uppsala: Scandinavian Institute of African Studies, 1983: 141-178. The author examined Nigeria-Brazil cultural affinity, race, trade and politics. Contains statistical data on Nigeria's trade with Brazil 1972-1979.

Opportunity knocks for Nigeria. *Africa*, March, 1979: 95-96. Describes new Trade pact between Nigeria and Brazil.

Problems both Nigeria and U.S. must solve. *Nigerian Herald*, 10 July, 1975. Argues that America's treatment of foreign students is unfair and highlights factors and pressures on the economy that gave rise to this inhuman treatment from the U.S. immigration officials.

Verger, Pierre: Nigeria, Brazil and Cuba. *Nigeria Magazine*, (*Special Independence Issue*) October 1960: 167-177.

INDIA

Co-operation Pact with India. *Africa Dairy; Weekly Record of Events in*

Africa, 19 (42) 15-21 Oct., 1979: 9719-9720.
See also: P. 9538. Nigeria and India signed an agreement on technical and economic co-operation.

JAPAN

Fajana, Olufemi: Trends and prospects of Nigeria-Japanese Trade *Journal of Modern African Studies*, 14 (1) March 1976: 127-36. Both Japan and Nigeria depend on International Trade for their survival and a substantial increase in the volume of Nigerian Japanese trade can be predicted.

Morrison, Godrey: Japan in Africa: Trade, investment marked by hunger for resources. *African Development*, 8 (6) June 1974: 3-17. Contends that Japan's lack of natural resources has spurned its advances in Africa.

Tsurumi, Iyohiko: Trade between Nigeria and Japan. *Nigerian Review*, Dec. 1968: 17-19.

THE AMERICAS

King, M.C.: Nigerian Foreign Policy and the African diaspora: The North American Region. Zaria: *Journal of the Nigerian Society for International Affairs*, January, 1979.

UNITED STATES OF AMERICA

Aderinola, Dapo: Carter will be responsive to African feelings. *Daily Times*, 10 December, 1977: 9. Assumes that Carter's Administration would exhibit some concern over the plight of Blacks in South Africa by emphasising such ideals as justice, decolonisation and independence and urging the American multinational corporations to be more active in challenging the status quo by exerting optimal pressure for peaceful change.

African Fisheries Development and U.S. Investment Potential. *Africa Business and Economic Review*, 16 June, 1980: 142-144. Fourth and final article in a series on African Fisheries, focusing on specific countries viz Ghana, Nigeria, Angola, Kenya, Mozambique and Sudan.

Akaraogun, Olu: Carter's Pilgrimage. Africa. May 1978: 15-17. An overview of Carter's March 1978 trip to Africa, suggesting that the trip was necessitated by American domestic pressure coupled with international considerations.

Dr. Akinyemi defends General Obasanjo's American trip. *The Nigerian Chronicle* 22 Nov., 1977: 3. The Director-General of NIIA concludes that contrary to the expectations of the critics of the visit of President Carter's impending visit to Nigeria, Obasanjo's visit is significant because of the blunt manner he told the American Government that the liberation of South Africa is the major preoccupation of Nigerian foreign policy.

Aluko, Isaac Agboola: A new image for Nigeria in the U.S. *Daily Times,* 4 July, 1977: 22. Critically examines the harm which might be inflicted on Nigeria-U.S. relations by the later's over-close identification with Apartheid, and maintains that it's the U.S. that can substantially change the racist and oppressive system in Rhodesia, Zimbabwe & Republic of South Africa.

Bamgbose, Sina: U.S. Visit: Climax of Safari. *Nigerian Tribune* 26 Oct., 1977: 4. The author offers an in-depth analysis of American Foreign Policy and global developments since World War II, ranging from Warsaw Pact, NATO, SEATO & Dominion principle and African Countries since attainment of political freedom.

Bertolin, Gordon: U.S. Economic interests in Africa: Investment, Trade and Raw Materials In: Whitaker, J.S. (ed.) *Africa and the U.S.* New York, 1978: 21-59. Analyses global interdependence and the increasing reliance of the U.S. on foreign sources of oil and the economic importance of Africa especially Nigeria to the U.S.

Carter's Visit 1 & 2, *Nigerian Chronicle,* 31 March, 1978: 3. Reviews the relationship between the two countries and the significance of the visit to the various conflicts in Africa.

Chima, William Ndubuisi: Perspectives of Nigeria-United States Relations 1960-1977: An Inquiry into the impact of economic interdependence upon the diplomatic relations of the two nations. Ph.D. Thesis Ann Arbor: University Microfilm International 1982. An inquiry into the influence of the economic interdependence on the diplomatic relations of the two nations.

Conference on U.S. Foreign Policy in Africa, 13 December, 1979, Detroit, Michigan. Sponsored by the U.S. Department of State and the Economic Club of Detroit. Contents include: U.S. Strategic Interest and Africa; Africa's International Role; African Economic

Prospects; Nigeria: America's New Trade; Energy and Investment Partner; Peace Efforts in Zimbabwe & Namibia.

Historical background of Nigeria-U.S. relations. *Nigerian Standard*, 4 Nov., 1980: 5.

See also: *Nigerian Herald,* 28 Oct., 1980: 6. Seeks to identify the crucial circumstances under which the relationship was built (Slave trade) and there from focussing on the bilateral—economic, commercial, and political relationships between them.

Impact of Obasanjo-Carter Detente. *Daily Times,* 3 Nov., 1977: 20. Attempts to estimate the success of the visit in terms of its immediate impact on and reaction from five sectors of the American Society: the government, the legislature, the press, business community and the general public with special emphasis on the black community.

Johnson, Paul: The Carter Milestone around Maggie's neck. *Daily Times,* 15 June, 1979: 3. (culled from the *London Evening Standard*). The author explores the implications for U.S. should she decide to abrogate the sanctions against South Africa, and a set of pragmatic policy options for Nigeria in countering any prospective U.S. policy which proves detrimental to her national interests and policy goals in Africa.

Johnson, T.A.: Nigeria and the U.S. *Africa* No. 76 Dec. 1977: 22-26.

Melbourne, Roy M.: The American Response to Nigerian Conflict. *Issue,* Summer 1973: 33-42. Discusses ways in which American politicians reacted to Nigerian Civil War with emphasis on relief aid to persons in rebel Biafra.

Ndifor, Asong: Nigeria: Friends again with U.S. *New African Development,* April 1977: 3111. Signs of ending U.S.-Nigerian relations during early Carter administration.

New Trends in Nigeria-America relations. *Sunday Observer,* 23 Oct., 1977: 5. Appraises the ties between the two countries and argues that trade expansion and co-operation in economic and technical fields, offer a surer route to economic growth of both countries. Considers simultaneously the Anglo-American Peace Plan in Zimbabwe.

Nigeria-America Economic relations—its growth, problems and prospects. *The New Nation.* 4 (28) Aug., 1981: 25-37. Examines economic relations between the two countries in recent years.

Nigeria and The USA—Carter's Secret plan for the future *New Africa,* Aug., 1978: 13-14.

Nigerian anxieties over U.S. policy. *West Africa,* No. 3339 27 July, 1981: 1687-1689.

Nigerian President visits U.S. *U.S. Department of State Bulletin,* 80 (2045) Dec. 1980: 24-26.

OBASANJO's visit to U.S. reviewed. *Sunday Sketch.* 23 Oct., 1977: 5. Considers the visit as another forum through which General Obasanjo succeeded in stating the basic objectives of Nigerian foreign policy, and observes a similarity between the disposition of the Carter Administration towards Africa and the African policy of the Federal Military Government.

Obasi, Nnamdi: Carter's second diplomatic trip. *Daily Sketch,* 25 March, 1978: 5. Sees Carter's administration as a deviation from Nixon-Ford-Kissinger approach to African affairs.

Ogunbadejo, Oye: A new turn in U.S.-Nigerian Relations. *The World Today,* March 1979: 117-126. Contrasts President Carter's policy towards Africa with that of his predecessors and suggests that the key to U.S.-Nigerian Relations is the U.S. Policy stance on Southern Africa.

Okediji, F.O. et al.: What attracts Nigerians to America. *Daily Sketch,* 29 March, 1973: Suggests that certain forces influence people's decision to migrate, for example career aspirations, lack of facilities for fulfiling their professional expectations and educational opportunities.

Okoli, Enukora Joe: Studying the system. *West Africa,* 10 March, 1980: 435. Discusses the recent visit of the Speaker of Nigerian House of Representatives who led a delegation of his colleagues to Washington to observe U.S. legislative processes.

Osuntokun, Jide: Obasanjo's visit to the U.S. To be or not to be. *Daily Express,* 5 Oct., 1977: 11.

See also: *Daily Sketch,* 10 Oct., 1977: 3. *Daily Standard,* 10 Oct., 1977: 3. Critical of America's South African policy on apartheid but was optimistic that President Carter's Administration would bring peaceful change in Southern Africa though the Anglo-American proposals are full of pitfalls.

Oudes, Bruce: The U.S. and the Nigerian Civil War. *West Africa,* 8 Sept. 1972: 1177. Discusses what stance U.S. Embassy in Lagos should have towards host government as an example of broader U.S. Government ambivalence on Nigerian Civil War.

Overseas Liaison Committee. Future Nigeria-U.S. linkages in Higher Education. Washington D.C., Agency for International Development,

1977. Contents include: Recommendations, for Nigeria-American university relations, issues in Nigeria-U.S. co-operation, staff recruitment in the U.S. Nigeria staff development and inter-University linkages.

President Carter's visit to Nigeria: Joint Communique. *The Nigerian Chronicle,* 7 April, 1978: 13. Identified the dominant bilateral and international economic avenues for co-operation, examined in detail the current state of affairs in Africa and the Middle East but with greater emphasis on South African situation.

Pwol, Joel: U.S.-Nigerian Relations—An Analysis. *Sunday Standard,* 30 Oct., 1977: 5. See also: *Sunday Standard,* 30 Oct., 1977. Examines America's foreign policy strategy as they relate to purely bilateral and African interest levels and concludes by observing that there is a political evolution in Africa of which Nigeria is a starting point which underlines the stature of her international image.

Reis, Toyin: The U.S. visit and Nigerian Foreign Policy. *Times International,* 24 Oct., 1977: 3. Explores the implications of United States Africa policy, the consequences for United States and with Nigeria in particular; and Africa in general, if U.S. does not support intensification of the Liberation Struggle in Angola, Namibia, Zimbabwe and South Africa.

Smith, Terence: Carter will begin 4-Nation trip today. *New York Times,* 28 March, 1978. Considers the trip as a way to dramatise his administration's interest in the developing world and the African trip is designed to underscore the administration's active role in solving the problems of Southern Africa.

Sobowale, Dayo: Jimmy Carter's visit to Nigeria. *Times International,* 27 March, 1978: 3. Contends that of all the issues affecting Nigeria-America relations none is as important for Nigeria as racial injustice in South Africa; international economic issues ranging from oil prices, law of the sea, Somalia-Ethiopian conflict and intrusion of Soviet and Cuban forces in African Affairs were also examined.

Super, Susan: Why U.S. gives aid to three OPEC Members. *Agenda,* July/August, 1979: 16-19. A survey of the poorest of poor nations.

Visit to West Africa. *U.S. Dept of State Bulletin* 80 (2042), Sept., 1980: 11-13. Vice President of United States of America's address at a dinner in Lagos.

INTERNATIONAL ORGANIZATIONS

Commonwealth of Nations

Anyaoku, Emeka: The Commonwealth. *Africa,* March 1974. Describes frustrations of African member states including Nigeria in the Commonwealth over inaction in addressing Southern African issues in a serious manner.

Commonwealth and Nigeria. *West Africa,* No. 1692, 4 Jan., 1969: 1-2.

Commonwealth Foundations. *Commonwealth African Directory of Aid Agencies.* London: The Commonwealth Foundation 1979. Provides information on 200 governmental and non-governmental agencies involved in technical assistance and other aids to African member countries of the Commonwealth.

Dudley, Billy J.: The Commonwealth and the Nigeria/Biafra conflict, In: Seminar Papers on the Impact of African Issues on the Commonwealth. London: Institute of Commonwealth Studies.

Foreign Policy Statement by the Minister of Foreign Affairs and Commonwealth Relations, Hon. Jaja Wachuku in the Federal Parliament on 4th September 1961. Nigeria's participation in the Commonwealth Parliamentary Association was before Independence. See O.A. Ojedokun: Nigeria's Relations with the Commonwealth with special reference to her relations with the United Kingdom 1960-66 (Ph.D. thesis presented at the University of London 1968) 614.

Ogar, Clexus: The role of the Commonwealth in the liberation of Southern Africa. *Nigerian Broadcasting Corporation Newstalk,* 15 May, 1976. The Head of State, Lt. General Olusegun Obasanjo spoke on the vital role which the Commonwealth could play in the Liberation of Southern Africa.

ECONOMIC COMMUNITY OF WEST AFRICAN STATES (ECOWAS)

Address by His Excellency General Olusegun Obasanjo, Head of the Federal Military Government, Commander-in-Chief of the Armed Forces of Nigeria and Chairman, Authority of Heads of State and Government of Ecowas at the Opening Session of the meeting held in Dakar, Senegal, 28-29 May, 1979.

Iya Abubakar: Aliens misunderstand Ecowas treaty. *New Nigerian* 22 Oct., 1981: 10. Ecowas nationals who entered illegally were taking undue advantage of the abolition of visas for short term visits as contained in the treaty. It is now the responsibility of immigration officers to flush out such aliens who have overstayed the stipulated time.

Alkema, E.A.: Association and the European Economic Community: some legal aspects with relation to Nigeria's association with the E.E.C. *Law in Society Proceedings,* 3, 1967: 1.

Aluko, Olajide: Nigeria's initiative in the West African Economic Community *Societe d'Etudes et d'Expansion, Revue, Liege,* Nov/Dec. 1973: 870-880.

Anana, Chris: Ciroma gives recipe to ECOWAS. *Nigerian Standard,* 25 August, 1976: 3. The Governor of Central Bank enumerated some of the problems the Community will face as some African member countries were too small to be able to create modern viable industrial structures within their national framework.

Anusiowu, E.: Towards rapid industrialisation of Africa (Part 1). *New Nigerian,* 27 June, 1978: 20. A review of some papers presented at the Inaugural Conference of the West African Economic Association, 13-15 April, 1978 in Lagos, Nigeria.

Arikpo, O.: Nigeria to benefit from ECOWAS *New Nigerian,* 26 June, 1978: 12.

Ashiru, Fola: ECOWAS leaders okay agreement on free movement now for citizens. *New Nigerian,* 31 May, 1979: 1. Citizens of the 16 member countries of ECOWAS are now free to move within the community without visas.

Ayeni, M.A.: Let's watch immigration procedures. *Sunday Sketch,* 8 October, 1978: 4. The pursuance of international diplomacy calls for internal vigilance. Nigeria should now be conscious of her internal security if her role of African leadership in political affairs is to continue unabated.

Businessmen told to equip themselves with Ecowas task. *New Nigerian,* 17 November, 1980: 12.

Campbell, Keith: Nigerian Foreign Policy and the ECOWAS. *The South African Institute of International Affairs,* Occasional Paper, 1978. Provides an outline of Nigeria's Foreign Policy with her neighbours—namely Cameroon, Chad, Niger, Benin and Togo including policy towards Africa and South Africa as well.

_____ Nigerian foreign policy and the Economic Community of

West African States (ECOWAS). Johannesburg: *South African Institute of International Affairs,* 1978.

Check foreign economic domination Obasanjo urges ECOWAS. *Nigerian Observer,* 3 November, 1976: 3. Lt.-General Obasanjo stated that ECOWAS effort is to rid Africa of foreign economic domination.

Coetze, David: Nigeria flexes its muscles and forms a new bloc. *African Development,* 8(3) March 1974: 11-13. Nigeria's increased economic weight in West Africa is having political consequences, apparent in her role is the proposed formation of an Economic Community.

Dagunduro, Sehinde: Nigeria, Togo make a pledge on ECOWAS. *New Nigerian,* 23 December, 1975: 1-2. In a joint communique, Nigeria and Togo pledged to make ECOWAS a veritable instrument for the achievement of total independence and unity in the continent.

Decraene, Philippe: UN sucies pour Dakar: la Confereration de Senegambia. *Le Monde Diplomatique,* December 1981: 5. A success for Dakar and the Senegambia Confederation.

ECOWAS: Adewoye sounds a note of warning. *The Punch,* 15 April, 1978: 11. The Chairman of the Council of Ministers, Omoniyi Adewoye has warned that Ecowas could break-up if the individual countries of the community place too much emphasis and importance on their separate sovereignties.

Ecowas Chief briefs Obasanjo. *Daily Times,* 25 January, 1979: 3. Exchanging views with the Chairman of the Ecowas fund, Lt.-General Obasanjo reiterated that member nations will not be judged by the number of meetings held but by the effectiveness of the organisation in influencing the condition of living of the people of the sub-region for good.

ECOWAS endorses four major recommendations. *Daily Sketch,* 21 July, 1977: 16. The Conference of Ministers held in Lagos unanimously endorsed four major recommendations—customs union, free movement of goods and people, transport system and telecommunication.

Ecowas member-countries urged to fulfil their financial obligations. *Federal Ministry of Information Press Release,* No. 1132, 28 May, 1980.

Ecowas member-countries urged to shed off neo-colonial propensities *Federal Ministry of Information Press Release,* No. 1708, 24 November, 1978. Dr. Adewoye appealed to ECOWAS member-countries to renounce conventions or agreements which tend to perpetuate their role as traditional suppliers of raw materials.

ECOWAS must live (Editorial) *Nigerian Herald,* 26 August, 1976: 5.

Sovereignty that lacks the strong backing of economic power cannot justify its claim to international integrity and respect. This is why all Ecowas member states must unite further for economic stability.

ECOWAS: Nigeria and Mali to champion objectives. *National Concord,* 29 May, 1981: 2.

Economic Community of West African States (ECOWAS) Nigerian support. *Africa Research Bulletin,* 12 (10) 3671A-B, 15 October—14 November, 1975.

ECOWAS: Nigeria's stand. *Nigerian Chronicle,* 6 November, 1975: 3. Nigeria's stand on Ecowas membership is that the community should be allowed to take off first before any country outside the region could join.

ECOWAS: No free movement yet. *Nigerian Chronicle,* 26 April, 1978: 16. At the summit conference just ended in Lagos, some Heads of States opposed the free movement into richer countries.

ECOWAS officials brief Obasanjo. *Nigerian Tribune,* 16 August, 1979: 7. Two Ecowas officials, Dr. Abubakar Ouattara, the Executive Secretary of Ecowas and Dr. Romes Horton, the Managing Director of ECOWAS Fund, briefed the Nigerian Head of State in his capacity as the current Chairman of the Heads of States of Ecowas.

ECOWAS still a reality. *New Nigerian,* 18 August, 1975: 1. Colonel Garba gave the assurance that the change in government in Nigeria would in no way interfere with the formation and continued existence of ECOWAS.

Ecowas summit expresses grave concern over Cameroon-Nigeria and Cameroon/Gabon incidents. Nigeria. *Federal Ministry of Information Press Release,* No. 866, 31 May, 1981. The Heads of State and Government of ECOWAS have expressed grave concern over the incidents between Cameroon and Gabon on the other hand.

Ecowas will start work after two years—Peter Afolabi. *The Nigerian Standard,* 28 February, 1977: 1.

ECOWAS: When? *Nigerian Tribune,* 20 April, 1976: 1-2. Even if Senegal succeeded in carrying away all the other French speaking states, the ECOWAS should go on all the same.

Ecowas to negotiate Headquarters agreement with Nigerian government Federal Ministry of Information *News Release,* No. 1311, 22 July, 1977. Nigeria as host country to the community is expected to grant certain privileges and immunities to the secretariat of the community vide Article 60, section 4 of the Treaty establishing community.

Edozien, Elfreda: ECOWAS: a bulwark against imperialism. *Nigerian Tide,* 9 December, 1976: 9.

Ekpu, Ray: Barriers off. *Nigerian Chronicle,* 1 June, 1979. Sequel to the signing by the authority of Heads of States of Ecowas in Dakar of a protocol of free movement of persons, right of residence and establishment, Nigeria may introduce a new passport to enable Nigerians who may wish travel to Ecowas countries.

Ekwueme restates government commitment to ECOWAS. *New Nigerian* 6 December, 1979: 1. Vice-President Ekwueme reiterated the commitment of the new Federal Government to the ideals and goals of ECOWAS.

Eminue, Okon: Are fears over Nigeria's size and prosperity justified? *Daily Times,* 21 January, 1982: 7.

Eze, Osita: Ecowas and freedom of movement: what prospects for Nigeria. *Nigerian Forum,* 1 (1) March 1981: 22-28. Stressed the importance of national security inspite of Ecowas freedom of movement law.

General Obasanjo outlines the progress and perspective of Ecowas. *Federal Ministry of Information Press Release No. 817,* 27 May, 1979. General Obasanjo described the documents of the Protocol signed and ratified by member states on free movement of persons, right of residence and establishment as important instruments that would make.ECOWAS more meaningful to the peoples of the sub-region.

Gold, Kenneth: Nigeria to set up communication links with Ecowas states. *Nigerian Standard,* 30 October, 1980: 1. To enhance trade relations, Nigeria is prepared to establish more telecommunication and transportation links with other Ecowas states.

Gowon congratulates ECOWAS. *Nigerian Observer,* 29 May, 1975: 13. General Gowon congratulated other Heads of States who have appended their signatures to the Ecowas Treaty.

Harrigan, Peter: West African Community—clearing the path. *African Development,* 8 (7) July, 1974: 21-23. Author analyses difficulties that lie ahead for integration in West Africa and concludes that Nigeria made initial campaigns successful.

Haruna, Mohammed: Towards a meaningful Ecowas. *New Nigerian,* 25 November, 1976. Once we have laid the democratic basis necessary for a meaningful ECOWAS, we can begin to restructure our various economies such that they can survive and thrive independently of the Western economies.

Head of State warns member-states of Ecowas over petty nationalisms *Federal Ministry of Information Press Release,* No. 819, 27 May, 1979. General Obasanjo warned Ecowas member-states in Dakar that 'We cannot keep jealously to our nationalisms and hope to survive in the scheme of things in the world economic order as it now exists'.

Helleiner, G.K.: Nigeria and the African Common Market. *Nigerian Journal of Economic and Social Studies,* 4 (3) November, 1962: 283-298.

Ifechukwu, J.A.O.: 17th anniversary of Nigeria's independence: Nigeria and the survival of Ecowas. *Nigerian Observer,* 1 October, 1977: 41.

Ikuniaye, Dan: Events of my time—Nigeria in Ecowas. *Nigerian Herald,* 22 Dec., 1977: 7.

Jukwey, James: ECOWAS must fight against counter-forces—Obasanjo. *New Nigerian,* 19 July, 1977: 24.

Kanu, Chijioke: Flashback: Ecowas summit in Lagos—translating dreams into reality. *Nigerian Chronicle,* 5 May, 1978: 7. Points out that Ecowas has made some progress in areas such as trade, transport and telecommunications. Joint development ventures like road projects are also in existence.

Measures taken to insure Ecowas institutions against abuse of power concentration in the hands of its executives. Federal Ministry of Information *Press Release* No. 2322, December, 1977. Dr. Adewoye enumerated measures taken by the council of Ministers to ensure that all Ecowas institutions are properly managed so that the laudable objectives could be achieved to the advantage of all its member-states.

Ndongko, Wilfred A.: The Economic implications of multimembership in Regional Groupings: The case of Cameroon and Nigeria. *Afrika Spectrum,* 11, 1976: 319-22. Analysis of multimembership of some countries in the 3 African Regional groupings—ECOWAS, LCBC and UDEAC; questions which could arise from such an Economic arrangement are posed with regard to Nigeria and Cameroon which are members. Finally some alternative trade arrangements are considered.

Nigeria: Federal Ministry of Information. Call for Economic Co-operation among West African Countries: An address by Mallam Adamu Ciroma, Governor, CBN. *News Release No. 1035,* 23 August, 1976.

Nigeria: Federal Ministry of Information.

Speech by the Hon. Federal Commissioner for Trade, Major-General M. Shuwa on the occasion of the signing of the Headquarter's agreement between Nigeria and the African Groundnut Council Lagos, March 28, 1976: *Press Release* No. 421, 30 March, 1976.

Nigeria: Federal Ministry of Information. Speech by the Hon. Federal Commissioner for Finance, Mr. A.E. Ekukinam on the Occasion of the formal launching of the West African Clearing House at the NIIA, Lagos, 1 July, 1976. *Press Release No. 792*, 1 July, 1976.

Nigeria's General Obasanjo on an Ecowas Tour. *New African*, November, 1978: 61-63. Report on Obasanjo's visit to Guinea, Benin and Togo and the consequent strengthening of West African Economic self reliance.

Nigeria is the back-bone of Ecowas. *Daily Sketch*, 23 Jan., 1979:11. Nigeria provides more than 31 percent of the annual budget while Ivory Coast, the next largest countributor gives 12.6 per cent.

Nigeria implements Ecowas accord. *Nigerian Statesman*, 3 June, 1980: 2. A large number of people from Ecowas member nations have been taking advantage of Nigeria's ratification of treaty on free movement to stream into the country.

Nigerian delegations visit Ecowas nations. *Nigerian Observer*, 11 September, 1976: 3. Two Nigerian delegates flew out of Lagos to various West African States on a special mission relating to Ecowas.

Nigeria ratifies Ecowas protocol. *Nigerian Chronicle*, 8 March, 1980: 14. Nigeria is to implement the provision of the protocol relating to free movement temporarily until it comes into force after ratification by at least seven member states.

Nigeria supports multilateral trade among Ecowas member states. *New Nigerian*, 3 Dec., 1977: 12. Lt-General Obasanjo has given the assurance that any multilateral arrangement which could promote transfer of goods and movement of people across the borders of member nations of Ecowas would be encouraged by Nigeria.

Nigeria and Togo satisfied with non-aggression agreement among Ecowas states. *Federal Ministry of Information Press Release*, No. 1279, 10 Sept., 1978. The two countries hope that the signing of non-aggression agreement by Ecowas member states will lead in the future to a common defence agreement within the organisation.

OBASANJO condemns detractors of Ecowas. *Federal Ministry of Information Press Release*, No. 818, 27 May, 1979. General Obasanjo has condemned the destructive comments in a number of foreign papers and periodicals on the efforts of the Ecowas.

Obi, Charles: Adhere to Ecowas Treaty. Shagari cautions against harassment of citizens in member countries. *National Concord,* 29 May, 1981: 1-11. President Shagari has warned against harassment of citizens and imposition of stiff entry – exit conditions by member nations of Ecowas.

Ofoegbu, Mazi Ray: The Relations between Nigeria and its Neighbours. *Nigerian Journal of International Studies.* 1 (1) July 1975: 28-40.

Also in: ODU: A Journal of West African Studies, 12 July, 1975: 3-24. This essay provides some background information on the feasibility of the Ecowas proposal.

Ojo, Olatunde J.B.: Nigeria and the formation of ECOWAS. *International Organisations,* 34 (4) Autumn 1980: 571-604. Highlights Nigeria's commitment to ECOWAS, the process of commitment, the diplomacy of bringing the organisation into being plus domestic and external factors responsible for Nigeria's leading role.

Ojo, Olatunde J.B.: The formation of Ecowas: some insights into Nigeria's African diplomacy. *Nigerian Society for International Affairs,* Zaria, 1979.

Okuboyejo, M.A.A.: Nigeria as a member of the proposed Economic Community of West African States. Mimeo. 12, Lagos, 1974.

Olofin, S.: Ecowas and the Lome Convention: an experiment in Complementary or conflicting Customs' Union arrangements? *Journal of Common Market Studies,* Sept, 1977: 53–72.

Opening address by the Head of the Federal Military Government, Lt. General Olusegun Obasanjo, delivered on his behalf by the Chief of Air Staff, Air Commodore Yisa-Diko at the second session of the Council of Ministers of Ecowas, Lagos, Nigeria, July 18, 1977.

An opportunity for development – Obasanjo in Senegal. *Nigerian Chronicle,* 29 May, 1979: 16.

In renewing his faith in the collective sovereignty being nurtured in the West African sub-region through Ecowas, General Obasanjo said 'It is the only viable leverage which can lift us from the morass of poverty, and make us count not merely as pawns but as a voice to reckon with in world affairs'.

Onwumere, Eugene.: Getting Ecowas into motion, *Daily Express,* 1 May, 1978: 3.

The position of all Ecowas members at present is that integration has to be built up gradually through economic and technical agreements before any lasting political union could be feasible.

————Nigeria and Ecowas. *Daily Times,* 20 Feb., 1980: 9.

Examines Nigeria's commitment to Ecowas, the strategy and tactics adopted in increasing supportive coalition that brought Ecowas into being and the future of the organisation.

President Shagari addresses Ecowas Summit in Lome. *Federal Ministry of Information Press Release,* No. 1137, 29 May, 1980.

Regional Economic Integration: the lessons of experience. An address by the Chairman of Ecowas Council of Ministers, Dr Omoniyi Adewoye delivered at the third meeting of the Council held in Lagos, April 14–17, 1978.

Time to review Ecowas. *Nigerian Tribune.* 26 Jan., 1981: 16.

Senator Obi Wali has called for a re-assessment of Nigeria's commitment to Ecowas with a view of assessing the question of security of individual states.

Udo, Amos. E.: Ecowas: The sides of the coin, *Nigerian Statesman,* 11 June, 1981: 3.

While it is hard to quarrel with this country's adherence to the agreement allowing the free movement of Ecowas member citizens, nevertheless one is disturbed by the fact that most of those coming to Nigeria under the Ecowas umbrella not only overstay, but illegally take up employment. One is also disturbed over the large influx of undesirable aliens, beggars for instance, who pour in from some Ecowas states.

————Effects of Ecowas Treaty on Nigeria. *Nigerian Chonicle,* 13 March, 1981: 3.

The Treaty on free movement may be doing Nigeria more harm than good. With the growing danger undersirable aliens pose for the security of this nation, their continued presence should be a matter of national concern.

Udokang. Okon.: Ecowas and the Problem of Regional Integration. Times International, 22 March, 1976: 2.

Udokang, Okon.: Nigeria and Ecowas: Economic and political Implications of Regional Integration. In Akinyemi A.B. (ed). *Nigeria and the World.* Ibadan, 1978: 57–81.

The problems and prospects of the newly formed Economic Community of West African States were examined.

Usim, Bob.: Ecowas Aliens. Nigerian Statesman, 25 May, 1981: 16.

Investigations show that about 3,000 Ghanains enter Nigeria daily without valid immigration documents as required by the Ecowas protocol agreement.

————Nigeria's commitment to the treaty and protocol of Ecowas.

Nigerian Statesman, 24 June, 1981: 3.

Nigerian stands to lose nothing by her commitment to the Ecowas Treaty and Protocol. Nigeria is one of the founding fathers of the community and indeed the prime mover of the accord. It would therefore be unreasonable for her to back out of a venture she considered a right and sound approach to African social and economic problems.

Yansane, A.Y.: State of economic integration in West African South of Sahara: the emergence of Ecowas. *African Studies Review,* 20(2) Sept., 1977.

European Economic Community

Agreement establishing an Association between the EEC and the Republic of Nigeria (Signed in Lagos, 16 July, 1966). *International Legal Materials,* Vol. 5, Sept., 1966: 828–858.

Akinsanya, A.: The European Common Market and Africa. *International Problems,* 16 (1 & 2), Spring 1977: 99–117. *Also in: Pakistan Horizon,* 28 (3), 1975: 38–55. *West African Journal of Sociology and Political Science,* 1 (2) Jan., 1976: 147–163.

The Lome Convention provides for a reliable supply of raw materials to the industrial and affluent States of Europe. It does not so clearly benefit the African States.

Aluko, Olajide.: Nigeria and the European Economic Community. *International Studies,* 13 July – 3 Sept., 1974: 465–474.

Nigeria served as a spokesman for Africa in the negotiations.

Okigbo, P.N.C.: Africa and the Common Market. *Evanston: North Western University Press, 1967.*

Contains chapters on the genesis of the EEC, the 1958 Association of African Countries, the 1968 Association of Independent African States, Nigeria and the EEC, the possibilities for African Common Market and prospects for the future.

Standard Bank of Nigeria. Economic Department. Commonwealth Africa and the enlarged European Community: Notes on the possible effects of Britains entry. *African Affairs,* 71 (285), Oct., 1972: 427–436.

Assesses the effects of UK entry into EEC on African member nations of the Commonwealth and pinpoints the safeguards which these territories will need to have included in any agreement with the enlarged Community.

Organization of African Unity

Aluko, Olajide.: Nigeria's role in Inter-African Relations with special reference to OAU. *African Affairs*, 72 (287), April 1973: 145–162.

An observation that since the end of the Civil War Nigeria has played a more active role in the continental and OAU affairs.

Arikpo, O.: Nigeria and the OAU. *Quarterly Journal of Administration*, 9 (11), Oct, 1974: 44–59. *Also in: Nigerian Journal of International Affairs*, 1(1) July, 1975: 1–11.

The text of a lecture presented on 31 July, 1974 by the Commissioner for External Affairs of Nigeria.

The Lagos Plan of Action in the field of Trade and Finance. *African trade*, 5 (1), June 1980.

Emphasizes the need to expand and promote closer economic relations at the intra-African level as a necessary step towards trade expansion with other developing regions.

Okolo, J.E. and Langley, W.E.: The Organisation of African Unity and Apartheid: Constraints on resolutions. *World Affairs*, 137 (3), 1974: 206–232.

Sen, Yima.: False start in Lagos. *West Africa*, 2 June, 1980: 962–63.

A controversial dissenting view of the usefulness of the OAU Special Summit on Economic matters.

United Nations

Adebo, Simeon O.: *Nigeria's foreign policy at the U.N.* Lagos: Voice of Africa, 1964, (Phonotape).

Akpan, Moses E.: *African goals and diplomatic strategies in the United Nations: an indepth analysis of African diplomacy:* North Quincy, Mass: Xtopher Publication House, 1976.

Discusses the elimination of racial discrimination at the United Nations.

Arikpo, Okoi.: *Nigeria and the United Nations:* an address made on the occasion of the 25th Anniversary of the United Nations. N.I.I.A., Lecture Series, No. 3, 1970.

Debate on Nuclear testing: Statement by Hon. M.O. Okilo, 22 Oct., 1963.

Foell, Earl.: The World's deadly silence on Nigeria. *Los Angeles Times*, 16 March, 1969: 3.

The UN impasse regarding the civil war and the extent of foreign involvement.

Herter, Christian A. et. al.: Federation of Nigeria admitted to U.N. Membership: Statements Oct., 7, 1960, *U.S. Department of State Bulletin,* Vol. 43, 24 October, 1960: 659–660.

Ogbu, Edwin Ogede et. al.: Calls for an end to all military co-operation with South Africa. New York: U.N. 1973. United Nations, *Unit on Apartheid,* Notes and documents No. 18/1973.

Ogbu, Edwin Ogede.: No compromise with Apartheid: United Nations Centre Against Apartheid, 1976.

Includes statements on the responsibility of International Community, implementation of the arms embargo, isolation of the South African regime, economic disengagement, no recognition of Bantustans etc.

———— Mission of the Special Committee against Apartheid to Nordic Countries, May 1975. Statements by. . . New York, United Nations, 1975. *United Nations Unit on Apartheid,* Notes and document No. 22/1972.

———— Mission to New Zealand. Statements by the Chairman of the Special Committee on Apartheid. New York: UN, 1974. United Nations. *Unit on Apartheid,* Notes and documents No. 29/1974.

Question of Cyprus: Statement in the First Committee by Alhaji Aminu Kano, Oct., 11. 1965.

Resume of the views, ideas and suggestions made by the Nigerian Delegation during the 1964 Sessions of the Conference of Eighteen Nation Committee on Disarmament.

Statement made in a plenary Session/Meeting of the 20th Session of the General Assembly 5 Oct., 1965 by the Hon. Nuhu Bamali, Deputy Minister of External Affairs of Nigeria.

Statement made by Ambassador Adebo, Permanent Representative of Nigeria in the Special Committee on Peace-Keeping Operations on 20 August, 1965.

Statement by H.E. Chief S.O. Adebo at the 78th Meeting of the United Nations Disarmament Commission, 11 May, 1965.

Statement made on 30 Sept. 1963 by Hon. Jaja Wachuku, Minister of External Affairs of the Federal Republic of Nigeria to the United Nations General Assembly Eighteenth Session 30 Sept., 1963.

Statement on the first Committee on the Inadmissibility of Intervention in the Domestic Affairs of States and the Protection of their Independence and Sovereignity by Aminu Kano in 1964.

Tukur, Mahmud.: Nigeria's External Relations: the United Nations as the Forum and Policy Medium in the Conduct of Foreign Policy, Oct., 1960 – Dec. 1965. Zaria: Ahamadu Bello University, Institute of Administration, 1969.

The United Nations role and African Interests. *West Africa.* No. 3299 13 October 1980: 2011–2013.

Enukora Joe Okoli, report on President Shagari's American visit and address at the United Nations.

Institute of Commonwealth Studies
Oxford